ON ARISTOTLE
AND
GREEK TRAGEDY

ON ARISTOTLE
AND
GREEK TRAGEDY

John Jones

STANFORD UNIVERSITY PRESS
STANFORD, CALIFORNIA

Originally published in 1962 by
Chatto and Windus Ltd
40 William IV Street
London

*

First published in the USA in 1962 by
Oxford University Press

*

Reissued 1980 by
Stanford University Press
Stanford, California
ISBN 0–8047–1092–9 (cloth)
0–8047–1093–7 (paper)
LC 80–50895

Printed in Great Britain by
Redwood Burn Ltd
Trowbridge and Esher

For
H. W. GARROD
1878-1960

CONTENTS

AUTHOR'S NOTE

I have imagined this book as the first part of a trilogy dealing with the presentation of the human self in western literature. It is also meant to stand on its own; but the reader will notice that a number of themes, broadly Shakespearean and Romantic, have been left unpursued, and he may wonder what is going on.

With Aeschylus and Euripides I follow Gilbert Murray's Oxford Text, the second edition in both cases; with Sophocles, Jebb's text; with Aristotle, the second edition of Rostagni's text. I indicate divergencies where these occur.

Mr T. C. W. Stinton put aside his own work in the summer of 1961 in order to read my manuscript and make detailed criticism of its argument.

Other friends and classical scholars have been variously kind. I should like to name Miss Anne Elliott, Professor Eduard Fraenkel, Mr W. F. Jackson Knight, Professor Constantine Trypanis and Mr D. M. Davin.

I: ARISTOTLE'S *POETICS*

1 New Fictions for Old

ARISTOTLE wrote the treatise *On the Art of Poetry* towards the end of his life, when Aeschylus had been dead for rather more than a century, and Sophocles and Euripides, who died within a few months of one another, for about seventy years. 335 B.C. is an acceptable approximation.

This work, which we always call the *Poetics*, has no rival among commentaries on the tragic drama of the Greeks. Its finish is rough, sometimes suggesting lecture notes rather than literary composition; and its second book has disappeared in which Aristotle dealt with Comedy and other subjects. But it is the only extended critical and theoretical record to survive from the civilisation that produced the plays. And that would be decisive, even if its intrinsic merit were less than it is.

The question of merit is an historically complicated one because the *Poetics* has exerted more influence through the ideas people have read into it than through those it contains. While, of course, this is not the only ancient text to be subjected to a series of misapplications, temporary, local, and mutually inconsistent, the *Poetics* must be distinguished by almost total failure of contact between Aristotle's argument and the successive traditions of exegesis. There is nothing very like the fate of this book in all the secular literature of the West.

The facts are well known, but we have been blind, as I think, to their application against ourselves. A kind of false security results from acknowledging the absurdities of neo-classicism. We contemplate that remote aesthetic tyranny imposed by Italian and French theorists who claimed to speak for Aristotle, and in his name expounded the Rules and mounted guard over Decorum; we try to conceive a world in which Corneille and Dryden could separately prostrate themselves before a ghost in order to urge that the rule (which is not a rule in Aristotle) requiring a play's action to be confined within twenty-four hours should be relaxed a little to admit an action of thirty hours: and then we settle into self-congratulation.

Our sense of superior enlightenment has one sound support, which is our immense advantage in scholarship over earlier times, and one rotten support, which is the unexamined assumption that our views about art—especially about the representation of human beings in art—are not only more just than those we call neo-classical, but also (because they are obviously right, because they are ours, because the neo-classical view has been refuted: there is a great nest of fallacy and mental inertia here) enjoy a natural, aboriginal, triumphant affinity with Aristotle's.

In the living situation what is rotten is, as always, intertwined with what is sound. The *Poetics* which we have appropriated to ourselves derives jointly from modern classical scholarship, principally nineteenth-century and German, and from Romanticism. Histories of literary criticism sometimes state that reverence for the *Poetics* was destroyed by the Romantic Movement, which is a misleading generalisation based on the scene in England where the hold of neo-classical theory had always been relatively weak, and where the younger men inclined simply to turn aside from Aristotle's treatise when they found the taste of it "for all the world like chopped hay"[1] in their mouths. In fact, the earlier European Romantics responded in an ambiguous way to the *Poetics*, and this was largely because their designs against French cultural hegemony could not be altogether reconciled with their wish to confirm the new enthusiasm for Greek civilisation associated with Winckelmann. Lessing, for example, was at once an implacable enemy to Baroque Tragedy and almost a traditionalist in his reading of the *Poetics*.

And later, when Romanticism became the new orthodoxy, the tendency was rather to re-interpret Aristotle than to reject him. Out of humour with the rules of art, people turned to those parts of the *Poetics* which seemed to promise human and psychological interest—to *katharsis*, and to the dramatic character who shall strike us as like ourselves, and to the idea of a fatal flaw or blunder (*hamartia*).

They turned most insistently to the tragic hero. Moreover, they still turn to him,[2] so that what Butcher wrote at the close of the last century remains true today: "With the exception of the definition of tragedy itself, probably no passage in the *Poetics*

[1] Thomas Gray, *Correspondence*, ed. Toynbee and Whibley, vol. I, p. 241.
[2] Max Kommerell (*Lessing und Aristoteles*, 1940) dropped an important hint in observing that the belief in a single hero for every tragedy rests on a mistranslation of Chapter Thirteen of the *Poetics*.

has given rise to so much criticism as the description of the ideal tragic hero in ch. xiii."[1] Now this is the point at which (I believe) modern gains in intellectual method are nullified by the gross unconscious prejudice with which that method is directed. Not merely has the importance which certain Romantic-sounding themes had for Aristotle been exaggerated; a much more serious consideration is our silent and innocent perverting of his book's main argument. I mean that we have imported the tragic hero into the *Poetics*, where the concept has no place.

The crucial passage occurs where Aristotle has been discussing different kinds of plot, and *hamartia*, and concludes:

> The well constructed plot must, therefore, have a single issue, and not (as some maintain) a double. The change of fortune must not be from bad to good but the other way round, from good to bad; and it must be caused, not by wickedness, but by some great error [*hamartia*] on the part of a man such as we have described, or of one better, not worse, than that.[2]

In detailed commentary and criticism, as in the broad outlines of interpretation, Aristotle's "change of fortune" has always been taken to mean, and indeed is often translated, "change in the hero's fortunes". This is the settled tradition to which must be offered the direct challenge that there is no evidence—not a shred—that Aristotle entertained the concept of the tragic hero.

At once it will be objected that we have here a quibble over terms: the word hero does not appear in the *Poetics*, as it happens (and there is nothing surprising about the absence of the Greek *hērōs*)[3]; but the idea of the protagonist, of the central figure— that very wide and flexible idea is obviously there in some form.

Everything depends on that "obviously". For someone who will not think of surrendering the hero, that "obviously" is a matter of what seems to be the most elementary common sense: if the change of fortune is caused by the *hamartia* of Aristotle's "man such as we have described", then surely Aristotle wants us to attach the change of fortune to that man, to call it his.

[1] These are the opening words of "The Ideal Tragic Hero", Chapter Eight in his *Aristotle's Theory of Poetry and Fine Art*.

[2] *Poetics*, 53a13-17.

[3] Because *hērōs* had not for Aristotle the developed literary-critical and dramatic associations that "hero" has for us.

That "obviously" is partly, too, for our opponent, a matter of aesthetic conviction: the change of fortune cannot, he assumes, be interesting or effective, cannot move us, unless we call it the hero's and feel it to be his. And finally it is a matter of the evident general truth that changes of fortune do not happen in the air, either in life or in art; they happen to human beings and are brought about by human beings.

Aristotle allows this last point, but his quirkish, roundabout way of doing so ought to make us suspect that he is not viewing the subject with our eyes:

> Being the imitation of an action, Tragedy involves a plurality of stage-figures who do the acting.[1]

And this leads to a second statement which constitutes his brief but decisive answer to both the other points:

> Tragedy is an imitation not of human beings but of action and life.[2]

Thus the obvious interpretation of Aristotle's "change of fortune" as "change in the hero's fortunes" is confronted by an apparent absurdity. What can it mean to say that Tragedy is not an imitation of, does not represent, human beings? The answer will become plain, I hope, in the argument that follows; at the outset it is worth remarking merely that Aristotle's strange assertion has failed to embarrass his critics and exponents. They often muffle its effect in translation (for example Bywater render *anthrōpōn*—"human beings"—by the dim and neutral "persons"); but their purpose in doing so has always been the honest one of producing an English version at once accurate and readable. The truth is, they are unable to ask themselves whether Aristotle means what he says; they are prevented by an almost invulnerable habit of mind which discredits the *situational* autonomy of his "change of fortune", forces a kind of human dependency on it, attaches it to the heroic, suffering solitary who is supposed to stand at the centre of the stage and of attention, like Hamlet.

Assuredly like Hamlet, for the Shakespearean drama is never far from consideration by the modern literature of the *Poetics*, because of the English writer's influence on German Romanti-

---

[1] 49b36-7.   [2] 50a16.

cism and on their humane learning,[1] and on ourselves of course, and on the world. This issue is a very wide one embracing all aspects of the literary presentation of human beings, and at the same time the tragic hero will be found at the heart of a number of apparently unrelated problems. Consider *hamartia*. Nearly all professional Aristotelians have felt obliged, in the face of related passages in the *Nicomachean Ethics* and the *Rhetoric*, to take this word to mean error of judgment, and to exclude any strong implication of moral fault or shortcoming. I believe that they are right, and that the strenuous efforts which were made during the nineteenth century, and occasionally since, to lend moral emphasis to *hamartia*[2] must be reckoned unavailing (although it is important to bear in mind that the Greeks did not distinguish wickedness and stupidity with anything like Christian definiteness). But the motive behind these efforts is easy to discover. If we let Oedipus command interest as a proud and obstinate and pathetic king like—even very remotely like —Lear, and if our Clytemnestra is a resolute, masculine-minded murderess from the same quarter of the aesthetic heaven as Lady Macbeth: then, as soon as a quasi-Shakespearean figure crosses the imagination's threshold, we resist the conclusion that Aristotle wanted tragic downfalls to result from mere, or almost mere, miscalculation. The poverty of this feels intolerable.

Or consider two leading terms of art in the *Poetics*, *peripeteia* and *anagnōrisis*, usually translated Reversal and Recognition. These, says Aristotle, are Tragedy's most effective means of working upon our emotions[3]; and the instinctive modern response to his pronouncement is to couple the tug of powerful feeling experienced by the spectator, his intense caring about what he sees, with the stage-portrayal of one man's vicissitude: so that if we could, we would understand *peripeteia* to mean a personal reversal (the prosperous man falls into adversity), and would interpret *anagnōrisis* as the recognition of an individual's identity. I say "if we could" because the text makes it plain

[1] See F. Gundolf (*alias* Gundelfinger), *Shakespeare und der deutsche Geist*. I believe there is nothing in English of any substance.

[2] In truth the moral sense of *hamartia* went almost unquestioned in the older tradition. William de Moerbeke, for example, was perfectly orthodox in translating it into the Latin *peccatum*. And five hundred years later (in 1789) Twining was still orthodox with his "frailty".

[3] 50a33.

that we can't; the centre of gravity of Aristotle's terms is situational and not personal; he is talking about a reversed state of
affairs and a recognition of, a discovering the truth about, a
state of affairs which was unknown before or misapprehended.
Of course the situation may be one of a prosperous man falling
into adversity; but nothing is gained by arguing that the substance of the situation *may* be personal when Aristotle's attention
is not directed to this point at all.

The source of disquiet is once again our imported tragic hero,
and the connection between the Aristotelian Reversal (which
we would like to personalise) and the Aristotelian change of
fortune (which we do render "change in the hero's fortunes")
is manifestly close and continuous. For the change on which
the action hinges is a recurring as well as a major theme of the
Poetics; the passage with which we began is one among several,[1]
and on each occasion we tether the change ignominiously to the
hero who is conceived to be suffering it. And finally, by introducing the hero we obscure the vital truth (to which I shall
return later, as I shall to other features of this preliminary
sketch) that it is the fact of change which Aristotle finds essentially tragic, not the direction of change. That is why he is
so careless and unemphatic in recommending whether the
change should be downward or upward. As we shall see, he
contradicts himself, once preferring the happy ending and once
the unhappy. Which remains hard to understand so long as we
suppose that the tragic change evoked in him, as it does in us,
an image of the hero and his individual fortune.

While the literature of Aristotle's tragic hero is considerable,
that of the hero in Greek Tragedy is immense. The same hero
who has been imposed on the *Poetics* is looked for in the plays
themselves, and he is found there of course: and sometimes, by
a nice irony, Aristotle incurs blame for failing to fit his theory
to the dramatic facts. Antigone, *pace* Hegel, is innocent (the
commentators protest) of *hamartia*. Oedipus's *hamartia* does not
cause his downfall. Philoctetes does not fall, he rises. How silly .
of Aristotle to demand that the hero shall be like ourselves. You
can see from his dry and thin account of the hero's character,
when he admired Sophocles and had the entire wealth of his

[1] See also 51a14, 52a16, 55b28.

creation to draw on, that Aristotle was more than a bit of a scientific pedant.

I am not suggesting that we have only to abandon the concept of the hero for everything to come right. Naturally Aristotle's *Poetics* still makes less than perfect sense after the hero has been excised, and parts of it still feel seriously inadequate to the Greek drama; while that drama itself remains desperately foreign. Nevertheless, the hero is a narrowing and distorting influence and nearly always baneful, and getting rid of him calls for bold action against a number of deep-rooted assumptions. We must open our minds to the possibility of an ancient —but Western—dramatic literature which cannot profitably be compared with Goethe's or Coleridge's Shakespeare. And we must not allow speculation about the origins of Tragedy to force the hero on us: Sir William Ridgeway's theory that Tragedy began in choral worship at the tombs of great individuals (heroes in the well-established sacral meaning of the word) was conceived as a direct challenge to the reconstructions made by Gilbert Murray and others on the basis of ritual celebration of the sufferings of a hypothetical Year-god; but Ridgeway's dead and glorified "hero" and the *Eniautos-Daimōn* of Cambridge anthropology both gratify the presupposition that Tragedy grew up around the doings of various grand solitaries.

In the event, none of these theories has worn well[1]; but the adverse judgment of scholars cannot be expected to reach so wide an audience as the errors or the unproved guesses that have been vigorously popularised. Murray himself spread the *Eniautos-Daimōn* gospel far beyond his own deservedly successful books, to Jane Harrison's *Themis*, and to the *Poetics* (by way of his Preface to Bywater's translation)and to the *Encyclopaedia Britannica*; so no wonder people write as if the *Daimōn* were a familar figure of Greek literature and life, and even as if a step-by-step correspondence between ritual form and tragic text had been established.[2]

---

[1] Sir Arthur Pickard-Cambridge's appraisal in *Dithyramb, Tragedy and Comedy*, pp. 174-208, is not over-severe.

[2] Thus in *The Idea of a Theater*, p. 26, Francis Fergusson writes that "the Cambridge School of Classical Anthropologists has shown in great detail that the form of Greek tragedy follows the form of a very ancient ritual, that of the *Eniautos-Daimōn*, or seasonal god".

And what is known gets twisted into support of the hero, as
well as what is guessed at. Tragedy began as a choral song and
dance, and only at a later stage did an actor appear who stood
outside the Chorus and engaged in dialogue with it: that is
certain, but it does not give the modern critic the right to cry
welcome to Thespis and his first actor on the ground that here,
in Tragedy's dim pre-history, some considerable time before
our earliest surviving play was written, the Greeks arrived simultaneously at the protagonist and at drama's true self. Without
denying that drama entails conflict or that it takes two to make
a quarrel, I would urge that the facts of Greek Tragedy—particularly the corporate consciousness of its Chorus in moments
of self-division—require us to manage the ideas of conflict and
duality with a flexible intelligence. Notice the helpless and
almost lunatic fixity of the sober academic comment (one could
cite a hundred like it) that Aeschylus's *Suppliant Women* "repre-
sents the primitive character of Greek tragedy. It has no 'hero'.
Chorus and heroine are one"; whereas his *Seven against Thebes*
"presents us with the first proper hero in the history of tragic
art".[1] (What is a proper hero?) This is the environment of the
long sterile debate as to whether Creon is the real hero of
Antigone's play and Odysseus of Ajax's, and Clytemnestra the
heroine of Agamemnon's; while *The Women of Trachis* has been
pulled in two between Deianeira and Heracles: one or other
has to be granted the heroic role; we must make our minds up.
Apparently it takes a critic of exceptional acuteness to rescue
himself from his own conviction that "Aristotle places firmly in
the centre of his ideal play the Tragic Hero, with his *hamartia*"
—as Professor Kitto does with the rejoinder that "the centre
of a play is not necessarily a Tragic Hero".[2]

Aristotle might have answered Professor Kitto and the rest:
"But I never mentioned the Tragic Hero in my *Poetics*. I defined
Tragedy—again and again—as the imitation of an action, and
I even went out of my way to insist that Tragedy does not
imitate human beings."

Here in its entirety, as Ingram Bywater translated it, is the
passage where Aristotle discusses *hamartia* (which he does only

[1] Herbert Weir Smyth, *Aeschylean Tragedy*, pp. 52, 131.
[2] *Form and Meaning in Drama*, p. 233.

once in the *Poetics*), and where he is always supposed to be talking about the Tragic Hero:

> It follows, therefore, that there are three forms of Plot to be avoided. (1) A good man must not be seen passing from happiness to misery, or (2) a bad man from misery to happiness. The first situation is not fear-inspiring or piteous, but
> 5 simply odious to us. The second is the most untragic that can be; it has no one of the requisites of Tragedy; it does not appeal either to the human feeling in us, or to our pity, or to our fears. Nor on the other hand should (3) an extremely bad man be seen falling from happiness into misery. Such a story
> 10 may arouse the human feeling in us, but it will not move us to either pity or fear; pity is occasioned by undeserved misfortune, and fear by that of one like ourselves; so that there will be nothing either piteous or fear-inspiring in the situation. There remains, then, the intermediate kind of personage, a
> 15 man not pre-eminently virtuous and just, whose misfortune, however, is brought upon him not by vice and depravity but by some error of judgment [*hamartia*], of the number of those in the enjoyment of great reputation and prosperity; e.g. Oedipus, Thyestes, and the men of note of similar families.
> 20 The perfect Plot, accordingly, must have a single, and not (as some tell us) a double issue; the change in the hero's fortunes must not be from misery to happiness, but on the contrary from happiness to misery; and the cause of it must lie not in any depravity, but in some great error [*hamartia*] on his part;
> 25 the man himself being either such as we have described, or better, not worse, than that. (52b34-53a16)

Bywater published his edition and translation of the *Poetics* in 1909, following Dacier, Twining, Tyrwhitt, Ritter (who seventy years earlier had exposed the shortcomings of the Aldine text), Spengel, the massive Vahlen, and other considerable scholars. Bywater's qualification should be stressed—he was an outstanding Regius Professor, a specialist of the highest technical accomplishment, an editor of great and enduring authority—because all sorts of ill-equipped amateurs have attempted the *Poetics*, and we must be clear that our discussion has nothing to do with what is usually meant by incompetence.

There are three discrepancies to be noted between Bywater's translation and the Greek original. Where he has "a good man"

(l. 2) the Greek has "good men"; where he has "a bad man" (l. 3) the Greek has "bad men"; and where he renders "the change in the hero's fortunes" (l. 21) the Greek has "the change of fortune". The first and second of his alterations are not quite as trivial as they seem, for they contrive jointly to suggest that Aristotle has in mind a single dominant figure throughout, when in fact his discourse shifts from plural to singular. These two alterations help pave the way for the third, which is, in the whole range of its implications, momentous.

If someone had asked him why he diverged from the Greek text at these points, Bywater, who was a man of the finest academic probity and of conservative instincts, would no doubt have said that his only concern was to make Aristotle's indisputable meaning plainer than it would otherwise have been. And thus we should be thrown back on the inescapable obviousness and correctness (as everyone has judged) of the traditional view. It remains only to reiterate that Aristotle's demand that the change of fortune shall be brought about by the *hamartia* of "the intermediate kind of personage" (l. 14) does not entitle us to style that personage the Tragic Hero; for to call him the hero can only mean that we put him at the centre of our ideal play —as commentator after commentator has alleged that Aristotle does, thrusting the hero on his treatise here and in those other places where the pivotal, situational change is mentioned. And if outraged common sense exclaims that Aristotle actually mentions Oedipus and Thyestes (l. 19), the first being the most famous of all tragic heroes, then we must add insult to injury by pointing to the apparently crazy topsy-turvydom of Aristotle's concession that Tragedy, since it imitates an action, needs people to do the acting.[1] The fact that he feels bound to admit that an action cannot act itself ought to be sufficient warning of the trials in store for common sense during a study of the *Poetics*.

---

[1] And as for Oedipus and Thyestes, Aristotle's continuation should be remarked: ". . . and the men of note of similar families". A heavy stress falls on *families*, as becomes clear immediately afterwards when he declares: "Nowadays the best tragedies are constructed on the story of a few houses" (53a19); and later again when he explains this concentration upon a few families by observing that these simply happen to be the families in which events peculiarly suitable for tragic treatment have occurred (54a9-13).

2 *Imitation and Action*

Then "Tragedy is an imitation of an action". This is the root-proposition of the *Poetics*. It is accompanied by the negative assertion that Tragedy does not imitate human beings, which deserves to be respected, and not brushed aside as an effect-seeking exaggeration, at least until Aristotle's imitation and action have been explored.

IMITATION

The *Poetics* is a textbook for dramatists and aspiring drama-tists, designed to teach them how to write good tragedies; and it is also a work of high theory, a Defence of Poetry. It is a defence against attacks scattered among the writings of Plato, who taught philosophy to Aristotle when he was a young man. Plato held it against poetry that its emotional appeal is a threat to the authority of reason, that it tells lies (simply, the stories told by poets are untrue, these things never happened[1]), and that works of imaginative literature are remote from reality—remote in a special philosophical sense.

Aristotle answered all three criticisms. A better psychologist than Plato, he believed that there is more to be gained by educating the emotions than by repressing them. The doctrine of *katharsis* is central to this argument.[2] As to telling lies, Plato's crude historical criterion is refined in the *Poetics* into a much more adequate analysis of the authority proper to poetic state-ment, an authority which is not dependent on the historical status of the events narrated by the poet. Plato's third criticism, and Aristotle's reply to it, involve the concept of imitation, of *mimēsis*.

In Book Ten of his *Republic* Plato argues roughly as follows.

---

[1] Plato modifies this objection when considering untrue but edifying stories.

[2] Aristotle promises (*Politics*, VIII, 7) to discuss *katharsis* in some detail. There is no such discussion in our extant sources, and it is probable that Aristotle offered one in the lost second book of the *Poetics*. It is also likely that his dialogue *Concerning the Poets* (also lost) had a lot to say about the emotions: see A. Rostagni, "Il dialogo aristotelico περὶ Ποιητῶν; *Rivista di Filologia*, 1926, 433-70; 1927, 145-75. We may be certain that Aristotle's views on this subject have reached us in a seriously incomplete form.

There are many tables in the world, but there is only one idea or form (Platonic Idea) of a table. When a carpenter makes a table he produces a mere semblance of this idea which is the one "real" table lying beyond all the tables which have been or can be made: so that the idea, for our present very general purpose, is outside the world altogether. And when an artist sits down in front of the carpenter's table to paint a picture of it, the picture that results is a copy of something which is itself a kind of shadow of the real object. Thus the artifact is removed at two stages from reality.

Plato's argument is so unworthy—of himself and of his subject—that one suspects him of knocking it hastily together in order to give himself a chance to attack art, *en passant*, from the standpoint of his central doctrine of ideas.[1] The sense in which he conceives of the painter copying the carpenter's product is grossly insufficient. Nevertheless Aristotle does not pause (at least in extant sources) to refute him.[2] Instead, he puts forward an alternative version of *mimēsis* in which he indicates, effectively if obliquely, the vulnerability of Plato's notion that painters set out to copy their subjects in the spirit of the advertisement which guarantees a likeness. No Greek would have denied that a picture of a table must be immediately recognisable as that, but many Greeks must have shared Aristotle's dissatisfaction with the attitude struck in Book Ten of the *Republic*.

Mimēsis is therefore very much in issue. We have just seen that Platonic *mimēsis* refers us to the doctrine of ideas, and so to the first principles of his metaphysic. Likewise with Aristotle's counter-thesis: the account of artistic representation, rendering, imitation, which we meet in the *Poetics* grows out of a philosophical system which Aristotle does not expound—we should not expect him to—in the present essay on poetry, but which

[1] Hostile critics have used the obvious illiberalism of Plato's remarks about art to help sustain a totalitarian account of his philosophy. Friendly critics are divided. Some allow that no coherent aesthetic can be spelt out of the *Republic*. Others try to make creditable sense of what Plato says—notably R. G. Collingwood, who argues (with small success in my judgment) that Plato meant us to understand from his very hesitant distinction between imitative and non-imitative art that he was only opposed to bad art.

[2] Aristotle's dialogue *Concerning the Poets*, according to the reconstruction offered by Rostagni, went to the root of the Socratic case against art by attacking the doctrine of ideas.

has to be constantly acknowledged in and behind his familiar talk of *mimēsis*: we must think of him lecturing to his pupils for whom the precise terms of agreement and division between Plato and Aristotle were the stuff of their intellectual life.

When, after long and strenuous thought, Aristotle came to reject the heaven of real forms which he had received at Plato's feet, he formulated in its place a principle of indwelling form. The carpenter's table which for Plato was an unreal semblance of the real idea is now reckoned to be partially real. Aristotle expressed this partial reality by saying that tables (and everything in the world) are matter-and-form compounds, matter being the brute stuff of their make-up and form their intelligible essence—that which I respond to in an object when I see and pronounce, "This is a table." In fact, all recognising of objects happens in this way, so that what instructed Aristotelians do with a certain philosophical awareness, ordinary men do unthinkingly.[1] We all know a table when we see one, but we do not all know what we are doing when we see-and-know a table. The artist, who may or may not know what he is doing, is concerned with the intelligible essence, the form, in a manner which distinguishes him both from philosophers and from ordinary men. His activity is the contemplation of a form followed by the rendering of it into the medium of his art.

And so Aristotle's painter does not produce a copy of a copy. He sits before the carpenter's table in brooding consideration of its form (or of the essential tableness which is its reality), and then he tries to coax the form on to his canvas: this is the struggle of composition. The difference between Aristotle's painter and Plato's is of cardinal importance since it marks the moment at which their estimates of the authority and value of art diverge. And the difference turns primarily upon *mimēsis*. Plato could quite well have said that the painter imitates the transcendent idea visible to his inward eye, not the table made by the carpenter. This obvious step is taken much later by neo-Platonism, never by Plato himself, and the fact that he does not do so is one ground for suspecting him of stubborn initial

---

[1] For Plato, too, recognition of objects must be in some sense a grasping of their reality. Hence the difficulty (exposed very honestly in his *Parmenides* dialogue) of maintaining either the transcendence of the ideas or the complete unreality of things in the world.

prejudice against art. When Aristotle comes to challenge his great master and speak up for art, his attitude to the work of imitation is altogether more respectful.

ACTION

The individual arts are distinguished from one another by the media in which their work of imitation is carried out, and in some cases by the form which is imitated. The medium of Tragedy, as of all poetry, is language, and the form which Tragedy imitates is an action, a *praxis*: "Tragedy is a *mimēsis* of a *praxis*." Aristotle makes this assertion more than once,[1] and makes it with careful emphasis. He may have feared that he would be misunderstood at this first vital stage of his argument, and if that was the case his fears have proved justified; from the outset we have to ride the exegetic tradition very light in order to follow him.

Action (*praxis*) cannot mean plot (*muthos*) in the *Poetics* because an action is a form which the tragedian contemplates, and it stands logically and chronologically before the business of composition. *Muthos* does not appear until the artist sets about rendering the apprehended form into the dramatic medium: hence, as Aristotle says, "the *muthos* is a *mimēsis* of the *praxis*".[2] This way of expressing himself involves him in a double use of *mimēsis*, since he has been saying repeatedly that Tragedy is a *mimēsis* of a *praxis*. But his meaning is sufficiently clear. On the one hand art is the imitation of a form, and the form which the tragic art imitates is an action.[3] On the other hand, that which is visible to the mind's eye as an action—a naked essence, like all forms—is not realised as a work of art until the dramatist articulates it on the stage in terms of plot. Thus there are two different representational correspondences: one between the tragic art and action, another between action and plot; and

---

[1] A bedrock association of *mimēsis* and *praxis* is found at 49b24, 49b36, 50a16, 50b3, 52a2; and the *Poetics*, we shall see, is built on it.

[2] 50a3-4. See also 51a31-2.

[3] Aristotle nowhere says that the *praxis* of a tragedy is its form, but I am contending that we must understand him to mean this in the *Poetics*, whereas in the *Nicomachean Ethics* the application of *praxis* is moral and generalised and there can be no question of its being conceived as a form. Nor are its generalised associations entirely absent from the *Poetics*; in fact we should acknowledge them at 50a16.

Aristotle speaks of both as a *mimēsis*—inadvisedly perhaps, but it may not be his fault that the workmanship of our text of the *Poetics* is rough.

With *muthos*, therefore, we leave aesthetic theory behind and approach the practical problems of playmaking: Aristotle calls *muthos* "the arrangement of the events"[1] in a play; the tone of his discussion becomes down to earth. And all the time we must respect his initial distinction between action and plot, while the *Poetics* pursues its textbook office with growing singleness and Aristotle has less to say about *praxis*, naturally, and more about *muthos*. Having asserted the primacy of *praxis* in his theory of Tragedy, he now tells would-be dramatists—and he is very insistent about it—that *muthos* is by far the most important part of a play.[2] In fact he has already guaranteed *muthos* its sovereign place by defining its task as the representation (to avoid the word imitation for his second sense of *mimēsis*) of the *praxis*, thus imposing the full burden of expression on it. Plainly, a playwright who fails to give dramatic expression to his idea has made the most general and fundamental blunder it is possible to conceive, at the level of execution. This account is not without its naïve aspect, but at least Aristotle's singling out of *muthos* is expected and almost predetermined.

When the *Poetics* is reiterating the importance of *muthos* we have to remember that the plot's ability to sustain its exalted role is determined by its success in representing the ideal tragic action. Aristotle does not forget this, but he does contrive to simplify his terminology in a manner that has bemused his interpreters. He often assumes that the plot has done its job perfectly, that the stage-articulation of the action is complete. The advantage of this assumption is that he can discard the awkward doubleness of *praxis* and *muthos*: he can dispense with the first term and use the second to mean the fully realised *praxis*, or *praxis* seen from the practising dramatist's standpoint, seen within the context of an imaginary perfect play. His procedure (which is a convenience to himself and in tune with the less theoretical interests of the *Poetics*) has led commentators to say that he is "deceived"[3] by his terms, or that his extraordinary preoccupation with plot is due to the fourth-century in-

---

[1] 50a4, 50a16, 50a32.   [2] 50a16.
[3] Gilbert Murray, Introduction to Bywater's Translation.

fluences of post-Euripidean melodramatic Tragedy and the early New Comedy, two genres which nursed a strong intrigue-interest.

The second of these errors is calamitous. It confounds Aristotle's leading distinction between the *a priori*, metaphysical principle of action and the dramaturgic principle of plot. It makes do with a rough synonym instead of asking whether, in a particular instance, Aristotle is using *muthos* to mean realised *praxis*; for only when the answer to this question is "yes" may we refer his observations about plot to action. It misconceives the felt ontological discontinuity, very near the heart of the *Poetics*, between the visionary form, lucid and necessarily beautiful, and mere aspiring stage-event. It even flatters the modern reader's expectation that the plot or story or myth (vaguely, *muthos*) shall lie behind, be prior to, the action of the play.

Then the action is a form, and Aristotle suggests what kind of form when he tells dramatists to give first consideration to the plot because "the plot"—here the realised *praxis*—"is the cardinal principle and, as it were, the soul of a tragedy".[1] The analogue of the soul (*psuchē*) is careful; Aristotle invites us to think of the plot-play relationship as parallel to the soul-body relationship in the human organism.[2] Now, in Aristotle's mature doctrine the soul is the form of the body, and the body is the matter in which the soul is immersed.[3] Therefore a human being bears a general likeness to a table in that both are form-matter compounds embraced in the single substance. But the soul is distinguished from the form of the table and all other forms by its quasi-purposive vitality, and this is why Aristotle invokes it for comparison with the realised *praxis*. He wants to indicate that the form of a tragedy is more than a principle of intelligibility. It is also a quickening and directing impulse, a kind of soul.

---

[1] 50a38.

[2] And perhaps in all animals. Aristotle's view of the animal *psuchē* is hard to determine.

[3] In an early dialogue, the *Eudemus*, Aristotle still shares Plato's belief in a pre-existent and immortal soul, separate from the body. Later, in his *De Anima*, he regards soul and body as a single substance related as form to matter. (And perhaps Book One of the *Nicomachean Ethics* shows Aristotle in mid-stride between these two attitudes.) This change probably falls within the more general one sketched above, from belief in something like Plato's ideas to belief in indwelling form.

Aristotle pauses, ultimately, in the face of a metaphor which he fetches from animate nature in order to indicate that mysterious life by which, as all of us feel, true art is informed (the verb has literal force for him). He is driven to the broad likeness of the "living creature",[1] and there, more than once, he lets the matter rest. While, therefore, the *Poetics* makes poor sense if its philosophy—which means first and foremost the metaphysical basis of the idea of tragic action—is ignored, it is also cheated of its final generous flexibility by commentators who fail to acknowledge the tact with which Aristotle says let be to theorising. He tells us that the tragic action is like a living creature; it is a single sufficient whole, "complete in itself"[2]; many things happen in life which cannot be reduced to the "one *praxis*"[3] of Tragedy; tragic action commands an exquisite taut economy beyond the reach of Epic[4]; there are some things which the creative writer must learn for himself, or find within himself, because they cannot be taught.[5] His gestures towards poetry are sometimes large and admiring and easy, rather than didactic.

We conclude that Aristotle's understanding of tragic action is not narrowly or even tidily philosophical: indeed a certain intellectual unsophistication is evident in his manner of gazing at the object, the realised *praxis* which in its perfection is proportioned like a beautiful animal, impressive in size but not so big that the eye cannot take the whole thing in.[6] Such talk suggests a dominantly visual aesthetic—an impression strengthened by the observable coarsening of *mimēsis* towards truth-to-

---

[1] 50b34, 51a3-4, 59a20. [2] 49b25, 50b25, 52a2, 59a19.
[3] 51a19. [4] Chapter XXVI.
[5] In order to give Aristotle his due we must discard Romantic ideas about inspiration and return to the Greek view, which was broadly that art is teachable. The unspoken reservations of the *Poetics* on this score seem to me to run deeper and wider than the famous admission that mastery of metaphor "is the one thing which cannot be learnt from somebody else" (59a6-7). Without saying anything about the tragedian's capacity to feel, Aristotle mentions the desirability of his experiencing the emotions he is trying to present convincingly on the stage (55a30-1—*of having experienced* would be better); and he lets fall the remarkably open and bottomless pronouncement that in art "a likely impossibility is always preferable to an unconvincing possibility" (60a26-7, restated at 61b11-12). I suspect he was aware that this crucial artistic plausibility cannot be entirely "learnt from somebody else".
[6] Chapter VII.

nature verisimilitude in neo-Aristotelian schools, and by the visual tenor of modern theory, after Kant. Nevertheless, Aristotle's aesthetic model can be thought of as visual only in a refined and inward sense, as we discover from the triple association of Tragedy, music and dance in the *Poetics*. Musical rhythm (*rhuthmos*) and dance-movement (*schēma*)[1] have a likeness to tragic action which was obvious to him and which becomes illuminating to us when we extend to Aristotelian *praxis* that stability of pattern underlying and containing flux which (as is well known) he and all Greeks recognised in *rhuthmos* and *schēma*. While it makes sense to us to speak of rhythmic form or pattern, we cannot, as a Greek could, apply "rhythm" to a statue without being conscious of using the word outside its normal semantic range; and similarly with *schēma*, when Aristotle considers the rhythm of a dancer's movements[2]—*schēma* also means form in painting and sculpture in the *Poetics*[3]—his thoughts dwell less upon the beautiful process than ours would, and more upon the executed figure.

This is a matter of relative emphasis, but important all the same, for it partly explains why the dynamic calm of Greek tragic action strikes profoundly alien to the reader who has eyes to see. It affords a general introduction to the plays and, more immediately, to the ground *praxis*-pattern of the *Poetics*. That pattern, Aristotle tells us, is apparent in the reading of a tragedy; it is independent of performance[4]. He probably feels philosophically committed to this view because his form-and-matter doctrine dooms to failure, or to approximate success, those arts whose medium is necessarily physical: the painter can stress the form lurking within the carpenter's table, but he

[1] One should not think of musical rhythm and dance-movement as the meanings of *rhuthmos* and *schēma*, but as particular applications of the two Greek words.

[2] 47a27.

[3] 47a19.

[4] 62a11-13. Aristotle does not pursue his argument in detail or perhaps with complete consistency. He holds (50b17) that *opsis* (usually translated "Spectacle", but it probably means the appearance of the stage-figures rather than the whole visual impression of the staged play) has little or nothing to do with the tragedian's art; and he also allows that "the effects of Spectacle" (62a16) are a considerable element in one's enjoyment of a tragedy. We recall that the *Poetics* inhabits both the world of theory and the world in which plays are acted and watched.

cannot rescue it altogether from its marriage to brute matter since he too is producing a physical object. Thus the theoretical perfection attainable by Tragedy depends on the self-sufficiency of the read text which Aristotle asserts on its behalf. To this extent the issue may be prejudged, and Aristotle's enemies have been quick to exploit, and over-exploit, the damaging implication of his belief that the tragic experience is only superficially connected with theatre-going. For what is this implication? That the intellectualism of Aristotle's indwelling form, the background doctrine, is inadequate to the facts of art. Not that his practical address to Tragedy is head-in-air. Not, above all, that the action which delights the inward eye is a philosopher's fancy.

3 Human Beings

Aristotle warns us in his own way that the tragic action advanced in the *Poetics* is not abstract and bloodless. Tragedy, he says, is an imitation "of action and life", and this coupling is supported by the analogue of the soul and by the reiterated metaphor of the living creature. Action, the soul-like form, is more than a principle of perfect intelligibility. But still it is a form, and if somebody had asked him what is action the form *of*, Aristotle would surely have reckoned the question fair. I believe he would have answered that the *praxis* contemplated by the tragedian is the form of an event in life, sometimes close in time and known immediately, but usually received from an historical or mythological source[1]: history and myth are never distinguished in the *Poetics*, there is no problem of relative authenticity. Thus tragic action presents the translucent and vital quiddity of a life-event; it makes sense of experience. Aristotle's treatise begins and ends, as any sane aesthetic might, with art confronting life in an effort of interpretation.

And yet he says that Tragedy is not an imitation of human

[1] This answer would have to be modified if it were to embrace tragedies with wholly fictitious plots; but there is no need to do so since Aristotle assumes that the material of Tragedy is mythico-historical—in spite of a glance at Agathon's *Antheus*, a tragedy in which "names and events are both fictitious" (51b22).

beings. By this he cannot mean that Tragedy lacks what we loosely call human interest; somehow the imitation of action and life must carry human interest without being an imitation of human beings. An abrupt and ugly passage explains, lecture-note fashion, how this is so:

> Tragedy is an imitation not of human beings but of action and life, of happiness and misery. Happiness and misery are realised in action; the goal of life is an action, not a quality. Men owe their qualities to their characters, but it is in their actions that they are happy or the reverse. And so the stage-figures do not act in order to represent their characters; they include their characters for the sake of their actions.[1]

Human interest enters the *Poetics* at this point, and the difference between its legitimate and illegitimate treatment in Tragedy is foreshadowed by "they include their characters for the sake of their actions". Here Aristotle switches from the action of the play to the actors in the play so that he can present us with the histrionic correlate of the dramaturgy that conceives and articulates an action rich in human interest, but does not imitate human beings. Actor and dramatist both include character for the sake of action, each in his separate sphere; and, shifting back again to the dramatist's standpoint, Aristotle likens his case to that of the painter:

> The analogy of painting is very close: if someone were to cover his canvas with the most beautiful colours laid on at random, he would please us less than if he drew a monochrome sketch on a white ground.[2]

Among the major issues raised by Aristotle's comparison, the most important is the service which one element in the artistic process renders to another, and through which its very existence is justified. Having said that character is included for the sake of action, and next that "a tragedy is impossible without an action, but there may be one without characters",[3] Aristotle now introduces a "very close" analogy in which the full literal

---

[1] 50a16-22. The received text is unsatisfactory. Vahlen's view of the passage has commended itself to nearly all editors (although not to Rostagni) and I follow Vahlen here.

[2] 50a39-b3.   [3] 50a23-4.

application of these assertions is unavoidable, thus making it as hard as possible for us to play them down in relation to Tragedy. As the monochrome sketch is to bare tragic action, colour is to character.[1] The painter who strives after a likeness of his subject can rest assured, however thin and poor the result, that he is working within the bounds of his art: not so the painter of a medley of beautiful colours, for no Greek could have denied (since all the painting he knew and dreamed of was representational) that the end-product is at best an agreeable chaos, not a work of art at all.

Similarly with the tragedian; and Aristotle's analogy bears mainly upon the function of character: he wants to make the proposition that character serves action seem no less assured than is (for a Greek) the proposition that the only legitimate use of colour in painting is to support the finished likeness. He is saying that character is included for the sake of the action; he is not saying, or he is saying only incidentally, that character is less important than action. This crucial inflexion of argument has not been acknowledged, either in close professional analysis, where stress falls on the "subordinate significance"[2] of character and on the "superiority of activities over states",[3] or in the general and popular expositions with their antithetical talk of Plot and Character, those capital-letter fixtures of commentary. It needs to be said that the plot-character dichotomy is radically false to Aristotle's understanding of Tragedy, that character, like colour, must be denied even the most primitive autonomy.

The task of a tragic plot (*muthos*) is, we recall, to render an ideal action in terms of stage-event; and it may succeed in this without having recourse to character. But the clear implication is that a tragedy is the richer for containing character, just as an executed likeness is the richer for being coloured. Not only is the analogy of colour and character firmly invoked; it is also less forced, more happy and natural, than is at once obvious to ourselves; for Aristotelian character (*ēthos*) is almost precisely

[1] Aristotle's plain and forceful analogy is obscured and weakened by Castelvetro's transposition of the painter-dramatist comparison to 50a33. Castelvetro's view, favoured by most nineteenth-century editors, is now generally and rightly abandoned.

[2] Bywater, note on 50a15.

[3] Gerald F. Else, *Aristotle's Poetics: the Argument*, p. 253.

ethical colouring. Its discriminations are exclusively moral, and it is applied two-dimensionally to the surface of the realised action.

Aristotle duly confines *ēthos* when he declares: "Character in a tragedy is that which reveals a moral choice."[1] All familiar thought of the characters of friends or the characters in books must be set aside, since *ēthos* is without the ambition of inclusiveness (character in its various modern contexts casts a net around personality), and it yields nothing to naturalistic expectation. We even find *ēthos* working against a general naturalistic tendency when Aristotle remarks that "the tragedies of most of our modern writers are characterless",[2] whereas "nearly all the early men"[3] had greater success with character than with action. The fuller psychology and relative closeness to nature of the post-Euripidean drama—the drama called modern in the *Poetics*—could and did go with extreme ethical poverty. Nor did the brilliant verisimilitude of Zeuxis's painting (the story survives from antiquity that he painted some grapes so like the life that the birds flew down and pecked at the paint) save his work from being, as Aristotle tells us, "empty of character".[4]

Again it is true that *ēthos*, this narrow moral spectrum, has an outwardness of application which brings it unexpectedly close to colour. When Aristotle defines *ēthos* as "that which reveals a moral choice" the modern reader anticipates an exposure of consciousness; instinctively he stresses *reveals*, because he has inherited—from Socratic-Platonic, Euripidean, Jewish, Roman, Christian, humanist and Romantic sources— an image of the human self and its working which he accepts for a universal *donnée* of life, and never questions. If he were to question it, he would observe that Aristotle has already issued a very emphatic warning against the mentality that unthinkingly stresses *reveals*. He would recall that the eye of Tragedy, according to the *Poetics*, rests on actions and not on qualities or states of mind and soul. He would understand, with a slow

---

[1] 50b7-8. Very occasionally Aristotle uses *ēthos* less narrowly: at 60a11 and in Chapter XV.

[2] 50a25.

[3] 50a37.

[4] 50a28. Zeuxis's work was not always or merely photographic. Elsewhere in the *Poetics* (61b13) we hear of him improving on his models.

dawning of general illumination, that Aristotle has founded his book on the distinction between false imitation of human beings and true imitation of actions because he reckons it his first responsibility, as early as the fourth century, to oppose the inward-turning of attention and interest that goes with a stress upon *reveals*.

The gulf between our preconceptions and the express doctrine of the *Poetics* can only be bridged through the recovery of some of the lost human relevancies of action. Aristotle is assaulting the now settled habit in which we see action issuing from a solitary focus of consciousness—secret, inward, interesting —and in which the status of action must always be adjectival: action qualifies; it tells us things we want to know about the individual promoting it; the life of action is our ceaseless, animating consideration of the state of affairs "inside" him who acts, without which action is empty and trivial, an effluvium. This movement from adjectival action to the substantive self would seem, were it conscious, not merely natural but inevitable. Were it conscious, however, we should have to admit that we are first rejecting Aristotle's injunction to make character serve action, and then replacing it with its opposite. Revealing a moral choice means, for Aristotle, declaring the moral character of an act in a situation where the act itself does not make this clear.[1] Reader and spectator are apprised of the ethical colour of the action at this point of the play. To our sense of characteristic conduct Aristotle opposes that of characterful action: the essence of conduct being that it is mine or yours; of action, that it is out there—an object for men to contemplate.

It matters supremely, of course, that the object should repay contemplation; hence Aristotle's insistence that happiness and its opposite are both realised in action, that action is the goal of life. He is saying that the human self is present in its acts— present, moreover, with a fullness and effectiveness attained nowhere else. And so his argument is two-sided: he holds that action, self-in-action, is rich with the wealth of realised humanity; and he holds that an inactive self is merely potential and unachieved.

[1] 50b7-10. I follow Rostagni's interpretation of this passage which presents difficulties of detail, none of them material to my argument.

C

The very abrupt statement in the *Poetics* should be set beside the judgment between "state of mind" and "activity" which Aristotle makes in the *Nicomachean Ethics*, concluding (with a hostile glance at Plato's intellectualist ethic) that "the good state of mind may exist without producing any good result, as in a man who is asleep or in some other way quite inactive, but the good activity cannot. . . ."[1] Many commentators, one soon discovers, have brought the two passages together, but with the result that the discussion has been handed over prisoner to academic categories. The fact that the statement in the *Nicomachean Ethics* is fuller than, and throws light upon, the one in the *Poetics* has encouraged the idea that the former is somehow the major text, and that what Aristotle is doing in his literary essay is to refer to a doctrine lying within his moral philosophy. There is comfort in this for us, since it confines within acceptable limits a situation which would otherwise appear intolerably alien. But it is a fraud. The moral argument, of course not denied in the *Poetics*, is suspended within the larger vision of the self presented there; and the vision is larger because it must be adequate to Aristotle's present subject, which is tragic imitation: he naturally supports his recommendations for Tragedy with his own version of what human beings are really like.

Once the width and depth of Aristotle's theme are recognised, a fine agility develops in his reader; in order to see the "quite inactive" self with Aristotle's eyes he sheds most of the interest that quiescent selfhood holds for a modern sensibility, allowing its haunting latencies—the home of much familiar and great art—to fall away and shrink into a low-burning flame that merely keeps alive the hope of ampler life. He excepts himself from the universal cult of consciousness, reduces the inward flow to a kind of sullen token, because he wants to awaken a compensating respect for the bare (as we should think them) doings of self, and thus make sense of the *Poetics*. The form of Aristotle's advice to the dramatist is at first sight very strange:

> So far as he can, the tragic poet should act out with the appropriate gestures the events of his play; for we are best convinced by those writers who are in the grip of the emotions they are seeking to convey dramatically, and who establish in consequence a

[1] *Nicomachean Ethics* I, 8, 1098b33.

natural sympathy with their stage-figures: distress and anger are
most fairly rendered by one who is feeling these emotions at the
time.[1]

Not, however, that the passage has excited much discussion;
the keen literal edge to Aristotle's discourse has simply been
dulled; commentators have made him sound mildly, almost
inoffensively silly. A long-standing exception is Gustav Teichmüller, who observed nearly a hundred years ago[2] that Aristotle is giving straightforward practical advice here, and
therefore (so this scholar argued) cannot possibly mean what
he has always been taken to mean. Professor Else, a lonely
follower of Teichmüller, now reaffirms the "inanity" of the
orthodox interpretation:

> We get a vivid mental picture of the poet-actor in his study, leap-
> ing alternately to his feet and back to his writing-table, throwing
> himself into each role in turn, miming regal scorn or blank horror,
> dropping to his knees as the suppliant Polynices only to rise as
> Oedipus and reject the plea. It is a lively picture, but not a con-
> vincing one. What has all this to do with the poet's task?[3]

The answer to Professor Else's concluding question is, everything. What makes him call the picture unconvincing is the
non-correspondence (exposed by his attack upon a sound but
inert tradition of commentary) between Aristotle's experience
of being creatively alive and that which we bring with us to the
study of the *Poetics*. Our version of selfhood is centripetal and
intensely inward; we expect to find Aristotle telling playwrights
to get inside their characters—and Professor Else does what he
can to convert Aristotle's strange picture into this familiar one
with his "throwing himself into each role in turn". Moreover,
this inward version of ours aspires to an ideal of perfect stability
and conservation; hence our talk of the real self underlying,
persisting through, action and suffering, and our inability to
conceive the expressive vitality of the discrete and centrifugal
self[4]—the vitality which promoted Aristotle's (and I believe the

---

[1] 55a29-32.

[2] *Aristotelische Forschungen* I, p. 100 ff. (1867).

[3] *Aristotle's Poetics: the Argument*, p. 489.

[4] "I can only suggest that Aristotle was perhaps something of an extra-
vert. Constantly he stresses activity" (F. L. Lucas, *Tragedy*, p. 140 in the
revised edition of 1957).

ordinary Athenian spectator's) sense of fulfilment and joy as they allowed the acts of the figures on the stage to trickle through the fingers of imagination. They found wealth where we find waste and evanescence, and where the classical specialist finds an altogether incredible picture of the poet-actor savouring the action of his play while he composes. Probably not much of the ancient tragic experience is recoverable by us, but we can avoid forcing upon Aristotle the local and no doubt transient self of the modern West.

Then Tragedy is the imitation of an action, and the difference now establishes itself in very broadest outline between imitating human beings and imitating an action in which humanity is effectively present. Aristotle's composing dramatist, acting out the events of his play, works himself into the pattern of the single distinct *praxis* visible to his mind's eye, struggles to get it physically and emotionally right: this is the process of translating action into plot, *praxis* into *muthos*. In the work of art, of course, his blueprint gestures and movements will be apportioned among a group of stage-figures; differentiation obviously matters, is unavoidable, and therefore falls among the subjects dealt with in Aristotle's textbook. He states the principle of differentiation thus:

> Being the imitation of an action, Tragedy involves a plurality of stage-figures who do the acting. These necessarily possess certain distinctive qualities both of character and thought, since it is by virtue of these distinctive qualities that we speak of their actions also as having certain qualities. . . .[1]

And then I think it must have struck him how difficult it is even to mention the people in the play without seeming to flout the rule against imitating human beings, because he proceeds to enunciate yet once more the leading tenet of the *Poetics*:

> Tragedy is indeed the imitation of an action, and for that reason, rather than any other, it imitates the stage-figures—[2]

this time, we note, with pointed reference to the people in the play, the stage-figures (*prattontes*, as in the earlier passage); so that his readers shall have no excuse for thinking that the place

[1] 49b36-50a1.   [2] 50b2-3.

of action as tragic object is affected by anything he may say about the individuated presentation of the stage-figure. His last general pronouncement draws together the actor who includes character for the sake of action, the painter-dramatist who brings ethical colour to the service of his work of imitation, the actor-dramatist who constructs a model of his plot, the realised *praxis*, by acting out the events of his tragedy.

Differentiation turns, then, upon the distinctive qualities of which Aristotle speaks. We have already encountered these qualities, strangely overshadowed by action: "Men owe their qualities to their characters, but it is in their actions that they are happy or the reverse"—a juxtaposition that warns us not to expect from the *Poetics* any firm repose upon mood, state of mind, consciousness. Aristotelian man cannot make a portentous gesture of "I have that within which passes show" because he is significantly himself only in what he says and does. Instead of "that within"—Hamlet's omnipresent consciousness —he has the qualities which he owes to his *ēthos*; these are his without being an inward possession; the self-maintained continuity of the modern ego is lacking, and the work of individual appropriation (through which we recognise the character and qualities as his) falls to the outward nexus of habit. The virtuous man—so runs the argument of the *Nicomachean Ethics*—is always one who has learned to be good through acting well: there are no natural saints.[1] And his learning to be good is not the kind of process we are likely to imagine, perhaps by picturing a growing inner resource of virtue, a reservoir upon which he draws in characteristic virtuous conduct. Learning to be good is the acquiring of a virtuous habit (*hexis*) of character through a succession of good acts. It is forming a style, and this invites comparison between Aristotle's account of the moral life and athletic stroke-play; the virtuous man is like the batsman whose full range of strokes has been so firmly grooved through practice that the bowler despairs of tempting him to make a mistake, or even of catching him momentarily in two minds.

Once again the moral philosophy sheds light on the literary

---

[1] "We acquire the virtues by first exercising them. . . . We become just by doing just acts, temperate by doing temperate acts, brave by doing brave acts" (*Nicomachean Ethics* II, 1, 1103a31).

essay, and again the light is wasted unless Aristotle's moral man is seen to be continuous with his tragic man, and his tragic man is acknowledged to be, for him, actual. Very suggestive is the gradual emergence of personality in a channelling of action-pattern; it directs us to the confident outward thrust and to the corresponding faintness of inner focus that separate self-definition through my habits from self-definition through my consciousness. *Hexis*, habit or bent of character, is the product of past actions; it is the present causal link between a man and his actions which enables an observer to judge whether he is being true to himself; it is the ground of the same observer's prediction as to his future actions. By the erosive flow of action the individual features are carved out, no potent shaping spirit lodges aboriginally behind the face; and thus the Aristotelian stage-figure receives his distinctive qualities. To see how the very primordia of his identity are acquired and sustained (becoming inactive is relapsing into a state that lacks all interesting differentiation) is to recognise the fitness of that shared "action and life" to deliver its own kind of human and tragic solitude.

Aristotle lays it down in his military fashion that the dramatist "has four points to aim at" in the realisation of his stage-figures: they should be consistent, lifelike, good and appropriate.[1]

Consistency pays homage to logic; it is a product of Greek aesthetic intellectualism, here tempered with the admission that some individuals are in fact inconsistent and that such a one may appear on the tragic stage: in which case, says Aristotle, he should be "consistently inconsistent".[2]

That the stage-figure shall be lifelike is a requirement—one among four—which has often been dragged out of its context and tortured into conformity with neo-classical and then with Romantic expectations, unGreek all of them. Aristotle merely

[1] Chapter XV. Aristotle still speaks of *ethos*, but no longer in the special ethical sense which we have already examined. The word character is therefore best avoided in the present discussion.

[2] Thus Aristotle anticipates a sophistical objection to the requirement of consistency: a student might come up to him after the lecture and ask "But what about the inconsistent people?" At the same time it may not be entirely fanciful to see him fumbling—and fumbling impressively—with the fact that a strand of chaos may be traced through the pattern and system of the sanest life.

states that this requirement is different from those of goodness
and appropriateness; he does not even make clear at this point
whether he is asking that the stage-figure shall be like us average
humanity, or whether he is asking that it shall be like its
mythico-historical original, the "real" Achilles or Darius of
tradition. His silence is not surprising; the necessary introduction has already been given in the course of his account of that
change of fortune which is for him the pattern of tragic action
and which is best brought about, he thinks, by error (*hamartia*)
rather than by vice or depravity.[1] Now it is essential that the
change of fortune shall happen to "one like ourselves" because
the emotion of fear, the emotion linked with pity[2] and specific
to Tragedy, is aroused in the reader or spectator by his thinking
"This might happen to me"; and he will not have that thought
if the most elementary correspondence is missing between the
stage-figure and himself. A little later, therefore, when he is
telling dramatists what to aim at in their human representation,
Aristotle reaffirms that the stage-figure shall be like ourselves.

The simple sufficiency of this has been obscured by our
imported tragic hero who hovers over Aristotle's continuous
argument and causes an unreal breach between the earlier
passage in which he is supposed to be talking about a stressed
dramatic solitary—the hero—and the present passage in which
(as no one can doubt) he is talking generally about the stage-
figures of Tragedy: with the result that the requirement of lifelikeness is allowed an independence, and hence an importance,
to which it is not entitled. We read into it a familiar cultivation
of the inwardness of self when in fact Aristotle is doing no more
than accept the consequence of his earlier dogmatic assertion
that the emotions of pity and fear are specifically tragic. The
lifelike stage-figure is annexed to an argument about the effects
of Tragedy upon its audience—an argument which is directed,
particularly in its reference to *katharsis*, against Plato's declared

[1] See p. 13 above.
[2] One should hyphenate Aristotelian pity-and-fear because it is a mistake
to think of pity in isolation and interpret it, as some have done, in a spirit
of Christian altruism. Aristotle's discussion of pity-and-fear in the *Rhetoric*
makes it clear that "there can be no pity in his view, where there is not also
fear. Both pity and fear are derived from the self-regarding instinct, and
pity springs from the feeling that a similar suffering might happen to ourselves" (Humphry House, *Aristotle's Poetics*, p. 101).

hostility to art. When denying that Tragedy is vicious in its emotional consequences, Aristotle affirms a stage-figure who shall be felt by us who watch him to be like ourselves.

And the sense of "like ourselves" is primitive, far removed from Coleridge's experience of fellow-feeling towards a vacillating Hamlet. Indeed, the Aristotelian equivalent to Romantic self-identification with the protagonist is not even to be looked for here, but rather in his advice to composing dramatists that they shall act out the events of their story and so enable themselves to impress us as "most convincing"—*pithanōtatoi*—in their rendering of the action's emotional tone. When he asks that the stage-figure shall be like ourselves, Aristotle is not looking beyond that point of primary human and situational correspondence at which the thought "This might happen to me" is born; his observation that the requirement of lifelikeness is not the same as those of goodness and appropriateness would be grotesquely otiose, nonsensical almost, if he were advancing towards a quasi-Coleridgean position. What in fact this telltale observation intends is a warning that "like ourselves" is not quite the same as "like reality". We shall see in a moment that the stage-figure becomes like reality through the appropriateness of its representation, and that the appropriate is the typical. Now there are two moments when Aristotle's type-dominated aesthetic has to admit a foreign particularity: one is when the spectator, who is a real individual, is touched through pity and fear by the fortunes of the stage-figure; and the other is when the stage-figure is recognised as the likeness of its mythico-historical original, of Achilles or Darius who are also real individuals. In both these cases the sense of "like" is, for Aristotle, peculiar. He has the first in mind when he declares that the requirement of lifelikeness is different from that of appropriateness; and he has the second in mind, I believe (and so I also believe that the commentators are wrong not to recognise a distinction here), when he returns to the question of lifelikeness at the end of Chapter XV, after he has been talking about other things, and remarks that the good dramatist, like the good portrait-painter, can render a man better than he is in life, without losing the likeness—"as Agathon"—an admired tragedian—"and Homer have rendered Achilles".

But his main concern is with appropriateness and the type.

"No art", so he declares in the *Rhetoric*, "has the particular in view"[1]; and this is a principle of illumination not merely for the *Poetics*, but for a persisting aesthetic attitude which is never effectively challenged in the West until Blake voices his crucial Romantic premonition: "To generalise is to be an idiot."[2] Aristotle had maintained against Plato that poetry is "more philosophic" than history; it tells us "what kinds of thing a man of a certain type will say or do"[3]; it offers the general.

In arguing thus, Aristotle redirects attention to the two opposed accounts of *mimēsis*. The painter in Book X of Plato's *Republic* aimed at a faithful presentation of the object in front of him, as if he hoped to deceive onlookers in the way Zeuxis deceived the birds with his painted grapes; while Aristotle's painter attempts to extract and render back the object's form. The Aristotelian ambition is to realise the type, which is not the dull, non-existent average—not the hypothetical fruit of Blake's very different and derided generalising—but reality. If one who is neither Platonist nor Aristotelian—if a modern man were standing with Aristotle in front of Van Gogh's rush-bottom chair, the first would apprehend, in and through the painting, a chair, this and no other, whose triumphant phenomenal identity (you could have seen this chair in this room at Arles) is affirmed time-defeatingly by art; while the second would experience all particular circumstance fall away and perish in the serene, intelligible form.

And so with the stage-figure. He also is the realised type. Type-definition pursues him beyond his bare humanity, of course, into the facts of his life; he is a king or slave or woman, as well as a human being—which Aristotle acknowledges by telling dramatists to make their stage-figures appropriate. Thus the dramatist who wishes to portray courage or cleverness must remember that it is not appropriate in a woman to be brave or clever.[4] Moreover, we observe the requirement of appropriateness intertwined with that of goodness in Aristotle's demand

---

[1] I, 2, 11.

[2] Annotation to Reynolds: *The Writings of William Blake*, ed. Geoffrey Keynes, vol. III, p. 13.

[3] *Poetics*, Chapter IX.

[4] 54a22-4. There are some textual difficulties here. I prefer Bywater's version to Rostagni's.

that the stage-figure, as well as being kept distinct in his type, shall be good of that type:

> Goodness may be found in each human type: there is such a thing as a good woman and such a thing as a good slave, although no doubt one of these types is inferior and the other wholly worthless.[1]

The stage-woman should possess the womanly virtues and the stage-slave the slavish virtue; the former should not be brave like a man nor the latter generous-tempered like a king, for this would produce an ultimate aesthetic anarchy. Respect for type-definition reaches beyond the apparent vulgar concern with predictability in "what kinds of thing a man of a certain type will say or do", towards the form which can be known and represented, and towards the philosophical authority, for Aristotle, of the poetic statement.

The resulting presentation of the human self is unsatisfactory, we should say, because rigidly hierarchical and insensitive. Our interest is awakened precisely when type-definition fails, when Eros is proved in his suicide "thrice nobler" than Antony. Where Aristotle typifies, the human and social articulation of type being made in the language of status, we ask for psychological individuation. We often go further and assume that there is only one way of effecting an interesting differentiation among the stage-figures—the way followed by Shakespeare (according to the Romantic critical tradition) when he made Hamlet charge the pronoun with his own singular nature in the words:

> *The time is out of joint. O cursed spite,*
> *That ever I was born to set it right!*

While Hamlet is extraordinary, his situation is commonplace in that many men—men of unremarkable capacities—could have handled it efficiently. Contrast the Aeschylean Orestes, whose situation is anything but commonplace. The ancient rules relating to crimes of blood within the family single him out, the son of his murdered father, to perform the act of vengeance. Nor does he stand alone primarily through his admission of a duty, but through the objective social fact that

[1] 54a19-21.

the vengeance-killing of Clytemnestra is only capable of commission at his hand; if somebody else steps forward and kills her, it is as if she fell ill and died: in that case Agamemnon is not avenged, and Orestes has failed in his religio-dramatic enterprise. And so Orestes has a task which only he can perform, while Hamlet has a task which almost anyone but him can perform. The one is isolated by his status-determined circumstances, the other by his *psyche*-determined incapacity to act. There is no saying which of these dramatic solitudes is the more extreme, or eloquent.

Aristotle's statement that Tragedy is not an imitation of human beings is balanced (and also made intelligible to us) by his confidence in the ability of tragic action, his *praxis*, to sustain all relevant human interest. He feels this confidence because he apprehends the actuality of the thing as outward and discrete and centrifugal, a continuous dying into the full life of self through the self's dissipation in action. And now, when he comes to discuss the presentation of the stage-figure, the same outward thrust is apparent in his carving of identity situationally, through status and the type: his exposition is all of a piece.

In dramatic and histrionic fact, Aristotle's stage-figure is the mask. He lays no stress on the mask in the *Poetics* because he assumes that any mature drama is bound to be masked; like the open-air theatre and the sacred character of Attic Tragedy, the mask is accepted, very much taken into account, but not discussed; for Aristotle it is simply there, a permanent feature of his dramatic universe. It is, then, a feature which we have to supply for ourselves. And in a sense we do. Great caution is needed, because nearly all the literary information about this perishable linen object is late, and the evidence of archaeology is often ambiguous: the masked figures of a vase or wall painting may or may not be actors in a play. But something can be said, and has been said. Moreover, the accounts, learned and popular, of the Greek tragic mask have most of them an important point in common, which is their emphasis on the practical advantages conferred by the mask under ancient stage conditions: the easy doubling of parts with a tiny cast; the taking of women's parts by men; the recognisability of a larger-than-life face from the back of a huge open-air theatre;

the amplification of the actor's voice through a megaphone built into the mask.

And these are genuine advantages. But they are also secondary in that they do not expose the *raison d'être* of masking; no theatre, no society, assumes the masking convention because it is seen to be convenient. To the question, why mask? social anthropology does not return a single answer: the mask worn by each in succession of the Benin kings is the visible presence of kingship; the mask very commonly associated with the cult of the dead[1] is the epiphany of the departed ancestor, and its weird hooting in the night is called the voice of the dead (the root function of the so-called megaphone in the Greek dramatic mask is surely to change the voice, not to amplify it); masking flourishes in totemistic societies—the mask, like the wooden body of the totem, shows forth the psycho-physical and institutional solidarity of the descent group—and as a means whereby intricate kinship relations may be articulated: North American shutter-masks, an inner mask being revealed when the shutter opens, are addressed to the fact of selfhood's simultaneous multiplicity. Masks state different truths for different people. There is no need to generalise about these truths, but simply to urge that the Greek tragic mask be taken seriously.

In the context of the *Poetics*, this means accepting the mask as integral to the stage-presentation of human beings envisaged there, in fact as more than a useful adjunct to the actor. *Prosōpon*, the Greek word for mask, also means face, aspect, person and stage-figure (*persona*); we should allow mask and face to draw semantically close together, and then we should enrich the face far beyond our own conception, until it is able to embrace (as it did for Greeks from the time of Homer) the look of the man together with the truth about him. The face is the total aspect; it presents the human individual, the person. Therefore to say that the mask is a kind of face is to take it very seriously indeed—and it is also to utter the platitude that the people of Tragedy are the people of life, as art perceives and renders them. The ancient actor wore this object upon which

---

[1] Sir William Ridgeway made almost no use of the mask in his worldwide search for material to support his theory that Tragedy originated in the worship of the dead. This neglect is typical of the learned tradition as a whole.

the audience could read a few simple, conventional signs determining rank and age and sex; the artifact surpassed nature in
its lucid isolation of essentials, which was as the Greek aesthetic
instinct demanded. But mask and face were at one in their
sufficiency; unlike the modern face and the modern mask, they
did not owe their interest to the further realities lying behind
them, because they declared the whole man. They stated; they
did not hint or hide. Aristotle's account of this statement
acquires its concrete point of reference when we direct his
outward self and its status-defined individuality towards the
painted surface of the mask—towards the nexus of clearly
ordered type-distinctions, and towards the face of Tragedy
which has and needs nothing behind itself.

Although he does not consider the mask, Aristotle gives an
oblique indication of its significance through the respect paid
to action in the *Poetics*. The work of art which begins with the
dramatist contemplating an ideal *praxis* ends with the actors
executing the prescribed stage-event. Acting is always acting
for Aristotle—acting through what had to be done in the play.
The task of the actors is to support the action by forming props
on which it can be spread out for the audience to contemplate.
Further, this modest office does not call for any suppression of
histrionic potential; on the contrary, it taxes the actor to his
limit because at the living heart of the tradition the actor is the
mask and the mask is an artifact-face with nothing to offer but
itself. It has—more important, it is known to have—no inside.
Its being is exhausted in its features. To think of the mask as an
appendage to the human actor is to destroy the basis of the
ancient masking convention by inviting the audience to peer
behind the mask and demand of the actor that he shall cease
merely to support the action, and shall begin instead to exploit
the action in the service of inwardness. The mask, as a casual
survey of masking cultures makes plain, can present all manner
of versions of the human self; it is almost inexhaustibly rich in
its presentational modes. But it is vulnerable at one point. It
cannot maintain itself against the thought that all presentational modes are inadequate to the truth. The situation in which
Duncan reflects:

> There's no art
> Can find the mind's construction in the face

destroys it, for the mind's construction must be found there if it is to be found at all. And when it cannot be found there, masking becomes pointless.

The central argument of the *Poetics*, that Tragedy is an imitation not of human beings but of action and life, receives here its histrionic complement. The distinction between the composing dramatist who imitates human beings and one who imitates an action rich in human interest is paralleled by a second distinction between the actor who impersonates his mythico-historical original and the actor-mask who appropriates to that original his share of the play's action. The actor-mask ·is tethered to his original lightly, to ensure recognition, while his masking energies drive him on through the stage-event. The distinction again seems flimsy, since I cannot mimic the actions of Oedipus without pretending to be Oedipus: and again the distinction is important.

4 Conspectus

Applying Aristotle's *Poetics* to the surviving Greek tragedies, or simply making satisfactory general sense of it, has involved commentators in a double process of rejection and re-writing. The interpolation of the tragic hero is the first step towards re-writing Aristotle's treatise, and a decisive one in that the most elementary loyalty to his principles is surrendered as soon as the hero appears and attracts to himself, as he automatically does, the idea of tragic error. Immediately, Aristotle's imitation of an action becomes the story of a hero's downfall, brought about by his *hamartia*. We have already noted that the promising inwardness of *hamartia*—a familiar world of temptation, self-division, the exposed pathos of struggling conscience—is proved impossible to sustain. It remains to add that the downfall has been imposed on Aristotle, as well as the hero and his moral shortcoming. And this is not merely because the personal implications of downfall are alien to him; it would still be false to assert that the *Poetics* expects or demands a downward movement of the action, that any link is established between tragic climax and disaster.

Aristotle's address to the question of happy and unhappy

resolution—a vital question for those who are thinking about
a hero's destiny—is utterly casual, and also self-contradictory.
Once he says unhappy resolutions are preferable, once he says
the opposite[1]; he does not pause over the problem, or show
himself at all concerned. And the obvious explanation is the
correct one—that the problem is unimportant. The Renaissance
distinction between Tragedy and Tragi-Comedy, which comes
to turn precisely upon the suffering or the aversion of a climactic disaster, is insignificant to him. Mutability is Aristotle's
tragic focus, not misfortune. Discussing the best length for a
plot (that is, for a realised action), he hits upon a "general
formula" which is a length that will allow "a change to take
place from bad fortune to good, or from good to bad"[2]; the
alternative of upward or downward movement is ultimately
open, what matters is that the action shall have room to display
life's bottomless instability. Only when we pin this "change" to
a single sufferer (Bywater translates: "a length which allows of
the hero passing . . . from misfortune to happiness, or from
happiness to misfortune") does Aristotle appear perplexingly
and rather brutally indifferent to the human issue.

[1] 53a9; 54a4. Of course there have been attempts to reconcile the two
statements, and of these Vahlen's is the least unimpressive. But Bywater is
right frankly to admit contradiction. I believe the second text (which prefers
an averted disaster) to represent Aristotle's settled and general opinion: it
accords with his distaste for all that is grossly spectacular in plotting and in
the staging of plays. The first text comes at a point where practical and
contemporary interest—how to write tragedies in the late fourth century—
is exceptionally marked. Aristotle has just asked the question: "What should
the poet aim at, and what should he avoid, in constructing his plots?"
(52b28). A context of contemporary play-writing is further impressed by the
observation that "in recent times the finest tragedies have dealt with the
history of a few noble houses" (53a18), and, in a more interesting though
less obvious way, by Aristotle's defence of Euripides against the critics who
censure him for making many of his plays end unhappily (53a23-6); for
while Aristotle's broad view of Euripides was hostile, he had the historical
sense to recognise that his dramaturgy was the fountainhead of later
practice.

These are not trivial considerations since the stage-figure's *hamartia* (which
appears nowhere else in the *Poetics*) is closely involved with the unhappy
ending, so that if Aristotle's argument for an unhappy ending (contradicted
in his next chapter) is uncharacteristically *ad hoc*, modern promoting of
hamartia becomes yet harder to justify.

[2] 51a11-15.

We are at grips, as we have been throughout, with the resonance which action had for Aristotle, which dominated his
thinking about Tragedy, and which is almost lost to modern
critical sympathies. The degrading of action in order to make
it reflect the light of a fond aesthetic concentration upon the
actor is an instinct we find difficult to oppose; for even when
the hero is expelled, there is still the human subject of Aristotle's
"change of fortune", the one whom the story is *about*. And our
transvaluations gain superficial plausibility from the fact that
Aristotle is quite aware, and takes the trouble to acknowledge,
that an action does not act itself either on the stage or in the
mind's eye: "Tragedy is an imitation of an action, and involves
certain stage-figures who perform the action . . ."[1]—indeed this
is why the presentation of the stage-figures satisfies the strict
criterion of relevance applied in the *Poetics*, why it is among the
subjects discussed there.

Thus it does not make nonsense to interpret *hamartia* as a
hero's fatal blunder, except within the *Poetics* where there is no
hero but instead an action with its surface painted in ethical
and intellectual colours. Likewise *peripeteia* (Reversal—"the
shift of the action towards the opposite pole"[2]) can be related,
vaguely, to a drama of frustrated expectation and intention, of
bitter personal ironies; but in Aristotle's hands it is an instrument for the finer analysis of that "change of fortune" in which
the universal fact of mutability is laid bare. He has his reason
for bringing both *hamartia* and *peripeteia* under the heading of
plot-analysis rather than analysis of stage-figures, and his reason
is reflected through each phase of argument in this very remote
but self-consistent work. Nevertheless, both these terms of art
from the *Poetics* will, out of context, submit—they constantly
are submitted—to a psychologising rule; and so, sometimes,
will the details of Aristotle's phrasing. The verb *mellein* is a case
in point. *Mellein* means to be about to do or to intend doing,
and it is worked hard by Aristotle in the interests of mutability
and the pity-and-fear response of the audience: the moment
when a sudden and unexpected circumstance alters a course of
action which had seemed firm and predictable to its end—
when a man is on the point of, is well set on the way towards,
doing something, and at the last minute does not do it—is one

[1] 49b36-7.   [2] 52a22-3. I adopt Professor Else's translation.

of singular tragic reach. Here are two occurrences of *mellein*, the second a double one:

> On his arrival he was seized, and *was on the point of* being slain sacrificially when he revealed who he was . . . and this disclosure led to his deliverance.[1]

> [The best shaping of the action is] that which we find in the *Cresphontes*, for example, where Merope, *on the point of* killing her son, does not kill him but recognises him in time; and in the *Iphigeneia*, where the sister recognises her brother; and in the *Helle* where the son recognises his mother when *on the point of* giving her up to the enemy.[2]

These two passages are exactly parallel; in fact the reference to the *Iphigeneia in Tauris* in the second passage indicates the very situation described in the first. But it so happens that Aristotle's narration shifts from the passive to the active voice, and this gives his translator—Professor Else is the most recent—the chance to offer us "intending to kill" and "intending to betray", and to develop psychological implications in his commentary. While not bluntly wrong (since all these situations arise from a course of action pursued intentionally, in ignorance of some vital fact: state of mind is relevant in that being on the point of contains an intending in ignorance), this shift of emphasis is enough to disturb Aristotle's action-focussed effect. Bywater, again, who justly adheres to "on the point of" in the second passage, elsewhere renders the present participle of *mellein* thus:

> A third possibility [among incidents calculated to arouse pity and fear] is for one *meditating* some deadly injury to another, in ignorance of his relationship, to make the discovery in time to draw back.[3]

And with that insidious "meditating" he conveys a falsely primary impression of concealed and very "dramatic" brooding. Bywater inclines the text towards, say, *Macbeth* because the action's elements—the steps leading up to the infliction of the "deadly injury": the visit to the chemist, the purchase of the arsenic, the poisoning of the coffee—lack aesthetic dignity in his sight, they are nothing without psychological fulfilment (whereas for Aristotle they are the essential monochrome surface of the action which will be the richer when it receives a two-

---

[1] 55b9-12. [2] 54a4-8. [3] 53b34-6.

D

dimensional differentiation through ethical and intellectual colouring). Perhaps these slight deflections of Aristotle's meaning are more effective, cumulatively, than the gross imposition of the hero.

I said that the *Poetics* has been rejected as well as re-written. It is widely felt, and sometimes stated, that Aristotle's theory of Tragedy cannot be fitted at all comfortably to the surviving fifth-century plays; and this discrepancy is usually explained in one of two ways: by stressing the time gap between the end of the classical drama and the writing of the *Poetics*, or by alleging that Aristotle was personally ill-qualified to be a literary critic and theorist.

The first argument would be more respectable if our ignorance of the great body of tragic literature were less extreme, and if we could point to opposing testimony. Aristotle is not a perfect witness, but he is very much the best we have.[1] The *Poetics* belongs as a whole to his last period at Athens, but most scholars believe he was working on it very much earlier, perhaps in mid-century. His older contemporaries will have been grown men when Sophocles and Euripides were writing and producing, and what was no longer alive in the fifth-century tradition must often have been recoverable, by asking questions and by reading plays—he may have read many hundreds[2]—which subsequently perished, and by going to revivals. By the standards we are forced to apply, Aristotle was well placed.

The question of personal qualifications is harder to decide. But one popular misconception is soon disposed of: that Aristotle was a "pure" philosopher who strayed momentarily outside his province when he wrote the *Poetics*. The extant titles of his lost literary works, when these are added to the *Poetics*, the *Rhetoric* and the fragmentary dialogue *Concerning the Poets*, show that his interest in poetry and poets—particularly in Homer— was anything but occasional. Which is not to invite us to forget

---

[1] Aristophanes is also an important witness, but the value of what he has to say about Tragedy is hard to assess since the conventions of Old Comedy permitted, and Aristophanes certainly indulged, a large measure of fantasy in discussing serious subjects. In any case I believe, and shall argue, that Aristophanes and Aristotle agree with each other.

[2] Dramatic texts were in wide circulation during the fourth century.

that the *Poetics* was written by a philosopher—by this philosopher: but rather to make obvious the need for discrimination. A certain doubleness has already shown itself within the concept of action: Aristotle's deployment of *praxis* is for the most part elliptical and esoteric, almost to fit the modern theory that our text of the *Poetics* is a set of notes intended primarily or solely for his own use; and yet he is perfectly capable of rendering the subtle heart of his thesis in a single broad statement:

> [The tragic poet] should first simplify and reduce his story to a universal form (whether that story be taken from the existing stock or of his own making), before proceeding to lengthen it out by the insertion of episodes.[1]

Aristotle's general reader, even if he was aware that here too, in the idea of reduction to a universal form (*ektithesthai katholou*), the discussion's ampler context is logical and metaphysical, will not have been troubled. He will have sensed a double appeal to the ideals of clarity and economy, and, being a Greek, he will have responded. While Aristotle's philosophical commitments sometimes isolate him (how many fellow Athenians will have agreed that the full tragic effect can be achieved without performance?), they do not importantly corrupt his sensibility; the ways in which the *Poetics* is a philosopher's book are by no means all hostile to art.

Another term heavy with philosophy is *mimēsis*, which shares with *praxis* a second kind of life in the *Poetics*, much broader than the first and quite untechnical:

> It seems clear that the general origin of poetry was due to two causes, both of them lying within ourselves. Imitation comes natural to man from his childhood; he is distinguished from the lower animals by the degree to which he is imitative and by his way of learning his first lessons about the world through imitation. It is also natural for all human beings to take delight in works of imitation. . . . The reason for this is that to be learning something is the greatest of pleasures not only to philosophers but to the rest of mankind, however small their capacity for it.[2]

Commentators are right to note that the conflict between Plato and Aristotle comes almost into the open in this passage: Plato had little confidence or even belief in the intellectuality of

---

[1] 55a34-b2.　　　　[2] 48b4-14.

ordinary men, and he despised art for its intellectual poverty. But they are wrong to leave it at that, with Aristotle's counter-attack, because it is much less interesting to record that he is answering Plato than that he is re-affirming a very ancient Greek attitude when he speaks of representing objects on the part of the artist, and of recognising these representations (and receiving instruction and pleasure through doing so) on the part of the artist's public. Apologies for the intellectualism of the *Poetics* are misleading as well as unnecessary. The Greeks knew no such subject as aesthetics; their art was knitted so closely into their religious and intellectual life that they felt very little significant separateness about it. With poetry this consideration is specially relevant since literary prose does not appear on the Greek mainland until early in the fifth century, at a time when Attic Tragedy reaches its first maturity with Aeschylus. Until then poetry had been the universal literary medium, associated with history, science and philosophy no less than with the kinds, like epic and lyric, which we should call poetic. Nor, within their literature, did they distinguish at all clearly between poetic and non-poetic functions and effects. Homer's authority as the educator of Hellas was utterly general: in a sixth-century political dispute over title to the island of Salamis, the Athenians based their claim on a verse of the Iliad which they interpreted as proving that Salamis had formerly belonged to them. Xenophanes, an early philosophical opponent of the anthropomorphic and immoral gods of Epic, acknowledged that "all have learnt from Homer since the beginning".[1]

Then Aristotle is reasserting a traditional and even a primitive view when he founds art on education—I say reasserting because Plato's attack falls between Aristotle and these ancient convictions. Plato is here the revolutionary, directing his polemic against the immemorial paedeutic role of poetry; whereas Aristotle, in the *Poetics*, expounds and defends a refined traditionalism. Only a sophisticated fourth-century student will have understood Aristotle's version of *mimēsis* as a rebuke to the superficialities of Book X of the *Republic*, but his simplest reader or listener cannot have failed to see that he was maintaining an old and familiar view of art when he spoke of learning through works of imitation.

[1] Diels-Kranz, fr. B 10.

The lessons which art teaches us are about types, not about individuals; Aristotle's statement in the *Rhetoric*, that art does not concern itself with the particular, has the complete metaphysical imponderability of the individual behind it: the individual is unknowable. Once again an important principle is stated simply, as if (which may be the truth) Aristotle was aware of the plain man in his audience:

> The reason why people enjoy seeing pictures is that they find themselves learning as they look, inferring what class each object belongs to: for example, that this individual is a so-and-so.[1]

And the recognisability of the object ("That picture is of a horse") is as fundamental to the artist's labour as it is to his public's response to the end-product:

> As regards criticisms that relate to the poet's art itself . . . we may pertinently ask whether any error in his representation of objects is in a matter necessarily or only accidentally connected with the art of poetry; for it is a lesser error not to know that a hind has no horns than to draw an unrecognisable picture of one.[2]

This *reductio* to the recognisable type, grotesque enough after the centuries have isolated and pondered the aesthetic experience for us, is meant to have a skeletal bareness about it in Aristotle's exposition, but it is not methodologically immature, not a provisional sketch of art's working which will be discarded when he comes to advise would-be dramatists how to write readable and actable tragedies. If we think of the pleasurable recognising of horses and hinds as a response to be grown out of, we shall end by missing the seriousness and sufficiency of type-definition in Aristotle's remarks about the presentation of the stage-figure. We may even commend, patronisingly, an injunction such as "Make your princes princely" on the ground that it shows Aristotle groping after the authentic personal fineness of Prince Hamlet or Prince Andrew. Mr Eliot's observation, *à propos* of Ben Jonson, of the difference between art that is of the surface and art that is superficial, deserves application

---

[1] 48b14-16. I accept Professor Else's emendation at b16 (b17 in his text): ἐκεῖνο for ἐκεῖνος. Of course my main argument is independent of this conjecture.

[2] 60b22-31.

to the *Poetics* as a whole, and far beyond. For Aristotle's stage-figure projects, we must assume, his "real" human being; and his action- and type-dominated psychology and morals—through these his apprehension of the "real" human being is refracted—disclose further reaches of the refined traditionalism which sets him over against Plato.

There is no need to go as far as Professor Jaeger does towards making Aristotle the conscious expounder of Homeric values[1] in order to establish the necessary general point about the *Poetics*. It suffices to place him, and with him the Greek mind through centuries, against the quietist and inward trend of Plato's writing. If we take our stand for a moment upon the tragic retribution that operates against the man whose trespass was both divinely foredoomed and committed in ignorance, as was Oedipus's, the challenge of enlightenment is to be felt far less in Aristotle's thinking than in the individual moral auto-nomy that may be spelt out of Socrates's (or Plato's) insistence on the rationality of ethics, and out of the voice of conscience—it is almost that—audible to him and to him alone through the medium of his famous *daimonion*. The Socratic vision is pro-foundly untraditional, and he died for it. Moreover it gives rise, in the Platonic *œuvre*, to questioning about personal destiny, about the immortality of the individual, which the Christian or simply the modern reader is likely to understress, since this is one of the great, and obvious, themes of the world for him, and he supposes it always has been—for everybody. But the Greeks present us with a most brilliant awareness of personal identity which by and large they did not pursue beyond the grave[2]; they just felt, and said, that death awaits life at the last. Their literature everywhere reflects this gesture of final self-surrender, so appealingly blithe and so strange. Therefore I find something a little perverse in the surprise with which some professional Aristotelians admit the difficulty or impossibility of attributing to him any doctrine of individual survival, however modest, or even of producing evidence to suggest that he was much inter-

---

[1] See especially Chapter I of his *Paideia*.

[2] The mystery religions and what Professor E. R. Dodds calls Greek Shamanism were busy about personal survival, but we do not know how strong their hold was on ordinary sensible men. In any case it is hard to how tell *personal*, in Greek conceiving, survival was.

ested in the problem. Here at least Aristotle is an ordinary Greek, and the Platonic debate culminating in the separate and immortal soul of the *Phaedo* is extraordinary.[1]

Usually, then, when the *Poetics* is insensitive to our dearest interests, we should blame the Greek rather than the philosopher. His urgencies are not ours, and it is against the broadest possible background of cultural difference that we should interpret his talk of learning through works of imitation; while the human self realised in action and recognised—intelligibly differentiated—through its truth to type is not solitary and inward like our own. Except perhaps in its reclining upon action, the *Poetics* is nowhere so instinctively Greek as in its coupling of the requirements of truth to type (appropriateness) and goodness. The oddly wooden, and apparently self-contradictory, recommendation that the stage-figure shall be at once true to his type and good of that type connects Aristotle with the ancient Mean. Now the Mean has nothing to do with mediocrity; and moderation in behaviour, although enormously important, is only its moral echo; the thing itself betokens an objective concurrence of form and function such as Aristotle demands here for the stage-figure. Goodness in Aristotle's stage-slave does not impel him towards the top of the class of slaves, and so make or threaten to make him untypical; on the contrary, it draws him towards the middle in the sense that the slave-type achieves its fullest articulation in him, the good slave. Excellence is not a threat to class membership but its fulfilment. Thus the paradox of the good yet typical stage-figure resolves itself in Aristotle's perception of an achieved unity of the normal and the ideal within the individual who is worthy to stand for his class. Indeed this is the imprint of the Greek Mean upon the *Poetics*, deeply entrenched in Aristotle's mentality. We should understand the Aristotelian version of the Mean better, and be more inclined to give it the prominence it merits, if the

[1] If the *Symposium* was written after the *Phaedo*, as some believe, Diotima's curiously negative discussion of immortality in that dialogue suggests that Plato was dissatisfied with the conclusions of the *Phaedo*. But our concern is with Plato's restless urgency, not his formulated doctrine. And individualism is not being offered as a master-key to Plato. It is rather, so I believe, a personal prompting which he reckoned a temptation to be resisted. Hence the corporate rigour of his political philosophy, and hence (in part) his hostility to art.

second book of his treatise had not been lost; for Book II, as we can deduce from references in the surviving book and in the *Rhetoric*, examined Comedy in detail; and we also know that Aristotle regarded Comedy as Tragedy's opposite, a departure from the Mean instead of a pursuit of it. He distinguishes Comedy by ruling that its proper study is men "worse than the average"—not worse in every way, but worse as regards "the Ridiculous (*to geloion*), which is a subdivision of the Ugly".[1] And this queer concept of the Ridiculous is illuminated, I believe, by a passage in the *Rhetoric* where Aristotle is discussing the Mean in relation to government. He observes that either excessive straining or excessive slackening of democracy weakens it and leads to oligarchy; and then he offers the following analogy:

> Similarly, not only does an aquiline or snub nose achieve the Mean (*to meson*) when one of these divergencies is mitigated, but when it reaches an extreme of aquilinity or its opposite, it becomes so removed from the Mean that even the likeness of a nose is lost.[2]

Comedy inhabits the world of long noses and big ears—the world of caricature; and Aristotle's complete text probably stated a thoroughgoing opposition of the good and the typical and the beautiful in Tragedy, to the bad and the atypic and the ugly in Comedy.

Of course the entire "human" structure of the *Poetics* would collapse if differentiation founded on status were primarily titular for Aristotle as it is for us, instead of being actual—on the ground and in the bone. This actuality has two important consequences. The first is that the main weight of the tragic action will be carried by stage-figures of high rank. Even in the late fourth century, the objective differences of status—differences in quality of life-stuff—are sufficiently patent and unchallenged for Aristotle to feel no need to make an explicit rule of stage nobility, in the self-conscious manner of later theory; but he does apply a single adjective, *spoudaios*, to the action and to the stage-figure.[3] *Spoudaios* is usually translated "serious" when it qualifies the action, and "good" when it

---

[1] *Poetics*, 49a32-4.   [2] I, 4, 12.
[3] 49b24; 48a2 (see the whole of Chapter II).

qualifies the stage-figure—a bifurcation of meaning which commentary has found embarrassing and yet unavoidable, since appraisal of Aristotelian usage establishes that the elevation of the figures of Tragedy is intended to be moral. But this conclusion only causes difficulty because of our post-Socratic, ethically sophisticated understanding of "good" where Aristotle has in mind a generalised, aristocratic, ancient and practical ideal of human excellence,[1] so broad that the latter-day doubleness of *spoudaios* disappears within it. Considerableness of tragic substance is his theme, and the inner identity of seriousness in the action with heroic worth in the stage-figure who proves true to the noble type is still so obvious that he can leave his reader to recognise it for himself. Aristotle never conceived a civilisation that would value the self's mere and common humanity above its rank, in the language of equality before God or even in the reverence shown by art and speculation, as towards the most solemn of mysteries.

Secondly, and because Tragedy imitates action and life, status is to be found in the texture of Aristotle's *praxis*, forming part of the reality to be imitated. Vertical movement, interplay between high and low, cannot be much in evidence since the inviolable primacy of the noble type virtually excludes it; but we observe Aristotle developing the potentialities of status laterally, within the noble type, by means of the situations which Greek kinship creates. His initial point is that the dramatist seeking to arouse the tragic emotions in his audience is most likely to succeed when the violent and terrible stage-event, enacted or threatened, matures between close kin:

> Whenever the deed of suffering is done within the family: I mean when murder or some similar outrage is committed, or is in prospect, by brother against brother, son against father, mother against son, or son against mother—these are the things one should look for.[2]

And he also introduces kinship into his much more detailed examination of the crucial phase or moment of "change" (*metabolē*) in which the root-fact of mutability is exposed. This he does through the concept of Recognition (*anagnōrisis*):

[1] Professor Else's discussion is admirable: pp. 71-8.
[2] 53b19-21.

A Recognition, as the word itself indicates, is a change from ignorance to knowledge, and thus to a state of nearness and dearness or to a state of enmity, on the part of those who have entered upon the action each with his situation defined in its initial happiness or unhappiness.[1]

The connecting link between these two passages is the term *philia* which I render, hideously, "state of nearness and dearness" in my determination to avoid "love", the word favoured by English translators. The objection to "love" is that it channels the status-determining fact of kinship into the subjective sentiment, thus continuing our remorseless psychologising of Aristotle's argument. As with *mellein*, which we have already considered, state of mind is contained within the situational complex (here, the complex of kinship—nearness and dearness[2]); and, as with *mellein*, Aristotle's precedences are inverted if state of mind is allowed to dominate the whole. Recognition is the concomitant, at the level of awareness in the stage-figure, of the "change" upon which the tragic action pivots—just as Aristotle's Reversal (*peripeteia*) is the concomitant, at the level of awareness in the audience,[3] of this same change. The *Poetics*, coupling Reversal and Recognition, invites the dramatist to attempt a double reflection of his focal change, in the consciousness of overthrown expectations on the part of the audience and in the stage-figure's new awareness of where he stands. These are the means of drawing out and arresting for contemplation the action's single swing, which may be itself no more—and no less—than a sudden knife-flash in the doing.

His regard for kinship shows Aristotle's theory growing out of the deep-set facts, corporate and psycho-physical, of Greek

---

[1] 52a30-2.

[2] Alone (I think) among commentators since Vahlen, Professor Else has grasped the nature of Aristotle's *philia* adequately: "So in our passage φιλίαν is not 'friendship' or 'love' or any other feeling, but *the objective state of being* φίλοι, 'dear ones' by virtue of blood ties. When Oedipus 'recognises' Laius —that is, realises who it was he killed at the cross roads—he changes from ignorance to knowledge, and at the same moment, since Laius was his father, he moves into the status of φιλία . . . his feelings do not count so much as the new *situation* into which he has moved with his shift from ignorance to awareness" (p. 349).

[3] The fearful shock attending Reversal is often attributed to the "hero".

life: this is a further aspect of the underestimated traditionalism of the *Poetics*, and it leads us to wonder how much of his main and positive conviction, that Tragedy imitates an action, was or had been common property. The untechnical and almost casual way he refers to a tragic action's distinctness, its completeness in itself, its quasi-organic inner coherence, argues a broad confidence in being judged to talk sense; he does not speak like a man who fears that ordinary imaginations will find some initial absurdity in his presenting a single, complete, serious action as an aesthetic object. Moreover, it would be strange if so firm a habit of casting the entire dramatic universe into action and acting were merely personal. Enough has been said about action, but a few words are needed to elucidate Aristotle's idea of acting in relation to the term "stage-figure". I have felt driven to this odd usage because Aristotle persistently ignores the distinction between the actor acting his part and the man in the story—between the actor playing Oedipus and Oedipus himself—when he is considering the process of drama. What he does, again and again, is to speak of the "enactors"— *prattontes* or *drōntes*,[1] the doers of what is done. Occasionally these passages incline towards the visual practicalities of stage-production, for example when he says that the physical get-up of the *prattontes* must be taken care of[2]; more often, as in his examination of the moral and intellectual qualities of the *prattontes*,[3] the theatre atmosphere is faint or non-existent: the significance of this single terminology rests in the merging (which I try to preserve in "stage-figure") of actor and what we loosely call character within one race of doers; Aristotelian acting is large enough to enfold them both.

And this is because Aristotle's actor is an actor-mask, and his bond with the man in the story is forged through acting, through repetition, and not through impersonation; what was done by the man in the story is done again by the mask. Or, we may say, the actor-mask is not a portrait, not a likeness; it presents, it does not re-present; it gives us King Oedipus. While all elaboration of the Greek tragic mask is, as scholars like to

---

[1] 48a1, 28, 29; 49b26, 31, 37; 50a6, b3; 60a15.
[2] 49b31. Note too his remark that the *prattontes* of Epic, unlike those of Tragedy, are not visible to one: 60a15.
[3] 50a6.

put it, fanciful, an outline may be traced which the logic and entire economy of the *Poetics* broadly presumes; the mask in which Aristotle's discrete and centrifugal and status-defined self assumes stage-presence is also the force uniting actor and dramatic character, those two kinds of doers.

Ultimately, perhaps, the sacred drama of the Greeks is like much ritual activity of other times and places in that it seeks, through a carefully ordered repetitive mode, to secure favourable conditions for the past's return.[1] There is nothing odd in setting about to recover the essential virtue of a time greater than the present, when men were heroically big and strong and beautiful, and the gods could be seen and touched. Even Christians have believed, and not during the early centuries only, that they were in the Upper Room "again" with their Lord each time they took the bread and wine; and they have been untroubled with questions of then and now and eternity, with the superstructure of sacramental theology, which a linear and inexorably progressive notion of time calls forth. I do not suppose the Greeks, for whom time's movement was cyclical,[2] would have felt their rationality insulted by the suggestion that the Oedipus-mask, in the dim pre-history of their art, was at once the doer again of an aboriginally potent action, and the King himself returned.[3]

[1] See Mircea Eliade, *Le mythe de l'éternel retour*.

[2] They were without the ideas of divine creation and teleological direction of the world. Once again Plato has to be partially excepted from our generalisation; and yet in our eagerness to claim intellectual descent from Plato we have probably missed, in the forms themselves, an unexpected temporal stress touching the departed archetypes of a greater time. Were the forms always outside nature?

The familiarity of the argument that defends historiography on the ground that "these things, or things like them, will happen again" (Thucydides, I. 22), is thoroughly deceptive. Thucydides is not really talking like a modern determinist. Nor ought we to conclude that he believed the same situation would come round again in the next ten- or thirty-thousand year cycle—unless when we say this we also feel in awe of the latent complexities of *the same* and *again*. See G. E. M. Anscombe, "The Reality of the Past" (in *Philosophical Analysis*, ed. M. Black).

[3] I am not (need it be said?) airing my views on the origin of Greek Tragedy. In historical fact the actor emerged from out the Chorus, and the mask may not be a very early development. But such considerations are irrelevant since the Chorus, dancing as they sing and clothed in animal skins, are most intensely actionful—and "masked".

A far cry, the distant object of such brooding, from the mature accomplishment of fifth-century Tragedy—remote and also powerfully linked. When we first encounter this literature it has moved into bright daylight, while language and physical setting and social context are still drenched in religion. Embedded in the plays, and especially in Aeschylus's, are forms of prayer and ritual cries and invocations with a religious significance which the audience must have taken immediately. The actors were sacred officers of the cult of Dionysus; the priest of the cult occupied the seat of honour in the theatre; the god himself watched every play in the person of his statue; an altar to the same god commanded the dancing floor. For an Athenian citizen to undertake the expense of training and equipping a tragic chorus was a memorable act of piety; and performance, after months of preparation, fell within, was dedicate to, a great religious festival. The catalogue is formidable, but still vitally incomplete until its items are ranged round an action of the kind handled over and over again by the older dramatists, their individual licence extending no further than the adjustment of the story's details.[1] Antiphanes, a comic poet of the generation before Aristotle, makes a character in one of his plays complain that the tragedian has an easier job than the comic poet because "the stories are known beforehand to the spectators, even before anyone speaks; so that the poet only has to remind them".[2] Conveyed with comic flourish is the truth that Tragedy tells people what they already know. Antiphanes might have added the fourth-century rider that nowadays fewer citizens knew the old stories and fewer tragedians stuck to them—a pattern of decadence discernible even in the *Poetics*,[3] at odds with its vestigial religious sense and with the other elements compounding Aristotle's subtle traditionalism.

This rapid and lightly documented survey raises some questions discussion of which is postponed. I call Aristotle a tradi-

---

[1] One of the ways in which Euripides offended conservative opinion was by treating the old stories more freely than his predecessors.

[2] T. Kock, *Comicorum Atticorum Fragmenta*, fr. 191.

[3] Aristotle says that the received stories are known "only to a few" (51b26). On his own account he admits invented plots alongside traditional ones, but—as we have seen—without effectively incorporating these into his exposition of Tragedy.

tionalist without naming his untraditional enemies in the drama. (The alignment of forces is implicit within his distinguishing of a tragic imitation of human beings from a tragic imitation of action and life: Euripides's plays will provide the material for a partial reconstruction.) My reading of the *Poetics* advances an action, single and complete in itself and hinged upon a "change", but I do not apply this interpretation to any extant plays. (Sophocles, especially in his *Oedipus the King*, presents Aristotle with his norm and standard of excellence: the commentators have always said so, but they have also assumed, with astonishing blandness, that Aristotle admired Sophocles for the wrong reasons. For us, approaching Sophocles, this last issue will be crucial.) If Aristotle's thesis is what I believe it to be, and if it shows insight into the Sophoclean drama, there are still important parts of Greek Tragedy to which it cannot be very relevant. (The connected trilogy of Aeschylus, three actions joined in one work of art, lies immediately ahead.)

II: AESCHYLUS

1 The Matter of a Date

IN 1951 was published Part XX of *The Oxyrhynchus Papyri*, and in it a fragment[1] which proves that Aeschylus's *Suppliant Women* (the first play of a trilogy of which the rest is lost) was written in the last fifteen years of his life. The proof is indirect in that the fragment records, without giving us the date, that Aeschylus won first prize at the annual dramatic festival with his *Suppliant Women* trilogy, and that on the same occasion Sophocles was second. We knew already that Sophocles won the first prize with his first production, in 468.[2] Therefore the *Suppliant Women* must have been presented after 468.

The late date now established for the *Suppliant Women* has brought surprise and consternation to a learned world which had hitherto felt sure the play was early; for every test applied to it—comparative study of metre,[3] diction, ideas, dramatic structure and technique—strengthened the belief that we had here a record of Aeschylus's immaturity, an interesting prologue to the other six extant and obviously later works. In short there was an agreed view of Aeschylus into which the *Suppliant Women* fitted perfectly. And now the *Suppliant Women* must be moved, which means altering the whole picture. One or two people have (almost inevitably) tried to deflect the sense of the new fragment, and in dismissing these attempts the conclusion of fair-minded scholarship is that nobody would waste his time challenging evidence of this quality were not the date which it supplies very embarrassing.

Not for the first time, a policy of extreme caution is vindicated in the discussion of Greek Tragedy. By a familiar and vicious process, what was never more than conjecture had hardened into certainty, and it was stated for certainty by writer after writer (by no means only in superficial popular

[1] Oxyrhynchus Papyrus 2256 fragment 3.

[2] This date is certainly correct within two or three years—which is all the certainty we need.

[3] E. C. Yorke's metrical observations (*Classical Quarterly*, 1936) were a notable exception, and a few other scholars placed the play in the sixties because of the political reference they thought they saw in it. The modern orthodoxy which the new fragment oversets was itself the result of a gradual hardening of opinion during the Nineteenth Century.

E

surveys; this was also the foundation of specialist debate) that the drama of the early fifth century is represented by a single play, Aeschylus's *Suppliant Women*—a text which provides the means to generalise about a maturing tradition. And so the present is a moment to take stock of modern ignorance; to recall that out of a large school of writers only three are known by complete plays[1]; and of the output of these three only a small fraction—of Aeschylus and Sophocles less than a tenth, of Euripides rather more—now survives. We know almost nothing about the pre-Aeschylean drama, and almost nothing about the huge tragic literature following Euripides; millions of lines have perished while a handful remain.

The restraining influence of these well-known facts should be more strongly felt after the re-dating of the *Suppliant Women*; if, as ought not to be doubted, the play was written after 470, then those tests which collectively indicate a much earlier date were misconceived or misapplied. Technical linguistic problems are involved, of course, which lie beyond our range and my capacities, but these happen to be less important than the broad tractable question of structure. Most compelling of the reasons for assigning an early date to the *Suppliant Women* was the prominence of its Chorus. The Chorus is prominent in the size of the part given to it and—what is more significant—in its degree of involvement, in the directness and immediacy of its participation, in the action. (The *Suppliant Women* concerns the flight of the fifty maiden daughters of Danaus, who form the play's Chorus, from the fifty sons of Aegyptus, brother of Danaus, who want to force marriage upon them: the Chorus have just landed at Argos when the play opens; they come as suppliants, seeking sanctuary; after long hesitation they are granted asylum and the suitors are repulsed.) This points to an early date because the trend of extant Greek Tragedy is towards increasing confinement of the Chorus to lyric commentary on the events of the play, and so towards increasing withdrawal from the action. The Chorus becomes less of an actor and more of a poetically articulate spectator.

Nobody doubts that the Greek tragic Chorus did in fact, if very roughly, follow the course just described. Moreover, the

---

[1] Unless Euripides did not write the *Rhesus*. In that case we have one tragedy by an unknown fourth writer.

change from actor to spectator is itself part of a larger general tendency which is also evidenced sufficiently. In its remote beginnings Greek Tragedy was a song and dance performed by a Chorus, nothing more; and at its later and decadent stages, after the death of Euripides, the choral song and dance had sunk to the status of interludes marking divisions in the action of the play and having, as Aristotle tells us, "as much to do with the plot of any other tragedy as the one they happen to occur in".[1] We are therefore able to fit the surviving fifth-century plays into a development reaching over a long period, and to see in the work of Aeschylus (who was unquestionably a great pioneer in matters of dramatic form) the part played by a single writer in this change.

Thus a late date for the *Suppliant Women* appears to raise very serious difficulties extending beyond Aeschylean criticism to the understanding of all Greek Tragedy. I say "appears" because I believe we have introduced the principal difficulty ourselves, through the concept of drama which we bring with us to the study of this literature; when we sketch the progress of ancient Tragedy—no more than a sketch is possible, so fragmentary is the record—we interpret its evolution in accordance with a dramatic ideal which the Greeks never held. Their Tragedy began, we have seen, with a choral song and dance. Later, but still at a very early stage, a rudimentary dialogue developed between the leader of the Chorus and his fellows. Later again an actor appeared who stood over against the Chorus and engaged in a more extended dialogue with them and their leader. A second actor was introduced early in the fifth century, by Aeschylus; and finally Sophocles introduced a third actor.[2]

---

[1] *Poetics*, 56a28-9. In the same passage Aristotle's traditionalist instinct leads him to state the principle of Chorus as actor, with a hostile glance at Euripides: "The Chorus should be regarded as one of the actors; it should be an integral part of the whole and take a share in the action: I mean the share it has in Sophocles, not in Euripides."

[2] We also possess a few skimpy accounts of ancient stage engineering. Something is known about the crane (*mēchanē*) which was used for bringing on and removing people—usually divinities—through the air, and about the small moveable stage (*ekkuklēma*: perhaps a platform on wheels) which could produce an effect of close-up and exposure by being pulled forward bearing on it a corpse or tableau of corpses, and then drawn back again. (Disposing of dead bodies is a problem for every curtainless theatre; Greek deaths usually happened off-stage.) Aristotle records (*Poetics*, 49a18) that

Surveying this process, and conscious that Greek Tragedy reached full maturity with Aeschylus and Sophocles, we think— and expound and argue with each other—in the shadow of a parochial aesthetic logic of dramatic intensification. The books interpret the innovations just mentioned, and particularly the advent, one after the other, of the three actors, as a movement towards true drama and away from something else; indeed the terms "pre-dramatic" and "choral" are constantly used of early Tragedy without qualification or the producing of evidence that the Greeks thought remotely as we do. An unstated rhetorical question suffices: how can a genuinely dramatic literature emerge, and the subtleties of human interaction be rendered, unless there is individuation of the kind that the introduction of single tragic actors makes possible?

Aristotle's *Poetics* is one reason, but not the only one, for calling this attitude blindly unintelligent. His observing that drama may be so called because in a play the stage-figures act the story[1] makes contact with what had been central to the art of Tragedy from the beginning; in the primitive Goat-Song (*tragōdia*), when the choral group dressed themselves in goat-skins and danced the events of some story telling, probably, of the god Dionysus,[2] their performance was for the Greek sensibility quintessentially dramatic. The mimetic dance cohered with the singing, in a corporate and highly stylised presentation of the sacred fact; we should imagine the goat-skins, whether or not the Chorus were priestly servants of Dionysus, as a sacral envelope which fulfilled the double office of asserting the performance's religious character (since the goat was a sacred animal of defined ritual association) and drowning all extra-dramatic significances in the group life of tragic dance and song.

Now the imported modern gulf between drama and pre-drama

Sophocles, as well as adding the third actor, was the first dramatist to use painted scenery. He probably means that Sophocles painted the façade (*skēnē*) which stood behind the actors; it is unlikely that Sophocles introduced sets of painted scenery. Other ancient authorities attribute painting of the *skēnē* to Aeschylus.

[1]. *Poetics*, 48a28. He is connecting *drama* with *dran*, to do.

[2] The favoured view is that Tragedy began as an offshoot of Dionysiac ritual; but my argument here, as throughout, is independent of the over-debated question of tragic origins.

is the main obstacle to acceptance of a late date for the *Suppliant Women*; that Aeschylus, late in his career, should write a play that was less of a play—less in the focal dramatic sense—than anything written earlier of which we have record, is scarcely credible. But the situation alters when it is recognised that we have no reason to assume that the *Suppliant Women* was less of a play for Aeschylus and his audience. Of course he and they must have thought it old-fashioned—and chiefly because of the prominent Chorus; but our difficulties abate as soon as the unwarranted logic of dramatic intensification is discarded. It is quite credible (although it reveals a surprising experimental flexibility) that Aeschylus should have turned his back on all manner of fifth-century developments, provided he did not regard these as vital in determining the character of the art he was practising. I am suggesting that there has been a crude and radical misapprehension of values in modern commentary, of the kind that an historian of Western music would be perpetrating if he persuaded himself that Brahms's orchestration was inherently more symphonic than Mozart's.

To offer a provisional dichotomy, Aeschylus is a literary but not a dramatic revert in the *Suppliant Women*. The Greek drama was always, and particularly before Euripides, far less of a literary art than modern comparisons indicate: it blended opera and ballet with a more narrowly literary-dramatic effect; the tragedian composed the music for his choral songs,[1] he had technical knowledge of the dance movements to be executed by his Chorus[2] and may well have helped to train them in their steps; he rehearsed the actors and normally acted in his own plays. Of this extraordinarily syncretic form, a text, sometimes very corrupt, is all that survives, and our approach to it is almost bound to be over-literary. Thus when the *Suppliant Women* is under consideration, the bare text isolates and emphasises the strand of singularity in Aeschylus's conscious archaism of workmanship, but give no more than a hint of the powerful continuities, musical and choreographic, which will have placed the work, for its first audience, intelligibly within

[1] It was held against Euripides that he sometimes delegated musical composition to others.

[2] Aeschylus was renowned in antiquity for his interest in choreography, and we hear of Sophocles as a boy dancer.

the living tradition, and may also have impressed them—-this
would be a precise inversion of the modern response—as tragic
drama at its purest and most economical; their eye following
the line of mimetic presentation, unusually clear, continuous
and simple in this play, traversing the Chorus's fear, hope,
supplication, despair and final pious joy.

One lesson to be learnt, or re-learnt, from the new papyrus
is the abiding dramatic centrality of the Aeschylean Chorus.
A second, less obvious but still intimate with the first, is the
critical folly of undervaluing Aeschylus's attachment to the
connected trilogy. Each of the competing dramatists at the
annual City Dionysia presented three tragedies before a very
large audience of Athenian citizens and others.[1] These three
plays might have no thematic connection with each other, or
they might be bound together into one trilogy by the single
story running through them; and general accounts of the subject often mislead non-specialists by suggesting that triads of
connected and independent tragedies were more or less equally
common. The likelihood is that all three principal dramatists
wrote trilogies, but whereas we hear of one by Sophocles and
perhaps two by Euripides,[2] Aeschylus wrote at least ten. The
record of antiquity invites our conclusion that Aeschylus
cultivated the trilogy far more assiduously than any other writer,
and even that this form was almost a preserve of his: that may
help to explain why Aristotle does not feel the need to reconcile
his "single action complete in itself" with the trilogy—it is an
Aeschylean phenomenon.

A Greek tragedy is seldom much longer than fifteen hundred
lines; the three tragedies entered by a competitor were performed in a single morning during the festival, and Aeschylus's
one surviving trilogy, the *Oresteia*, ought certainly to be seen
and read as a three-act play. In that work a connection between
the dominant Chorus and trilogy form is evident almost at once,
for the opening choral song, the longest and surely the most
splendid in all extant tragedy (which reminds us that we have
no other trilogy with which to compare the *Oresteia*), has a

[1] The winner was determined by a panel of ten citizen judges.

[2] The connection between the component tragedies of a Euripidean
trilogy was probably very loose, and the evidence for trilogy-composition
by Sophocles is not conclusive.

refrain, "Cry 'Sorrow, sorrow!'—but may the good prevail!"
wherein a duologue of human hope with the known moral and
religious nature of the world is lyrically floated, and a specific
tragic atmosphere affirmed. That "May the good prevail!" is
echoed and re-echoed, in direct and oblique statement, ironic-
ally, pathetically, devoutly, blasphemously, and even hope-
lessly; and when, at the end of the third play, the Chorus of
Furies veer round from their threat of curse and bless Athens,
Aeschylus's command of tonal relationships perfects the recovered beginning of the trilogy through our awareness that
the good has in sacred and public fact prevailed.

Thus his direction of choral forces, slow and massive, betrays
one at the outset into the language of atmosphere and tone,
and into musical analogy: when Athena "argues" with the
Furies and "persuades" them to abandon their malign resolve
against her city, the exchange between them—through a
hundred lines there is no meeting of minds[1]; the Furies aim
against Athens two long outbursts of rage and shame, both of
which are word for word repeated—sends the fumbling critical
intelligence to the slow movement of Beethoven's G major piano
concerto rather than to anything in literary drama. And such
impressionism is perhaps harmless so long as it attempts only
the immediate truth that Aeschylus needed the time and space
which trilogy form gave him. This is our introduction to the
unique importance of the *Oresteia*, an entity, not three plays out
of seven surviving; and also to the lack of autonomy which
makes the remnant outside the *Oresteia* peculiarly scattered and
undependable. The *Seven against Thebes* ends with a sudden
division of the Chorus: one half go with Antigone who has this
moment resolved to bury her brother Polyneices, an act forbidden by the City's government; while the other half follow
the corpse of Eteocles who has been granted burial. This reads
perfunctory and rather strange. But the *Seven against Thebes* is
the last play in a trilogy of which the rest is lost, and this renders
us critically blind. Similarly with the religious postures of
the *Prometheus Bound* which are sometimes so Sophistic that
Aeschylus's authorship has been denied[2]: the thesis cries out

---

[1] *Eumenides*, ll. 778-880.
[2] Then so has his authorship of the end of the *Seven against Thebes*—but
for other reasons.

for its antithesis, we have only the trilogy's first part. Of those engaged in the controversy over the *Suppliant Women*, not many are made cautious by the thought that we have no idea what the rest of the trilogy was like. This only leaves the *Persians*, an independent tragedy with a self-sufficiency found nowhere in Aeschylus outside the *Oresteia*. The *Persians* is the one play in the entire extant literature—not just in Aeschylus—which is genuinely and fully founded upon *hubris*, and the story of the failure of the Persian expedition against Greece is at one with the work of art's morality—at one in prophecy[1] and in the deed itself[2] and in the quality of the poet's single insights. When the survivors of the Persian defeat are straggling northward they find their way home through Thrace barred by the newly frozen river Strymon, and Aeschylus tells that "many a man who had held the gods in no esteem until that moment"[3] now fell down on his knees and said his prayers before venturing on the ice. The effect is complete adequacy, without the portentous, teasing superfluities of the other plays. This makes the *Persians* in some respects our most precious Aeschylean relic, of course after the *Oresteia*.

2 Agamemnon's Murder

Aeschylus presented his *Oresteia* at the festival of 458, two years before he died. This date is certain and has always satisfied orthodox views about Aeschylus's mature dramaturgy: a third actor is needed, which shows him late in life adopting Sophocles's innovation; his brilliant manipulation of the ancient technique of stichomythia (line-by-line dialogue) has often been remarked; spectacle is ambitiously elaborate[4]; the Chorus,

[1] The ghost of Darius, Persia's wise ruler, foretells the military disaster of Plataea. This is "punishment for their *hubris* and impious thinking" (l. 808), and he goes on to say that the invading Persians have destroyed Greek altars and temples and the statues of their gods.

[2] Xerxes's throwing a bridge of boats across the Hellespont at the start of the expedition is a good example. The presumptuous "setting a yoke upon the neck of the sea" is a hubristic thread running through the play: ll. 65-72, 100-6, 130-2, 721-6, 744-50.

[3] ll. 497-8.

[4] The huge procession at the end of the trilogy must have taxed physical resources and called for great efficiency in production. The appearance of

while displaying the poet's lyric invention at full flood, participate in the action in an intermittent and altogether more shallow way than the actors. This last contrast of Chorus and actors concerns us most. It happens that the strongest, most positive and decisive intervention by a Chorus in all Greek Tragedy occurs in this trilogy,[1] when Orestes has returned to avenge his father and the Chorus intercept Clytemnestra's message to Aegisthus bidding him come at once with his escort of spearmen, and alter it so that he comes alone, unsuspecting, to die. But this is extraordinary, and does not affect the opposing of dramatic action to choral commentary which is largely responsible for the accumulation of a vast critical literature round the three principal figures of the trilogy: the returning king, the adulterous queen and the avenger son. Theirs is the drama, we say.

The first play, the *Agamemnon*, enacts the return of Agamemnon, king of Mycenae and commander in chief of the Greek expedition against Troy, to his home at Argos after ten years of war. He is welcomed with lies by Clytemnestra, his wife, who has made a plan with Aegisthus (the lover she has taken in Agamemnon's absence) to murder him. The murder of Agamemnon is the play's climax. In the second play, the *Libation-Bearers*,[2] Clytemnestra and Aegisthus are killed by Orestes, her son and Agamemnon's. Orestes was a child at the time of his father's murder; he has grown up in exile and now returns from abroad, disguised, to surprise his mother and kill her together with her lover. The last play is the *Eumenides*.[3] Orestes is formally brought to trial for his act of vengeance, and the trilogy ends with his acquittal.

Particularly close attention has been paid to the event which dominates the first play, which impels Orestes's action in the

---

the Chorus of Furies was so terrible that a panic, famous in later antiquity, seized Aeschylus's first audience. Most scholars recognise an impressive use of the *ekkuklēma* (see p. 67 above) in this work.

[1] *Libation-Bearers*, ll. 766-80.

[2] So called because the Chorus of slave-women, domestics of the royal palace at Argos, enter carrying drink-offerings for the spirit of the dead Agamemnon.

[3] The Furies, who are the Chorus, adopt this name (meaning "the gracious ones") at the close.

second, and which grounds his legal defence in the third: the murder of Agamemnon. It may be observed at the outset that the killing is not a mere or clear outrage, as one might speak of the killing of Duncan in *Macbeth* as an outrage, because Agamemnon is not innocent in relation either to Clytemnestra or to Aegisthus. The latter's cause of complaint, foreign to our morality and logic, is an offence committed by Agamemnon's father, Atreus, against his own father, Thyestes; Atreus had secretly killed Thyestes's children and had served them up to him at a feast, so that he ate them in horrible ignorance of what he was doing.[1] Aegisthus defiantly acknowledges his part in the murder ("I am the one who planned this killing, and I had right on my side"[2]) and justifies himself by appealing to the principle of inherited guilt:

> At last the moment has come when I can say that the divine avengers of men look down from above upon the sufferings of earth—now I see this man lying here, to my joy, caught up in the robe the Furies spun for him, paying in full for his father's treacherous crime.[3]

In planning Agamemnon's murder Aegisthus is visiting the wrong done by Atreus on the head of his son. Nowhere in the trilogy (if we may isolate the issue of inherited guilt for a moment) is it suggested that Aegisthus is here advancing an invalid argument, and this resting of his case on the affairs of an earlier generation gives a certain coherence and simplicity to his position throughout.

Clytemnestra's grievance against her husband is quite different from Aegisthus's, but on first inspection it is equally specific and at the same time much easier for a modern reader to respect, since it rests on something Agamemnon himself has done. At the start of the Trojan war the Greek expedition was delayed by adverse winds, and in order to secure a favourable change Agamemnon made a sacrificial offering of Clytemnestra's and his daughter, Iphigeneia. Therefore Clytemnestra presents her killing of her husband as a matter of "justice exacted for my child",[4] and she refers more than once to the

---

[1] Many later writers have used this story, notably Seneca in his *Thyestes* and Shakespeare in *Titus Andronicus*.

[2] *Agamemnon*, l. 1604.   [3] *Ibid.*, ll. 1578-82.   [4] *Ibid.*, l. 1432.

sacrifice as a sufficient vindication of her own action.[1] Like
Aegisthus, and with greater force to our conceiving, she says
that Agamemnon deserves to die:

> For did he not himself bring ruin on his house, by treachery? And
> now his suffering is equal to the suffering he inflicted on my child,
> and his, the much-lamented Iphigeneia; so he had better not talk
> big in Hades, since the sword that killed him only paid him back
> for what he did.[2]

And so the murder of Agamemnon is by no means a mere
outrage, and Clytemnestra's action—it was she who actually
dealt the two mortal blows—sends us back to the earlier killing
of their daughter. But Iphigeneia's death in its turn is not a
mere outrage, as the first choral song of the *Agamemnon* makes
plain. The Chorus, reviewing past events, narrate how the
Trojan war was occasioned by the elopement of Helen with
Paris while the latter was staying in Greece, at Argos, the guest
of Agamemnon and of Menelaus, Helen's husband and Agamemnon's brother. This escapade was of course an offence
against the brothers (a double offence against Menelaus who
was husband as well as host) and would have provided a sufficient *casus belli* on purely human grounds, but the Chorus stress
the fact that the Trojan Paris angered Zeus, chief of the gods
and guardian of the rights of hospitality ("Zeus whose power
is over all, Zeus lord of host and guest"[3]), and caused him to
send the Greeks against Troy. The punitive expedition led by
the two brothers was thus divinely enjoined against the city and
people of one who had dishonoured "the guest-table, and Zeus,
guardian of those who share the same hearth".[4] This has a
direct bearing on the position of Agamemnon when, once the
army had been assembled, its sailing for Troy was prevented by
adverse winds. He was now informed by Calchas, the seer
attached to the Greek army, that the goddess Artemis was
responsible; she was angry with him, and he must sacrifice
Iphigeneia in order to placate her. Agamemnon is caught in a

---

[1] *Ibid.*, ll. 1412-21, 1431-6.

[2] *Ibid.*, ll. 1523-9, reading Porson's πολυκλαύτην at 1526.

[3] *Ibid.*, l. 60.

[4] *Ibid.*, l. 701. See Denniston-Page's edition of the *Agamemnon*, Introduction xxiii, for further references.

trap; the expedition required by Zeus is now thwarted by
Artemis, and he must either abandon his fleet and army or kill
his daughter.[1] The Chorus report Agamemnon's words on the
dilemma now facing him:

> "Disobedience means utter, bitter ruin; but so does killing my
> child, my house's joy, and defiling my hands—her father's hands
> —with the streaming blood of a virgin slaughtered at the altar-
> side. Which of these courses is without evil? How can I become a
> deserter to the fleet and fail our alliance? For they are within their
> right when they hunger passionately, with an immoderate passion,
> for a sacrifice.to lull the winds: when they hunger for a virgin's
> blood. May all be for the best."[2]

Behind his predicament is a conflict of divine wills; and at
this point one's attempt to investigate Agamemnon's specific
culpability in relation to the general moral structure of the
trilogy is brought to a halt: Aeschylus has no word to say about
the fact that Artemis is frustrating the purpose of Zeus while
she prevents the Greeks from sailing, and he does not tell us
why Artemis is angry with Agamemnon. Commentators have
ignored the first of these large omissions almost entirely, but
they have been anxious to explain or rectify the second because
of their consuming interest in the king. To allow his downfall
to depend on the unmotivated malice of a deity in compelling
him to kill his own daughter (or in some hideous collusion of
deities, since we must suppose that Zeus could have stepped
forward in defence of his servant, had he wished) is obviously
unsatisfactory.

One expedient has been to invoke an earlier episode in
Agamemnon's adventures which Aeschylus fails to mention but
which does explain why Artemis is angry with him. Aeschylus
(some commentators have maintained) could afford to ignore
the initial insult which provoked the goddess to her action
because his audience was familiar with this part of the story
and would have supplied it for themselves. This argument fails
to impress, partly because the story of Artemis and Agamemnon,

---

[1] And we have no reason to suppose he would have saved Iphigeneia by
abandoning the expedition. The other chiefs would surely have sacrificed
her and sailed to Troy.

[2] *Ibid.*, ll. 206-17.

although certainly well known in its main outlines, was circulating during the fifth century in versions which differed very materially from one another over the crucial issue of the offence offered to Artemis,[1] and partly because of a rule of critical methodology which is none the less venerable for being constantly infringed: "It must be regarded as an established and indeed a guiding principle for any interpretation of Aeschylus that the poet does not want us to take into account any feature of a tradition which he does not mention."[2]

Forced simply to accept Aeschylus's silence on this point, others have turned, not always reluctantly, towards psychology. The train of thought here is not entirely clear, but it appears to run as follows: Aeschylus's failure to explain why Agamemnon is punished by Artemis, so far from being an embarrassment, is precisely the kind of thing a discerning reader welcomes as evidence of his civilised values and dramatic subtlety. It would be crudely external, mechanical, and unworthy of his advanced theology, if Aeschylus were to base Agamemnon's tragedy upon a naïve epic narrative of divine anger and vengeance; he is deliberately unspecific about the offence which occurred before the action of the trilogy opens, in order to direct attention (in the oblique and suggestive way proper to art) upon the consciousness and voluntary actions of the tragic hero.

The result of this approach is chaos. To ignore the religious offence—to dismiss the wrath of Artemis and her retaliation against the expedition as mere dramatic scaffolding which is thrown away when we come to regard the completed trilogy—is to make appraisal of the work harder rather than easier. If Aeschylus intended his story to achieve moral coherence on the plane of human relations, then from one point of view he has not said enough about fault and culpability, and from another point of view he has said too much.

These difficulties emerge immediately, in the first choral song of the *Agamemnon*. The Chorus of old men of Argos comment upon the king's decision to sacrifice Iphigeneia:

[1] Thus extant Tragedy offers two quite different accounts, in Sophocles's *Electra* and Euripides's *Iphigeneia in Tauris*; and traces of others survive. We even hear of Atreus being the offender, and not his son Agamemnon.

[2] Eduard Fraenkel, Aeschylus "*Agamemnon*", vol. II, p. 97.

And when he had slipped his neck through the strap of Necessity's yoke, and the wind of his resolve had veered towards impiety, impurity, unsanctity—from that hour his purpose shifted to embrace the top of reckless daring. . . . And so he hardened his heart and became his daughter's sacrificial murderer, to further a war waged to avenge the loss of a woman, and as a preliminary offering for the fleet's voyage.[1]

They indict him on two counts: his decision to sacrifice Iphigeneia was impious, and he waged a long and bloody war to avenge Paris's abduction of Helen. There is comfort of a sort here for psychologising commentary, but of a strange and unfruitful sort since the Chorus's silence about the cause of Artemis's anger is swallowed up in their much larger silence about the whole supernatural theme; nobody would argue that the Aeschylean Zeus is mere scaffolding. Moreover, this larger silence is only local. The Chorus have already told us that Zeus sent Agamemnon and his brother against Troy,[2] and that the intervention of Artemis presented him with a desperate choice: "Which of these courses is without evil?" The Chorus never suggest that Agamemnon should have faced Zeus's displeasure, or that he should have done anything other than what he did. They simply condemn him. And although the natural and supernatural themes are not separable in the single act—abandonment of the expedition would have brought down Zeus's wrath on his head, at the same time involving him in a betrayal of allies and subordinates—they behave as if they were.

In fact a double standard is applied to Iphigeneia's sacrifice and the Trojan war, and applied with thoroughness and mutual exclusion. We might expect Clytemnestra to be blind to wider and higher issues since it is her child who has been sacrificed; and when she says death is Agamemnon's desert and asks Zeus to fulfil her prayer for vengeance,[3] we have no reason to suppose her insincere. But there is no blood-tie binding the Chorus to Iphigeneia. Their denunciation of the sacrifice, the necessity for which they can see, is independent and religiously grave, while their clear hint that Greek soldiers' lives should not have been wasted over Helen fails to engage with the stated and stressed fact of Zeus's interest; by repeatedly applying to Zeus

---

[1] *Agamemnon*, ll. 218-27.   [2] *Ibid.*, l. 60 ff.
[3] *Ibid.*, ll. 973-4.

the adjective *xenios*[1] ("guardian of the rights of hospitality"), Aeschylus renders Paris's offence precise and impossible to ignore. The worth (or worthlessness) of Helen is entirely irrelevant to this, since it was never open to Agamemnon to propose that Paris should be allowed to keep her.

Nevertheless, and because of the persistent doubleness in choral and other moralising,[2] selective critical argument has constructed an hubristic Agamemnon who finds Nemesis in an ignoble death, murdered in his bath by a woman. He has been judged proud, cold, sensuous, boastful, cowardly, cruel, vain, weak, "boundlessly ignorant of human nature",[3] "feebly superstitious"[4] even; he has been clothed in "repulsive stateliness"[5]; indicted by "le sang d'innombrables victimes de son ambition"[6]; held desirous, in his "unconscious mind", of "the splendour of an oriental homecoming"[7]—found guilty in a wide variety—a suspiciously wide variety—of ways of offence to gods and men. This hostile account is based partly on selection, partly on the exploiting of genuine difficulties of interpretation,[8] and partly on what Agamemnon says and does

---

[1] *Ibid.*, ll. 61, 362, 748. And at l. 704 Zeus is called *xunestios*—"guardian of the hearth".

[2] A useful concept here is that of "over-determination", developed by Professor E. R. Dodds in his *Greeks and the Irrational*.

[3] Herbert Weir Smyth, *Aeschylean Tragedy*, p. 163.

[4] W. Headlam, *Agamemnon of Aeschylus*, p. 34.

[5] A. W. Verrall, *The Agamemnon of Aeschylus*, xvii.

[6] H. Weil, *Études sur le drame antique*, p. 43.

[7] *The Complete Plays of Aeschylus*, translated by Gilbert Murray: *Agamemnon*, pp. 121-2.

[1] I believe there is only one important instance, which centres on the argument that Zeus, while sending Agamemnon to Troy, did not license everything that was done there. Undoubtedly Agamemnon's mission was one of retributive justice, and he is welcomed home as Zeus's servant when the victory has been won: "Then give him fair welcome, as it is fitting you should, since he has uprooted Troy with the mattock of avenging Zeus . . ." (ll. 524-6). The correlate of this is the universal assumption that the Trojans are collectively guilty for Paris's wrongdoing; and nobody questions the overall justice, or particular severities, of the fate that overtakes Priam's city.

On the other hand, "the gods have their eye upon men of blood" (ll. 461-2); and the herald who arrives ahead of Agamemnon to announce the victory lets fall in a single line of verse (527) that Troy's "altars are destroyed, and so are the shrines of her gods", which marks the frustration of Clytemnestra's hope that the Greeks will "respect the Trojan gods" (338),

when at last, half way through the play bearing his name, he
appears before us. He makes a speech on arrival, and is persuaded by Clytemnestra in the famous carpet scene to walk
along a path strewn with costly tapestries, from his chariot to
the royal palace. The speech, for a flourishing tradition of
commentary, is "haughty and repulsive",[1] and the carpet scene
is a "process of temptation"[2] through which the inner "faiblesse
et vanité"[3] of the great commander are revealed. These are
Agamemnon's opening words:

> It is right that I should first greet Argos, and the gods of Argos
> who have helped me to a safe homecoming, as they have to my
> just punishment of Priam's city.[4]

His acknowledgment of nothing more than help from the
gods at a moment when one might expect a humbler address
and expressions of deeper obligation is primarily responsible
for the charge that Agamemnon is arrogant. Once it is shown
(as it has been shown)[5] that his manner towards his country's
gods is entirely in keeping with Greek notions of piety, the
foundations of this interpretation are shaken and it becomes
apparent that hostile readings of the speech as a whole rest
upon faith in the doctrine of the flawed nature of the tragic

---

and which recalls Aeschylus's earlier play, the *Persians*, in which the *hubris*
of the invading Persian army is indicated by its irreverence towards the
native Greek gods.

It is hard to feel sure that Aeschylus wants us to think about this. Some
scholars have maintained that l. 527 is spurious, but their reasons seem to
me flimsy. And yet the probability that Aeschylus wrote this line does not
justify the inflating of Agamemnon's personal ambition into a major theme
of the play, still less of the trilogy. The herald's statement is never developed,
and there is no attempt to bring the desecration of Trojan sanctities home
to Agamemnon. The herald, of course, is doing the opposite of hold it
against him.

[1] Verrall, note on ll. 801-45.

[2] *The Complete Plays of Aeschylus*, translated by Gilbert Murray: *Agamemnon*, p. 121.

[3] M. Croiset, *Eschyle*, p. 191 ("Faiblesse et vanité tout à la fois prévalent
en lui").

[4] *Agamemnon*, ll. 810-13.

[5] Professor Fraenkel's discussion (vol. II, pp. 371-4) seems to me conclusive. Misunderstandings of this passage arise through the application of
Judaeo-Christian divine transcendence and omnipotence to a society which
was without these concepts.

hero. Of course, there is also the carpet scene. After Agamemnon has spoken, Clytemnestra enters attended by servant-women carrying purple tapestries. She welcomes him home, declaring her faithfulness in her lord's long absence, and then orders her women to strew Agamemnon's path to the palace with the tapestries. He says it would be wrong to tread on this precious work and refuses to do so. Argument ensues between husband and wife at the end of which Agamemnon gives way and walks along the tapestries into his house, there to meet his death.

Why does Agamemnon yield? The question has been most strenuously debated, in the conviction that its answer will affect our estimate of the work's "message" decisively. The process-of-temptation school presents the familiar figure (students of English literature establish contact with Andrew Bradley's Shakespearean tragic hero) of the outstanding, gifted individual with a weakness in his nature—a weakness which is exposed to attack through play of circumstance or character, and which causes his downfall.[1] Unfortunately, Aeschylus's text can only be made to yield this general sense, or something like it, by a process of argument from silence and by reference to Agamemnon's secret desires, and even to the state of his subconscious. What we know of ancient dramatic convention is against any resorting to inference over important issues, and what we know of the society of the mid fifth century for which Aeschylus was writing is against the psychological bent of the inferences here called for. Scholarly opinion has hardened against the process-of-temptation school during the last few decades, to such an extent that it is no longer possible to name a critical orthodoxy. The counter-thesis, that Agamemnon "appears as the true gentleman he always is"[2] in the carpet scene, is more respectable, certainly; but it operates at the same level of individualistic humanism as its opponent, and this robs its superior honesty with the text of any great significance. We ought not to embrace it; rather rest satisfied, at this stage, with the provisional and largely negative conclusion that all attempts to spell out of the *Oresteia* a fault personal to Agamemnon and intelligibly related to his fate are misdirected. We are concerned

---

[1] "He would not have walked on the tapestries if left to himself, but secretly he longs to do so": Gilbert Murray, *Aeschylus*, p. 218.

[2] Fraenkel, vol. II, p. 429.

F

with something more fundamental than even the most complete
failure of moral imagination in the critic—than failure of the
sort that once read poetic justice into Desdemona's death
through the argument that she should have taken greater care
of her handkerchief. There is something wrong in our critical
isolation of the protagonist,[1] and something wrong in our
sealing-off of the principal figures—husband, wife, and son—
from the atmosphere of lyric commentary they live in. Futile,
too, is the common study of the *Agamemnon*, which is a First Act,
at the expense of the *Oresteia's* triadic unity.

3 The House of Atreus

A watchman lies stretched out on the roof of Agamemnon's
palace, propped on his elbows, scanning the horizon for the
prearranged beacon-fire which will announce the capture of
Troy.[2] The physical and visible situation delivers the *Oresteia's*
opening complete, full-formed; it were an absurd inadequacy
to speak of this disposition as having dramatic point. The
watchman lying on top of the building (represented by the
permanent *skēnē* before which the action takes place) is the eye
and tongue and consciousness of the household asleep beneath
him, and the poet's means of communicating its mood. "I
weep," he says, recounting his weary watch,

> and I groan over the troubles of this house of ours, no longer
> ordered for the best as it once was. And tonight I pray for a happy
> release from my task: may the beacon-fire carry its glad news
> through the darkness.[3]

[1] Professor E. R. Dodds (*Proceedings of the Cambridge Philological Society*,
1960) challenges Fraenkel's view of Agamemnon by appealing to "the
painful impression of mingled arrogance and stupidity which he makes on
most readers". I find that "painful" doubly interesting; it illuminates both
the larger-than-personal, sleepwalking horror of the carpet scene, and also
the modern reader's distress at being unable to make sense of Agamemnon.

[2] "Propped on his elbows" is open to question: see Denniston-Page's
note on l. 3. But it is absurd to deny (with more than one commentator)
that the watchman is lying on the roof. Here and throughout, I shall ignore
doubts which seem to me altogether ill-founded.

[3] *Agamemnon*, ll. 18-21.

And at that moment, in a congruence of wish and fact found throughout Greek Tragedy,[1] the fire burns up in the distance. He rouses the palace:

> Hullo! Hullo then! This loud cry of mine gives Agamemnon's wife the signal to rise from her couch with all speed and send a shout of thankful joy ringing through the house, in welcome to this fire. . . .[2]

And his speech ends with a sudden shift from joy at Troy's capture to anxious concern for the house and its affairs:

> Ah well, may he come home, the master of our house; and may I hold his dear hand in mine. But for the rest—I'm dumb: a great ox is standing on my tongue.[3] And yet the house itself, could it but speak, would have a plain tale to tell. . . .[4]

This short opening scene gets across to the audience (in a world without theatre programmes) necessary background information as to the time and place and people of the action, and it also asserts an intense, unremitting focus on the "house", the fortunes of which will be followed through the play and through the trilogy, into the next generation. The note of tragic disquiet in the watchman's speech issues from the house (observe the delicate and arrested movement towards personification in "the house itself, could it but speak") and concerns itself; the human individuals are apprehended only in relation to the household which contains them—not merely the watchman-servant perched up there on the roof for everyone to see, but those chief people of the story to whom he refers: the absent king is not "Agamemnon" but "the master of the house", his queen is not "Clytemnestra" but "Agamemnon's wife"—both of them designated by their household status and function. "House" (the Greek *oikos* and its synonyms) is at once house and household, building and family, land and chattels, slaves and domestic animals, hearth and ancestral grave: a

---

[1] And more deeply embedded than we suppose in remote, naturalistic techniques. Thus the Baker Street convention: "And there is our client, Watson, if I am not mistaken."

[2] *Agamemnon*, ll. 25-9.

[3] A vivid and no doubt vulgar expression for enforced silence.

[4] *Agamemnon*, ll. 34-8.

psycho-physical community of the living and the dead and the unborn. The master of the house is priest in charge of the family cult (in which slaves attached to the *oikos* participate) as well as its secular head, and his wife is bound to him through the *oikos* which she joins at marriage. Marriage is not primarily a business of personal relations—still less of romantic love—but of securing the continuity of the *oikos*.

Aeschylus's first audience will have been more receptive than we can hope to be of the image of this *oikos*—the house of Atreus —which the watchman establishes. For us it is a conscious but necessary effort to accept this image for what it is, and to retain it while the watchman descends and disappears from sight, and the Chorus file into the *orchēstra* and sing their opening song. They narrate the mustering of the expedition to punish Paris and his city, the anger of Artemis and Agamemnon's sacrifice of Iphigeneia; and as they are finishing their song Clytemnestra enters to give them the news of Troy's capture. There follows a long dialogue between queen and Chorus, at the end of which, in the second choral song, credit for the Greek victory is given to Zeus and just retribution is held to have visited Paris "who entered the house of the sons of Atreus and dishonoured his hosts' table by stealing the wife away".[1]

The plural "sons of Atreus" is remarkable. Aeschylus has altered the traditional form of the story (and violated the laws of human probability as the Greeks understood them) by making Agamemnon and Menelaus share a house. By this deviation he gives Agamemnon a claim against Paris alongside that of his brother, Helen's husband, and—more important than the legal issue—he avoids the dissipation of interest that would result if the web of action and reaction, crime and retribution, were extended beyond the one *oikos* which he wishes to keep in the dramatic foreground throughout. Still greater concentration is achieved by disposing of the Trojan war before Agamemnon returns. The herald, arriving ahead of his king, delivers an extended quasi-epic narrative of the fighting and its hardships; and now the time is ripe for Agamemnon's entry. The war is a dying theme, and an extreme simplicity of situation prevails. We are witnessing a homecoming.

Agamemnon greets his country and his country's gods, pro-

[1] *Ibid.*, ll. 399-402.

claims that he will appoint assemblies to consider matters of state and public worship, and concludes:

> And now I will enter my palace and approach my household hearth, first of all saluting the gods who sped me forth and have brought me home. Victory has attended me; may she stay with me always.[1]

No word of Clytemnestra. The focus is the *focus*—the socio-religious hearth of Indo-European societies and a living force to Aeschylus and his audience—now to be approached after long absence by the household's master who is also its priest. To feel the moment in this way is the first step towards a just reading of the carpet scene. The carpet lies between Agamemnon and his hearth: this is the situation which commentators have obscured in two closely related ways, by psychologising the meeting of husband and wife into a process of temptation, and by spiritualising a quarrel about treading upon a carpet into something supposedly more exalted.[2] Their joint effect is to reduce the carpet to a physical pawn in a mental conflict.

When Clytemnestra's women have strewn the purple tapestries in front of him, Agamemnon declares that he will not be pampered like a woman or grovelled to like a barbarian king:

> and do not draw down Envy upon my path by strewing it with tapestries. Such honours are for gods; I think with dread of a mortal man treading on fine embroidered work. Pay me the respect due a man, not a god.[3]

Mortal *hubris* and divine jealousy or envy (*phthonos*) are here, as so often, interlocked. And when Agamemnon says that to tread on the tapestries would be an act of insolent pride and folly likely to incur retribution from above, it is important to recognise that he is shrinking from something wider than almost

---

[1] *Ibid.*, ll. 851-4.

[2] A popular method of elevating the carpet scene has been to refer it to the murder of Iphigeneia. Thus Professor George Thomson states (*Aeschylus and Athens*. p. 259) that Clytemnestra's "purpose" in tempting Agamemnon "is to induce him to commit an overt act of pride which will symbolise the sin he is about to expiate". See also, among writers in English, John H. Finley, *Pindar and Aeschylus*, p. 260 (a good book), and Professor H. D. F. Kitto, *Greek Tragedy*, p. 108 in the revised edition of 1950.

[3] *Agamemnon*, ll. 921-5.

any modern formulation of impiety. *Hubris* embraces the familiar impieties as an offshoot of its wide-branching central meaning of doing deeds and thinking thoughts "greater" than those which a human being ought to do and think. Everywhere in Greek Tragedy we find *hubris*, and the fear of *hubris*, arising in contexts which are not obviously religious; and in the carpet scene our sense of impiety should be muted to the point of integration within this broad ancient concept: in fact it is a mistake to think of the tapestries as dedicated to religious uses, because we shall thus be led into the false precision that conceives of Clytemnestra urging Agamemnon to commit an act of clear-cut sacrilege. Faced with the tapestries, Agamemnon says it would ill become a human being to tread on them. Why? He suggests the answer himself: "I think with dread of a mortal man treading on fine embroidered work." The tapestries are precious; a lot of work has gone into them. No further reason is offered in the course of the ensuing dialogue[1] (it is said that people in general will disapprove, which merely leads us to ask why they should) until, at last, Agamemnon suddenly yields:

> Well, if you will have it so—let someone undo my shoes, and quickly. . . . And may no god glance malignly on me from afar as I tread upon these purple dyes. It awakes the deepest shame, this wasting of our house's substance with my feet and spoiling of costly woven fabrics.[2]

The suggestion contained in "fine embroidered work" is now fully explicit; Agamemnon's initial rebuke to Clytemnestra was rooted in his unwillingness to waste the substance of the *oikos*. His "Pay me the respect due a man, not a god" was directed to the truth that it would be fitting for a god to be offered some element of the household's wealth (this is of course the point of

---

[1] It is possible, but by no means certain, that Aeschylus is hinting at the oriental habit of strewing tapestries before the feet of potentates; his *Persians* makes play with the absurdities and the *hubris* (from the Greek standpoint) of barbarian conduct. If we admit this dramatic intention, it must remain subordinate to the economic theme.

[2] *Agamemnon*, ll. 944-9. A minority of commentators would render: "these purple dyes of the gods". This has the specious attraction of making Agamemnon's offence more precisely religious, by stressing what has already been admitted at l. 922. But there is also an argument of substance, based on word-order, for the minority view.

sacrificial destruction of objects), but to address that kind of service to a man could only result in a wanton wounding of the body of the house. One must be ready, and glad, to admit a certain largeness of poetic treatment. Aeschylus is not pressing upon us the thought of tapestries being sacrificed to gods. He is concentrating on the destruction of *oikos*-substance, and distinguishing the kinds of respect proper towards gods and towards men. (A near-absurdity arises when we stress, as I believe all commentators have done, the narrow transgression of walking on the tapestries rather than the broad *hubris* of wasting the house's wealth: we find ourselves regarding the tapestries as somehow reserved for the feet of gods. Indeed Agamemnon himself admits, according to the better interpretation of the controversial ll. 931-4, that for a man to walk upon tapestries like the ones now in his path is not necessarily an impious action.)

And again, while a servant is taking off his shoes—a gesture of modesty and of respect for the precious stuff, and also an attempt to minimise damage—Agamemnon declares his fear of divine *phthonos* ("may no god glance malignly on me"), now in direct association with the religious "shame" (*aidōs*) of the wealth-wasting. And he sets foot on the tapestries. And thus his homecoming is a harming of his house, the lucid externality of this equivalence presenting a complete and painful dramatic sense: the thing is done, it shows itself.

If any doubt remains as to where interpretative emphasis should rest, it is dispelled by Clytemnestra's words at the moment when Agamemnon gives way to her:

> The sea—who shall drain the sea?—is at hand with its store of purple stain for dyeing fine things, abundant, precious as silver, eternally renewed. And of fine things, my king, there is no lack in our house—by the god's grace: our house does not know how to be poor. I would have devoted many such to be trodden underfoot, if some oracle had required this tribute of the house when I was casting about for means to secure your safe return.[1]

She directs her attention (as, from behind her, Aeschylus directs ours) towards the household's wealth; she counters her husband's scruples with the argument that the *oikos* can afford

[1] *Ibid.*, ll. 958-65, reading Abresch's μηχανωμένη at 965.

the waste that is taking place at this moment, as Agamemnon walks along the tapestries into the palace. The religious fear which prompted his rebuke of Clytemnestra and his initial refusal to tread on the tapestries now moves into the dramatic foreground, for Clytemnestra's sentiment that the *oikos* is so rich that it need not bother about this kind of extravagance, while trivial-seeming to us, will have struck a fifth-century audience as recklessly hubristic; and they will have observed a vital distinction between the senseless wantonness taking place in front of them and the hypothetical circumstances envisaged by Clytemnestra of the same destruction following an oracle's command. Great wealth linked with high station had been from early times the subject of moral reflection on the virtues of moderation and restraint. Eminence did not arouse in the Greeks a narrow hostility or envy, but it did seem to them singularly vulnerable; they never tired of saying, in their tragic literature and elsewhere, that to be prominent and prosperous and at the same time to avoid *hubris* is exquisitely difficult. The old men of the *Agamemnon's* Chorus show a timidity and eagerness for a life obscure enough to escape heaven's jealous eye which one might parallel in almost any extant Greek Tragedy. Nevertheless, the choral songs of this play are exceptional in the degree to which they isolate and dwell upon material prosperity. I am saying that the great tragic subject of Excess is being given economic point.

An important function of choral meditation is to create and sustain atmosphere, to foster thematic affinities. Early in the play, after Clytemnestra has told them of Troy's capture, they reflect:

> Disaster, the child of reckless folly, is with us for all to see, when the house of the proud-hearted is crammed with wealth in excess, beyond what is best. Our prayer is for sufficiency without sorrow, for that share which the wise man calls enough. There is no escape for him who, wanton in his wealth, thrusts the exalted seat of Justice out of sight, out of mind.[1]

Their burden is Paris's guilt and just punishment, but the link between his abduction of Helen and their large moralising upon

---

[1] *Ibid.*, ll. 374-84. The first few words look desperately corrupt and I have attempted only a very rough indication of the probable sense.

riches is extremely tenuous—although we ought not to forget
that Paris has enriched his household and his city by this theft.
Aeschylus is availing himself of the opportunity given in the
Chorus's lyrical elaborations—the intrusive author's voice of
Victorian fiction achieves a similar end more blatantly—to
provide reader and spectator with an ultimate objectivity of
reference, like a key signature. This reaches us as a religio-moral
drift in which the action is suspended. When he gives the
following passage to the Chorus at the long-awaited moment
of Agamemnon's entry:

> Justice sets store by a righteous life, and her light shines in the
> smoky dwellings of the poor. But she departs with averted eyes
> from gold-encrusted halls where men's hands are defiled, taking
> her way to innocent homes. She does not bow to the power of
> wealth stamped false with idle praise; she guides all things to their
> fulfilment.
>
> Hail, my King, stormer of Troy, Atreus's son. . . .[1]

it is no accident that Agamemnon appears when he does: but
this is not to say that the words are directed at him in the form
of personal indictment. Indeed they are not directed *at* him at
all; we must allow the theme of unholy wealth and the visible
figure of the king simply to co-exist in our reception of the
scene. The Chorus's remarks are suitably general in tone since
their application is collective. They anticipate the self-wounding
of the *oikos* which is soon to be presented in the spoiling of
the tapestries.

Aeschylus has thus made careful preparation for the carpet
scene, to insure that its sense shall not be misapprehended. Nor
can one doubt the *hubris* entailed in Clytemnestra's defending of
waste by an appeal to wealth; the Chorus's religio-moral
brooding has produced a state of attentiveness in which doubt
is impossible. Furthermore, the choral song which follows her
speech contains an indirect refutation of its argument:

> The ship of human fortune, holding a straight course onward,
> strikes a hidden reef. Then, if a well-judged heave tips part of the
> cargo overboard, the wisely fearful captain saves his ship from
> foundering: and a house too, no longer over-freighted, escapes
> total wreck.[2]

---

[1] *Ibid.*, ll. 773-81.   [2] *Ibid.*, ll. 1005-13.

The *oikos*—any *oikos*—is being likened in a forcefully collective quasi-simile (the likeness sliding characteristically towards identification) to a ship at sea, and the Chorus are envisaging circumstances in which it would be a blameless and prudent decision to sacrifice part of the corporate wealth in order to save the rest. A comparison between purposeful surrender and purposeless waste emerges into consciousness almost unprompted. Clytemnestra is not directly challenged, but the economic bias of her *hubris* cannot be overlooked. We have noted a similar oblique commentary investing Agamemnon; the Chorus's words immediately before his entry are not directed at him, but they are felt to have been thrown round him; and when, in the song which comes to an end with his dying cry, they affirm: "Mankind never has its fill of prosperity"[1]—an unattached piece of moralising, even by the standards of Greek Tragedy—one experiences an *oikos*-focussed rightness of context which occupies the place both of causation (Agamemnon isn't killed because he walked on the tapestries) and of personal justice (he doesn't deserve to die for walking on the tapestries). Likewise when Clytemnestra turns to Cassandra, the captive Trojan seer whom Agamemnon has brought home with him, and orders her to go inside the house and take her stand "with many another slave at the altar of the god who guards its wealth", adding that she has "reason to be deeply thankful for having masters old in wealth",[2] the bitterness of Cassandra's situation (she is being sent inside to be murdered, which she knows through her seer's gift but cannot prevent) stands in the kind of relation we are considering—thematically pointed but causally remote—to the *hubris* of her new mistress.

I am not trying to subordinate Agamemnon's murder to the carpet scene, but to understand both in the light of Aeschylus's intention to dramatise the troubles of the house of Atreus. The point of immediate relevance is the dwarfing of all other consideration by the corporate consequences of these two outrages committed within the *oikos*, against itself. The Chorus's response to Agamemnon's death-cry is public and institutional[3]; they talk of "a plot to set up a tyranny in the city" on the part of the two "defilers of the house" ("murderers" would be too narrow a designation of those who have killed the king and master of the

---

[1] *Ibid.*, ll. 1331-2.   [2] *Ibid.*, ll. 1037-8, 1043.   [3] *Ibid.*, ll. 1346-71.

oikos), and when Clytemnestra appears before them to justify her action they reply to her with waverings and contrapuntal blendings of opinion, blaming her, admitting Agamemnon's guilt, confessing themselves unable to judge between the adversaries; but the dominant strain is their dismay, which is the corporate dismay of the stricken *oikos*:

> I am at a loss what to think and where to turn, now the house is tottering; I fear the pelting storm of blood that shakes the house. . . .[1]

and their horror of the evil spirit (*daimōn*) which has been seen through successive generations of the house of Atreus, and which is now at work again. The potency of the family *daimōn* and its central place in the trilogy is shown in the way it unites accusers and accused in a search for some means of appeasement: the Chorus and Clytemnestra in this play; Orestes, Electra, Clytemnestra, and the Chorus of household slavewomen in the next; the parties to the judicial proceedings in the last. Even more terrible is its power of lending opposed individuals a deeper harmony in wrong-doing; when Agamemnon is walking along the tapestries and Clytemnestra is saying there are plenty more where those came from, the greatness of the scene touches us through our haunting awareness of conspiracy. The *daimōn* is felt by all, and presented by Aeschylus, as bigger than the human beings; we should not take Clytemnestra's assertion that the "evil genius of Atreus"[2] assumed her shape in order to kill Agamemnon merely on the plane of self-excuse. The Chorus, who are not her friends, see more in it than that. They refuse to believe that she had no part in the murder, but they admit "a spirit of vengeance, provoked by his father's crime, might help you in this".[3] The shadow of the family *daimōn* falls across the generations and across the whole of this long dialogue, most darkly in the speech of Clytemnestra which closes it:

[1] *Ibid.*, ll. 1530-4.
[2] *Ibid.*, ll. 1501-2. *Alastōr* (the word translated "evil genius") is here very close to *daimōn*.
[3] *Ibid.*, ll. 1507-8. They refer to the crime of Atreus (Agamemnon's father), who killed Thyestes's children, as we recall, and served them up to him at a feast.

This is the covenant which I, for my part, am ready to make with the *daimōn* of the house of Pleisthenes: I will accept—not an easy thing for me—all that has been done and suffered, if from now on he will leave our house and drag down some other family by kinsmen's murdering of kinsmen. I shall be content with a small part of the household wealth, once I have rid this palace of the madness of family bloodshed.[1]

The *daimōn* is a persecuting quasi-physical presence which Clytemnestra hopes to divert from the house of Atreus towards another family—it doesn't matter which. And she hopes to achieve her object by buying the *daimōn* off. Now, near the end of the *Agamemnon*, the apparently disparate themes of economic *hubris* and the family *daimōn* draw close together. There is nothing unnatural or violent in this, because Aeschylus's *daimōn* spreads beyond the exclusive spirituality of our "hereditary guilt", while his *oikos*-substance, unlike our "wealth", does not feel the tug of a gravitational materiality. On the one hand, guilt is or is not extinguished; it cannot be diverted, as Clytemnestra plans to divert the *daimōn*. On the other, goods and money are not material objects attaching to the *oikos*; they inhere in its psycho-physical body. We therefore find the (for us) tired metaphor of unholy wealth exerting an immediate literal force throughout the *Oresteia*. Unholy wealth is more than unjustly acquired wealth; it is wealth which has lost its virtue and efficacy, described by the Chorus in a passage already quoted as "wealth stamped false with idle praise"— seeming-wealth, a counterfeit, not real wealth at all. And so the principal conclusion to be drawn from Clytemnestra's speech, in the light of choral commentary and subsequent event, is not that the *daimōn* cannot be bribed[2] but that she has nothing to

---

[1] *Ibid.*, ll. 1568-76. Pleisthenes is another of Agamemnon's ancestors, and so a member (we might say) of the house of Atreus.

[2] The question whether Aeschylus believes that the *daimōn* can be bribed has been phrased misleadingly by commentators anxious to credit the great poet with what they recognise as civilised views on guilt and atonement. It is possible here, as it is with Aeschylus's "monotheism" and his "refined" version of the savage Greek idea of divine jealousy (*phthonos*), to cite a few passages in which he may be pictured looking down reprovingly on popular belief and practice. There is one in the *Agamemnon*: "Neither by burnt offering nor by libation, nor by tears, shall a man soothe the fierce anger engendered by sacrifices which are hateful to the gods (ll. 69-71, referring

bribe it with. Once the situation is seen in terms of the internal relations of the *oikos*, and once we cease to force on Aeschylus a rigid separation of physical and mental, the tragic futility becomes evident of Clytemnestra's plan to appease the family *daimōn* by offering it the defiled and reduced substance of the family: stress upon her plan being lighter than upon the family's helplessness.

The family's privation demonstrates its guilt, and its guilt is scarcely touched upon in the personalistic debate about Agamemnon's deserving in relation to his murder. The vagaries, contradictions and obscurities which (we saw) frustrate the search for an intelligible, and not merely for an acceptable, morality or rationale of guilt and innocence, are not there for Aeschylus because Agamemnon himself—the Agamemnon of the critics, the autonomous, self-sustaining modern man—is not there. Aeschylus's Agamemnon draws his life, and with his life his guilts and innocences, from the *oikos*: "when a house is righteous the lot of its children is blessed for ever"[1] is the truth. The converse also holds, and no protest of outraged individuality follows the receiving of guilt from outside. Why should it? Life is fostered and transmitted by the *oikos* (the *oikos* contains the individual because it sustains him—not because of any social doctrine to that effect), so there can be no thought of sealing oneself off from whatever flows suspended in life's stream.

Vagueness in presenting guilt and the absence of the outraged individual are dramatically intrinsicate. No need asserts itself, or desire, to be precise about guilt when guilt is circumambient, atmospheric, blood-borne, often untethered to personal act or

---

to the sacrificial murder of Iphigeneia). Against these, nobody in Aeschylean Tragedy hesitates to appeal openly to a divinity's or a dead hero's greed for material gain. We read in an extant fragment of his lost play, the *Niobe*: "Death alone among the gods does not love gifts; neither by sacrifice nor by libation can you prevail upon him. . . ." The other gods are fond of gifts, and men are quick to offer gifts to them.

But all this is beside the point. Our lodestar must be the psychic impregnation of material objects, for this makes nonsense of both sides of the argument over Aeschylus's advanced or primitive theology—at least in the form in which it is usually conducted.

[1] *Agamemnon*, ll. 761-2.

omission; where in the nature of things there can be no knowing how a man stands with his gods. The palpitating unease of Greek Tragedy springs from a world in which to be sure your hands are clean is to convict yourself of *hubris*. In the *Oresteia*, Aeschylus dramatises this large aspect of his society's *Weltanschauung* by investing the house of Atreus with a murky, incompletely comprehended web of religio-legal culpability, and by making the chain-reaction of crime and fresh crime recede into a totally obscure past. It is repeatedly stated, with varied inflection, that Agamemnon's father tricked his brother Thyestes into eating his own children; but we also learn from Cassandra that Atreus's action was not unprovoked: Thyestes had committed adultery with his brother's wife. Cassandra also speaks of a "primal sin"[1] lying at the root of present calamities, but she does not specify its nature. The resulting disagreement among scholars (some refer her words to Thyestes's adultery, others to even more remote crimes within the family[2]) in their attempts to remove this doubt does homage to Aeschylus's achievement in weaving round the body of the *oikos* a seamless garment of sin-begotten and sin-begetting action in which the individual threads lose themselves within the whole. Family guilt is as much collective as inherited, in that the dead of the group form one enduring community with the living; both are prominent in the *Oresteia*, and both are fully endorsed by Aeschylus. The final settlement of the *Eumenides* expressly upholds the Furies' right to pursue a man for his ancestor's wrongdoing: "It is the sins of bygone generations that bring him before them for judgment, and Destruction strikes him down—silently, in dreadful wrath."[3]

The morality of the *Oresteia*—moralising in a vacuum has been the special vice of Anglo-Saxon commentators—is one with the great arc which its action describes, from the watchman perched on the palace roof to the acquitted Orestes whose

---

[1] *Ibid.*, l. 1192, following the reading of the manuscripts, where the Oxford Text admits Maas's emendation (ἄτης). ἄτη does not quite mean "sin", but it is not easy to render this word "which comprises mental blindness, guilt, and harm or damage" (Fraenkel, vol. III, p. 545, quoting O. Schroeder).

[2] It has been argued that Aeschylus mentions (l. 1469) the name of Tantalus, who is yet another ancestor, in order to remind his audience of that king's famous act of *hubris*.   [3] *Eumenides*, ll. 934-7.

response to deliverance from the Furies is a corporate thanksgiving: "O Pallas, O saviour of my house!"[1]—ample and lively enough to carry the individual's gratitude. We have paused over the murder of Agamemnon to indicate the gross distortion caused by the severance of morality from *oikos*-focussed action in an attempt to make it serve the king's single fate. It remains to say that the genuine moral chaos which ensues is less unfortunate than the false dramatic clarity of a climactic death in which the two defilers of the house become murderers above all else, and in which the vital pulse of the trilogy is lost. As the self-wounding of the house in the carpet scene moves towards the cutting off of its head, so the cutting off of its head moves towards the *de facto* transfer of authority which gives the close of the *Agamemnon* its subtle questioning lift. "I and thou," Clytemnestra tells Aegisthus, "ruling this house together, will make all well."[2] How? We recall her plan to buy off the family *daimōn*. Aegisthus's assertion: "I shall try to control the people with his [Agamemnon's] wealth"[3] accompanies the economic *hubris* of his more important partner and helps define the openness of the ending. The two lovers are no less deeply committed to the house of Atreus than was its master whom they have just killed. When the Chorus threaten Clytemnestra with reprisals after the murder, she answers, untranslatably: "For me, Hope does not set foot within the house of Fear so long as the fire upon my hearth is kindled by Aegisthus",[4] thus throwing herself on his protection, not in virtue of the personal and erotic relation between them, but of his socio-religious headship of the *oikos*, as she hopes to see it asserted and maintained. But Aegisthus's task is impossible; in the same sense that unholy wealth is a false appearance of wealth, the household hearth tended by the usurper remains cold.[5] We have already seen enough to know that the seizure of authority initiated through Agamemnon's murder is but part of a larger

---

[1] *Ibid.*, l. 754. Pallas is the goddess Athena.

[2] *Agamemnon*, ll. 1672-3.

[3] *Ibid.*, ll. 1638-9.

[4] *Ibid.*, ll. 1434-6.

[5] If Wilamowitz's doubtful interpretation of ἀθέρμαντον ἑστίαν δόμων at *Libation-Bearers*, l. 629, is correct (Fraenkel accepts it without question and without mention of W.: vol. III, p. 677), then the theme of the cold usurper-tended hearth becomes explicit in the second play of the trilogy.

and as yet undetermined whole. This settlement is shallow-rooted: "the house is tottering".

The means of salvation for the self-tormented *oikos* is hinted in the *Agamemnon* by the passing mention of Orestes. We learn he has been sent away during Agamemnon's absence to the house of a friendly prince; Cassandra has a prophetic vision of Clytemnestra's death at her son's hand, and the Chorus express the hope, very near the end of the play, that a superhuman power "guiding Orestes shall bring him home again".[1] Orestes is both of the house, being son to the murdered king, and at the same time no party to the action of the first play of the trilogy, being then absent and a child. He is singled out by blood and status for the task of restoration, and when the *Libation-Bearers* opens with the arrival of Orestes from abroad at Agamemnon's tomb, near the palace, we are witnessing the return of hope—of "the eye of the house"[2] as the Chorus of domestic slave-women call him, its leading and most precious faculty.

The story of the *Libation-Bearers* is Orestes's fulfilment of his mission, and it is important to understand what this mission is. Too much emphasis, in the prevailing critical tradition, has been placed on Orestes's duty to avenge his father: this is a continuance of the spiritualised and personalistic interpretation which we have noted in the *Agamemnon*, and the kind of damage which results is similar. Just as Agamemnon's murder falls within a context of transfer (or attempted transfer) of authority within the *oikos*, so the retributive killing of Clytemnestra must be referred to a larger scheme of corporate restitution and amendment. The Chorus of the *Agamemnon* threaten Clytemnestra with exile[3] and Aegisthus with death by stoning[4]—punishments inflicted by the community for an offence against itself and peculiarly noxious to itself. The Chorus of the *Libation-Bearers* welcome Orestes as the restorer of health to this same community; the self-wounding of the *oikos* presented in the *Agamemnon* is followed after many years by its self-healing:

The house has a cure to heal these troubles: not from outside, at alien hands, but from itself. . . .[5]

[1] *Ibid.*, l. 1667.   [2] *Libation-Bearers*, l. 934.   [3] *Agamemnon*, ll. 1410-1.
[4] *Ibid.*, ll. 1615-16.   [5] *Libation-Bearers*, ll. 471-3.

On his return, Orestes finds his sister Electra in helpless subjection to the tyranny of Clytemnestra and Aegisthus, but passively allied with the Chorus through "the common hatred we are nursing within the house".[1] They lament the pollution of the hearth—the household's altar and centre of its corporate life—and the long drawn out wasting of wealth; and when Orestes has made himself known, the Chorus anticipate the result of his encounter with their enemies by extending to him and his sister—the one who watched and hated as well as the one who is about to act—the very broad title of "saviours of your father's hearth".[2]

No murdered father's ghost appears in the *Libation-Bearers*, to speak and be seen, to cry Revenge, like old Hamlet. But Agamemnon's spirit is believed to haunt his tomb, and Orestes and Electra both pray to it, asking for help and intensifying the "common hatred" which is as yet their only weapon. The object of the following savage exchange:

> ORESTES: Father, remember the bath which gave your mur-
> derers their moment.
> ELECTRA: Remember the cloak—the strange casting-net they
> devised for you.
> OR.: They shackled you, my father, with fetters of thread, not
> metal-forged.
> EL.: They wound about you a wrapping shamefully contrived.
> OR.: Father, are you not roused by these taunts of ours?[3]

is to achieve even greater psychic concentration against the two defilers and wasters of wealth: the revenge-motif, in so far as we may formally distinguish it, serves the group's solidarity in hating. And fostering the hatred of the group is itself ancillary to demonstrating the group's unity in fact, its single interest. Orestes and Electra pray to Agamemnon:

> EL.: Listen, father, to this last cry; look on us your children
> crouched before your tomb; and pity us both, the woman and
> the man too.
> OR.: Do not allow the family of Pelops to be blotted out. Save us
> —and then, in spite of death, you are not dead; for children are
> a man's living name and fame, though he be gone; they are

---

[1] *Ibid.*, l. 101.   [2] *Ibid.*, l. 264.
[3] *Ibid.*, ll. 491-5.

like the corks that buoy up a fisherman's net, saving his knotted lines from sinking deep.

EL.: Listen! It is in your behalf that we cry out. Answer our prayer and you save yourself.[1]

Agamemnon in his grave has the most urgent of reasons to be concerned for the success of Orestes's enterprise: his life depends on it. The *oikos* must be rescued from a corporate extinction which will sweep away living and dead together. Therefore the price of failure is death—a sinking into cold, hungry oblivion for Agamemnon,[2] and for Orestes the annihilation of the childless exile who "dies" absolutely, outside his family:

Unhonoured of all men, friendless, he perishes at last shrivelled pitifully by a death that wastes him utterly away.[3]

If Orestes fails to recover the headship of the house of Atreus he will be, as he says elsewhere, "an alien utterly, for ever",[4] cut off from the collective life apart from which the idea of personal destiny is meaningless: his image of the lopped-off member slowly withering to nothing is well chosen. He looks to the family and the family looks to him, for he is its "hope of a seed that shall not perish, longed for with tears"[5]; together they live, and apart they die. This one great death threatening all brings us to acknowledge the foundations of social solidarity on which the *Oresteia* is built. It has nothing in common with single deaths which are events within the life of the group, lived through by the group, and of interest for Greek Tragedy only exceptionally, because of the forms they take. Death is prominent in the *Antigone* of Sophocles because burial has been refused to Polyneices's body; in his *Oedipus at Colonus* because the processes of death have been altered for the sanctified old king, and a mystery surrounds his leaving life on earth; in the *Agamemnon* because the head of a great house, king and military commander, has been butchered by a woman with an axe, and then mourning rites have been withheld from him. Shorn of

---

[1] *Ibid.*, ll. 500-9.
[2] It matters greatly that nobody should survive to present offerings, which are a kind of sustenance, at the dead man's tomb.
[3] *Libation-Bearers*, ll. 295-6.
[4] *Ibid.*, l. 684.   [5] *Ibid.*, l. 236.

special public circumstances, the death of a man does not hold great power over Greek intelligence and imagination; and this is not surprising since death does not present them with the fearful alternative of personal immortality and personal annihilation. It is the perfect solitude brought upon each of us by the thought of dying that makes death the tragic fact we know.

But Orestes, in the great scene in which he kills Aegisthus off-stage and then enters to confront his mother, carries a collective destiny which it is the function of the ever-present Chorus to hold before us throughout. Their fear recalls the earlier image of a ship in danger of foundering, and their resentment the later one of a horse held in by its rider's "great curb-chain".[1] When at last a man's cry sounds from inside the palace, they ask: "How goes it? How has the issue been determined for the house?"[2] (which makes hideous English; but such translations as Professor George Thomson's "How does it go within?" weaken the corporate focus unacceptably)—and Orestes emerges victorious to face Clytemnestra. She urges the mother-son relation upon him:

> CL.: Your life I cherished, and with you I wish to live out my own.
> OR.: What! Kill my father and then share my house?[3]

His retort exposes the *oikos*-rooted impossibility of sparing her life. She and Aegisthus are a "polluted pair",[4] and the killing of them is a kind of surgical operation in which the diseased part of the household's body is cut away. With Aegisthus there is no more to it than that: he has "suffered the adulterer's punishment as the law allows".[5] But Clytemnestra's case is different. She is Orestes's mother and he cannot kill her without bringing upon himself a singularly heinous form of blood-guilt: "my victory", as he neatly puts it, "is a pollution".[6]

We see a pattern established early in the *Agamemnon* reappearing at the end of the second play of the trilogy. Agamemnon had either to sacrifice his daughter or abandon the Trojan

---

[1] *Ibid.*, l. 962.   [2] *Ibid.*, l. 871.   [3] *Ibid.*, ll. 908-9.
[4] *Ibid.*, l. 944.   [5] *Ibid.*, l. 990.
[6] *Ibid.*, l. 1017. And his last words to his mother, before he forced her indoors to kill her, were "you murdered whom you should not; suffer now what should not be" (l. 930).

expedition—both courses involving him in guilt. Orestes, in the next generation, has to kill his mother, but he cannot do this without making himself answerable to the Furies, the pre-Olympian chthonic goddesses whose chief office is to punish those who have shed kindred blood. This second dilemma of the trilogy falls inside the action, unlike the first, and is more fully articulated. Orestes's compulsion to matricide is urged throughout at the level of the house's present desperate sickness; he comes as the healer from within. And to this necessity Aeschylus adds a second, of duty towards Agamemnon performed in obedience to divine command; Apollo has charged Orestes to kill his father's murderers, warning him that he will be pursued by the Furies who have been roused by this earlier killing within the family, if he fails in his duty[1]: so that he must offend his mother's Furies by acting and his father's Furies by doing nothing. We find, as in the *Agamemnon*, a parallel working of human and superhuman logics, and Aeschylus shows wonderful art in his disclosure of the full religio-social complex during the few lines of dialogue which culminate in Orestes forcing Clytemnestra into the palace for the vengeance-killing. Orestes has a companion in the *Libation-Bearers*, a young man of about his own age called Pylades. Pylades is quite unlike any stage-figure in Greek Tragedy. He enters with Orestes and remains on-stage almost continuously; but he says nothing. The silence of Orestes's friend is something we grow used to; it has become a settled feature of the dramatic scene long before Orestes confronts his mother; and now, four-fifths of the way through the play, Clytemnestra and Orestes are talking and Pylades is standing by, and Orestes turns to Pylades and asks: "What shall I do, Pylades? Shall reverence for motherhood hold me back? Shall I spare her?" And Pylades speaks for the first and only time:

> Then what will become of Apollo's Pythian oracles? And of our covenants pledged on oath? Count all men your enemies rather than the gods.[2]

Our shock at this unexpected finding of voice is a pale reflection of what a fifth-century audience must have felt. Their theatre worked with three actors, and a sharp distinction was inevitable, in dramaturgy and in play-watching, between speak-

---

[1] *Ibid.*, ll. 269-305.　　　　[2] *Ibid.*, ll. 899-902.

ing parts (taken by the actors, with necessary doublings) and mutes. Some of the mutes of Greek Tragedy are impressive presences—but they are mute. Conversely, some of the speaking parts are very slight, but there are no half measures over their speaking: you do not find characters with only two or three lines to utter. Pylades is the only exception to this rule; he begins and continues like a mute, and nobody watching the *Libation-Bearers* from within the Greek convention, as Pylades is introduced and repeatedly indicated without responding, can doubt that he is a mute; so that Aeschylus has secured the most complete arrest of attention, a stopping of dramatic time, for Orestes's direct, inescapable question: "What shall I do, Pylades?"

Commentators, finding a touch of nature here, explain that Orestes has been moved by his mother's appeal, face to face, and is faltering in his resolve to kill her; and they remain strangely uninterested in the unique pseudo-mute who is being thrust into speech. "What shall I do?" flows not from inner uncertainty but from the need to achieve full exposure of the Oresteian dilemma; we should conceive the thing from the standpoint of dramaturgic policy, situationally. The dialogue between mother and son sustains the *oikos*-theme in the generalising way of Aeschylean stichomythia:

CL.: But you must not mention my sins without mentioning your father's too.
OR.: But you must not accuse one who laboured while you were sitting idle at home.
CL.: It is a hard thing, my child, for women to be deprived of a husband.
OR.: Yet it is the man's effort which supports them while they stay at home.[1]

and states the simple and, at this stage, ultimate opposition of mother's Furies to father's:

CL.: Watch out! Beware the hounds that avenge a mother.
OR.: And the hounds that avenge a father—how shall I escape them if I leave this deed undone?[2]

But Apollo's command—the Olympian echo, as it were, of the human and chthonian debates—does not arise between them.

[1] *Ibid.*, ll. 918-21.　　　　[2] *Ibid.*, ll. 924-5.

That is left to Pylades; and in his one utterance we sense an
awful authority, as if the god had possessed the seeming-mute
and spoken through him.

Questions like this "What shall I do?", building up the
dramatic moment *ab extra*, are common in Aeschylus. Earlier in
the *Libation-Bearers* the Chorus are telling Orestes that Clytemnestra has had an ill-omened dream:

> OR.: Have you heard what the dream was? Can you tell it right?
> CH.: She dreamt she gave birth to a snake—that is her own
>   account.
> OR.: What followed? How does the story end?
> CH.: She swaddled it and laid it to rest like a little child.
> OR.: What food did it crave, the new-born venomous brute?
> CH.: In her dream she offered it her breast.
> OR.: Surely her nipple was wounded by the loathsome thing?
> CH.: Yes; with the milk it drew forth clots of blood.[1]

Orestes is very plainly prompting, he is not asking, and the
function of a line like "What food did it crave . . .", cast in
question form, is to coax into the open an aspect of Clytemnestra's dream which the dramatist wants mentioned. This kind
of exchange is first cousin to epic narrative in that the information that emerges serves the unfolding tale and not the questioner's ignorance. Which is not, of course, to argue that the
questioner knows the answer, that Orestes turns to Pylades with
his mind irrevocably made up: rather, that the modern critical
sensibility grasping at a Hamletish indecision finds itself empty-
handed. We have to direct outward and institutionalise the
horror and disgust and contempt of Shakespeare's "Almost as
bad, good mother, As kill a king and marry with his brother"
in order to understand where Aeschylus is laying his finger in
"What! Kill my father and then share my house?"; and
similarly, when Orestes asks "What shall I do, Pylades?", we
can only follow the question into the contemplated and im-
minent deed, a further facet of which Pylades is about to
illuminate and where poetry and meaning reside. It will be
objected that "contemplated" admits the play of consciousness
upon possibilities of action, and in a way this is just. But the
consciousness here admitted refers us to the watchman's thought

[1] *Ibid.*, ll. 526-33.

at the beginning of the trilogy: "And yet the house itself, could it but speak, would have a plain tale to tell"; the voices of humanity are the fragmented voice of the house of Atreus, and for the outraged and judging *oikos* the vengeance-killing of Clytemnestra is both a necessity and another terrible self-wounding. If we think of Orestes contemplating his deed, we must also remember that he is "the eye of the house". The Chorus's vision of him coming as the healer from within was, they now see, premature. Not proved false, of course, but judgment waits on the event as he defiles his hands with kindred blood, doing what must be done. The image of a storm beating against the house reappears.[1] Orestes rushes out, pursued by the Furies. He goes to seek ritual cleansing from Apollo, and the Chorus are left wondering, in the closing lines of the *Libation-Bearers*, whether Orestes is in truth "a deliverer—or shall I say a doom?"[2]

This question is answered in the *Eumenides* where Orestes is formally brought to trial by the Furies and acquitted by a court of law constituted for this occasion. Apollo, divine counsel for the defence, urges an honest count of votes with the solemn insistence: "the cast of a single vote has been known to raise a fallen house".[3] Thus the issue proves happy in which the single and the corporate fates are united, and Orestes's self-pollution through killing his mother is not finally ruinous. Aeschylus binds his third play to his second by means of Orestes's pollution, presenting a full life-cycle, from its inception at Clytemnestra's killing—the criminal duty, the "victory" which is also "a pollution"—to its departure confirmed (or perhaps effected) by the trial verdict. The staging of its initial attachment to Orestes deserves close attention. He follows his mother's death with a statement of his doubts and fears to the Chorus. They reply, firmly: "No, you have done well . . ."[4]; and at once he gives a shout of terror, for he has seen the Furies. Then this dialogue takes place:

CH.: What fancies are troubling you, best of sons to Agamemnon?
    Bear up; you must not let fear completely get the better of you.

---

[1] *Ibid.*, ll. 1065-7.   [2] *Ibid.*, ll. 1073-4.
[3] *Eumenides*, l. 751.   [4] *Libation-Bearers*, l. 1044.

or.: No fancies, these troubles—not to me. The hounds that
avenge mother-slaying are here, plain for me to see.

ch.: The blood on your hands is still fresh: that explains your
deranged mind.

or.: More and more—O lord Apollo—swarms of them. Look!
And their eyes weep bloody pus.

ch.: You have one way of being cleansed: Apollo's touch will rid
you of this affliction.

or.: You do not see them—but I do. They are after me; I must
escape.[1]

[Orestes rushes out

Orestes sees the Furies because his mother's blood is fresh on
his hands, and when he has been cleansed by Apollo he will
cease to see them. The Furies are subjective manifestations in
the sense that they appear only to Orestes, but they have
objective status in that their visible presence is grounded in the
material human blood on his hands: they cannot be called
figments of his imagination any more than the blood can be so
called. It is most important to respect the relation between
blood and Furies established in this dialogue because we are
thus warned to eschew the subject/object dichotomy whereby
we normally interpret such appearances (old Hamlet's ghost
is objective, Banquo's is subjective) and which is prevalent in
modern Aeschylean criticism. To summarise, commentators
conceive the Furies to exist at some point on a line extending
from pure subjective fantasy to pure objective fact; they dis-
agree as to the location of this point (those who believe in a
primitive Aeschylus place it near the objective extreme, those
who see him attaining or groping towards the idea of the
troubled conscience place it towards the other end), but they
do not doubt that the image of the subject-object line is a
satisfactory one for the conduct of their argument.[2] Nevertheless, the coupling of blood and Furies indicates that this image
provides a false frame of reference, or, if it is to be retained, that
the objective correlate of Orestes's solitary vision compels us to
place the Furies at both ends of the line simultaneously; for the
solitude of his vision is not the solitude of an unshared hallucination, but the solitude of this one pair of bloody hands.

[1] Ibid., ll. 1051-62, retaining αἷμα at 1058.

[2] Wilamowitz lent his authority to the "guilty conscience" interpretation;
Murray believed Orestes to be temporarily mad.

In fact we may avoid all these complexities by allowing Orestes's physical defilement and his seeing of the Furies to make their impact together, in a naively immediate way, as they do at the end of the *Libation-Bearers*. Seeing the Furies is proof of a kind of guilt, and having bloody hands evidences defilement; the culpable state of being is continuous with its manifestations, and Aeschylus and his society provide us with a single term embracing both: pollution. Moreover, the logic of pollution, the defilement-guilt unity, applies to the Furies as well as to Orestes; they pursue him (that is, they react to the mother-slaying) because of the physical taint, being represented in the *Eumenides* as tracking him down by the scent of blood upon him.

The reader of the *Oresteia* is under pressure—from himself as well as from the critical tradition—to convert pollution into something more familiar; it comes easier to make the Chorus tell Orestes that the shock and horror of the killing have produced an hallucination—the vision is "mental", the Furies aren't really there—than to follow Aeschylus in a simple going-together of defiled hands and apparition-assaulted consciousness. The more comfortable idea matches a double standard of inward guilt and outward defilement, the less comfortable and the correct, a single standard of pollution; and the need to discriminate between the more and the less comfortable idea is proved by the false double standard leading to a wilderness of subject/object dissensions[1] and to a near-systematic rewriting of the *Eumenides*. The rending in two of Aeschylean pollution has focussed attention on a contradiction which the most casual reader cannot fail to notice. At the end of the *Libation-Bearers* Orestes rushes out, bloody-handed and pursued by the Furies, to present himself at the shrine of Apollo for ritual cleansing. The opening of the *Eumenides* finds him at the shrine where the god receives him as a suppliant for purification and where the ceremony duly takes place. In consequence of this Orestes maintains firmly throughout the play that he is no longer polluted. Apollo supports him in this argument,[2] and Athena, the goddess-judge of the case, expressly recognises that the rites

---

[1] Are we considering primitive contagion or sophisticated guilt? We have to make up our minds about this so long as we apply what I call "the false double standard".

[2] *Eumenides*, ll. 576-8.

have been effective.[1] All would be clear and consistent did not Aeschylus give us an Orestes who is still, in dramatic fact, polluted—still dripping blood, still drawing the Furies after him by its smell, still (in the Furies' words) with a dark cloud of pollution hanging over him[2] which makes it impossible for him to return to his house or take part in common worship.[3]

This is the collision of facts—of effective cleansing with continuing pollution—which has exercised commentators. Some of Verrall's furthest flights were inspired by his unwillingness to believe that so mature a thinker as Aeschylus would have Orestes dripping with his mother's blood months after he has killed her. Verrall explained the blood at one point—there is no denying that it is there in the text—as that of animals Orestes has sacrificed, and at another as Orestes's own; the wandering exile has cut his feet on the long walk from Apollo's shrine at Delphi to Athens, or his exhaustion has brought on an internal haemorrhage and he is bleeding at the mouth.[4] These theories would not resolve the contradiction even if they were acceptable (since they fail to explain why Orestes is still polluted), but they do reveal the false double standard at work. They buy a sophisticated interpretation of Orestes's guilt or innocence at the cost of a primitive interpretation of the Furies and the defiling blood; the guilty state is severed from the bloodstained hands, leaving the commentator free to spiritualise the former and banish the latter to a world of crude material superstitions in which blood—any blood—attracts the Furies who are to be found following each and every trail with the abandon of ill-trained hounds. We end by supposing that Aeschylus and other enlightened spirits understood the *Oresteia* at the level of guilt and innocence, and the fifth-century groundlings at the level of defilement and purgation.

The sophisticated and the primitive worlds are both fictions erected on the grave of Aeschylean pollution; they bear no relation to his text, and so the text is manipulated into rough and ready conformity to the fictions. We are told that " 'purgation' is a survival and has little reality"[5] in Aeschylus's story because the commentator has trapped himself into maintaining that purgation has nothing more serious than defilement, noth-

---

[1] *Ibid.* ll. 473-5. [2] *Ibid.*, l. 377. [3] *Ibid.*, ll. 653-6.
[4] Notes on ll. 41, 244. [5] Verrall, xvii.

ing more pregnant with mind, to which it can minister. And although the contradiction between Orestes's ritual purgation and his continuing pollution is not resolved in this way, it is rendered tolerable by being assigned to that part of the story or to a level of treatment which Aeschylus did not greatly care about. Thus the issue is cheapened by a procedure which is as slovenly as it is dishonest. Paradoxically, it is by giving the contradiction its full value that its dramatic function becomes intelligible. What must remain an absurdity on the plane of defilement (how can Orestes be both clean and unclean?) grows into a sudden imaginative harmony on that of psycho-physical pollution where the relation of unclean hands and soul is one of continuity, and not of primitive and sophisticated levels of dramaturgy or of symbolic parallelism or of anything else. Indeed, the famous contradiction is our assurance that Aeschylus accepts and respects this simple continuity, that he lives within it and imagines through it; for the terrible doubleness of Orestes's position is faithfully rendered in the actuality of his cleansed and still-polluted hands.

With Orestes as with Agamemnon, Aeschylus returns the answer yes and no to our question "Is he guilty?"; and again we have to purge the question of all individualistic preconceiving in order to read the answer right. This means, primarily, a resolute containment of revenge when we regard Orestes's act, and, when we study its consequences, an ability to see him with the household's eyes—to stand with the domestic slave-women of the Chorus, waiting to see whether he will prove a deliverer or a doom—before we call the tragedy his. It is a mistake to suppose that the Furies' persecution of him is inspired by personal malignity, very much as it is a mistake to give a Hamletish twist to "What! Kill my father and then share my house?" Their statement at the trial, in answer to Apollo's defence of Orestes, has the same foundation of social and institutional impossibility as his retort to his mother:

> Just consider the meaning of your plea for his acquittal. Shall one who has spilt blood of kin, his mother's blood, on the ground—shall he afterwards live in his father's house in Argos? Shall he take part in public worship, at altars and where kinsfolk wash in holy water?[1]

[1] *Eumenides*, ll. 652-6.

The house cannot keep the mother or recover the son: this is the centre of distress and the full significance of the threat to the life, or life-in-death, of the wandering exile. The *montage* of the choral lyric is not random:

> Dark is the cloud of pollution hovering over the man, and rumour carried on voices of mourning proclaims that a mist-thick gloom covers his house.[1]

The false critical refinement that spiritualises psycho-physical pollution into a more tractable notion of guilt attenuates the dramatic object miserably, and recalls the fate of the carpet scene in the *Agamemnon*. We may venture the general observation that the boundaries of the self in Greek and especially Aeschylean Tragedy are more fluid than we allow. In the *Libation-Bearers*, when Electra discovers a lock of hair which Orestes has cut off as a religious offering,[2] when she holds it up and notes its likeness to her own hair and dares to wonder if it might be her brother's, the scene somehow confounds our sense of the pathetic; and insight into this strangeness comes later in the play when Orestes produces the robe in which Agamemnon was murdered, has it spread out, indicts Clytemnestra by it, ponders what name to call it ("a trap for a wild beast . . . a corpse's shroud . . . a hunting-net") and brings it into the foreground of his lament for his father, by which he sets right the denial of observances at his death: "Now at last I am here to speak his praises, to make lament for my father as I address the robe that brought death to him."[3] The Penguin translator does right to bring out the stand-in function of the robe—as the translator with a critical axe to grind does not feel entitled to attempt:

> *I offer now my lament, since I may not see his body,*
> *To this treacherous web that caught and killed my father.*

For he thus exposes the source of the incident's mysterious power (to which many who have seen the trilogy will testify) in the robe's effective communion with the long-dead king its

---

[1] *Ibid.*, ll. 377-80.
[2] ll. 164-204.
[3] ll. 980-1015. I do not follow the Oxford Text's pointing of 1015.

wearer.[1] The scene is a beckoning forward of the murdered man, to which we respond through our vestigial awareness of the communion under discussion—an awareness evidenced by the fascination of the personal possessions of the dead or absent,[2] and even by that obscure sense of a falling away from self, mixed with a lingering self-identity, which a man experiences at the sight of his hair on the floor of a barber's shop. Aeschylus affects us in this hidden way, through an exploitation of the nebulous fringe of selfhood which is very much more eloquent than anything we are able to summon from within ourselves: confident in its articulation, not in any sense fugitive or irrational. We leave our world of subjective pathos—of Constance's "Grief fills the room up of my absent child. . . . Stuffs out his vacant garments with his form"[3]—for a new, and immeasurably old, literalism.

We respond more readily to Orestes's lock of hair and Agamemnon's robe, where the communion of self with object is individual, than we do to the purple carpet of the *Agamemnon* whose capacity to suffer outrage is commensurate with its *oikos*-determined dignity. A carpet is a carpet until it is shown to be something more—and the something more being in this case the body, the psycho-physical substance, of the house of Atreus, we do not experience the same degree of subliminal receptiveness. The consequent undervaluing of Clytemnestra's economic *hubris* and the self-wounding of the house in the *Agamemnon* is matched by the personalistic, revenge-dominated view of Orestes's exploit in the *Libation-Bearers*. Against this we have urged the corporate fight for health and life, and the single great death threatening all. But the persistence of the economic strand ought also to be noted. Orestes's account of himself "turned brute-savage by the forfeiture of my inheritance"[4] has embarrassed commentators and led to fanciful

---

[1] Compare the extraordinary prominence of Xerxes's tattered clothes in the *Persians*. When his mother learns about his defeat, she says (ll. 846-8): "What pains me most is to hear of the shameful clothes in which my son is dressed."

[2] The worldwide habit of burying possessions with their dead owner is often explained as directed to their serving him in the next world. This obscures the essential fact of their communion with, or continuity with, his *persona*.

[3] *King John*, III, 4, 93.   [4] *Libation-Bearers*, l. 275.

glossing of its plain sense because it looks unworthy, selfish, greedy, to the eye that can only follow the material and spiritual strands in separation. For Orestes, there is nothing incongruous in coupling the incentives of "the god's command and my great grief for my father and with these the pinch of poverty"[1]; nor for Electra in expressing the pity of her brother's plight through his "being held from his patrimony".[2] The *oikos*-theme is one.

And a certain consistency appears also in the present discussion. For the robe and lock of hair and carpet and whole family wealth, saturated in individual or corporate selfhood, acquire their value through the same apprehension of outward and inward continuity that produces the moral logic of pollution. The thrusting outward of the self into a world of "mere" objects reciprocates the power of blood on the hands to taint the soul. Indeed the earlier warning against imposing a subject-object dichotomy on Aeschylus ought to be framed more widely, until his entire dramatic universe is placed in a middleground of the imagination where not only are objects *psyche*-drenched but human subjects objectify, externalise themselves—at first sight very strangely. Electra greets Orestes, when he has revealed himself to her after years of separation and misery, with a declaration of love. This takes the form of a statement that she has "four shares"[3] or parts of love to bestow on him— the share her father would have had were he alive, the share her mother has forfeited, the share that would have gone to her sister Iphigeneia, and his own share as her brother. It is as if her love, or herself loving, were made up into four undelivered parcels which Orestes now appropriates. This picture of the individual's emotional life (which would not have surprised Aristotle) strikes quaint and cold to us who are strangers, almost, to the multiple self,[4] and who take an inward concentration (our Electra would nurse a single flame of love deep within her) for selfhood's principle. Nor have we the containing *oikos* to vivify Electra's dry scheme of family relations, and to counterbalance the faint personal self with the strength of the collective consciousness. The house is a horse reined in by a

---

[1] *Ibid.*, ll. 300-1.   [2] *Ibid.*, ll. 135-6.   [3] *Ibid.*, l. 238.

[4] Orestes's contention at the trial (*Eumenides*, ll. 600-2) that Clytemnestra stands doubly attainted because she killed both her husband and his father is not a mere sophistry.

cruel rider; it is a ship weltering in heavy seas; it is a building in a storm; it is a human being lifting up her eyes in joy to welcome the deliverer. Aeschylus gives to Clytemnestra (silencing consideration of her sincerity as he does so) the image, only very gently roused and then as gently parted from, of a tree whose life has shrunk back into its root in Agamemnon's absence, now nourished and brought to its full being by his return:

> The root still lives, and the leaves return to spread over the house a shade against the dog-star: such is your homecoming to your house's hearth—a sign of warmth in winter. Yes, and when Zeus is making wine from the bitter grape, then at once there is coolness in the house when its undoubted lord moves about his halls.[1]

A fitting commentary on the *oikos*-theme, and on the poetic dramatist's power to render the house clear through (not in spite of) an extreme conceptual imprecision—a unity of elements whose co-operative diversity is its life.

4 The Aeschylean Norm

Those (and they are many) who look to the trial of Orestes for a solution to the troubles of the house of Atreus will always be disappointed. The trial solves nothing; there is no discoverable argument or attitude which the court accepts; in any case, the votes are equally divided, and all Athena, the court's divine president, does by finding for Orestes is to cut the knot: her "vote is (in modern language) not judicial; it merely determines (by arbitrary choice) the practical question necessarily raised by the non-decision of the court".[2]

---

[1] *Agamemnon*, ll. 966-72. Note the reiteration of the Greek: *domous, dōmatitin, domois, dōma*. And note the dreadful things that happen when the *oikos* is subordinated by the critic: "While the root of the vine (the root of sin—the slaughter of Iphigeneia) lives, foliage comes to the house . . . but when, in the autumn, Zeus draws wine (blood) from the young grape (virgin), then at last there is coolness about the house. . . ." (p. 101 of Professor George Thomson's commentary).

[2] Verrall, note on l. 737. Aeschylus does not make it entirely clear whether Athena gives her own vote, or whether she declares, without voting herself, that the effect of an equal division of the votes of the human jurymen will be to acquit Orestes. The second alternative is preferable.

But the trial does present us with a dramatic image of dead-lock, which liberalising commentators spoil by reading into the *Eumenides*, and the whole trilogy, an Aeschylean intention to oppose civilised principles of equity and morals to the savagery of blood-guilt, pollution and ritual purgation. Now it should not be doubted that Aeschylus intended his stage-trial to evoke memories of recent and not so recent Athenian history. In the distant past a court had been instituted, the very ancient Council of Areopagus, for the trial of persons charged with murder; and when Aeschylus shows Athena establishing this "tribunal to last for all time"[1] and then dramatises "the first trial ever held for bloodshed",[2] he is plainly commending, *ex post facto*, the assumption by the State of jurisdiction over a matter which had previously been left for the family to deal with by the immemorial methods of self-help and offer of amends.[3] He is celebrating the victory of State justice over family justice, and it may be supposed that his reason for satisfaction is the obvious one: a properly constituted court of law, with rules of evidence and judges bound by oath and enforceable decisions, makes a more efficient juridical instrument than the bloody and protracted vendetta. But further than that one ought not to go. Aeschylus's text, soaked as it is in a profound collective horror of pollution and in respect for ritual cleansing, renders untenable all suggestion of conscious archaising in his treatment of the myth; he is not looking down from a position of superior enlightenment upon the urgencies of the *Oresteia*, and this is the sense in which the trial affords no solution. It *decides* something certainly; a verdict is reached, the knot is cut. But it solves nothing.

[1] *Eumenides*, l. 484.

[2] *Ibid.*, l. 682.

[3] It is also historically important that trial for homicide was the oldest function of the Areopagus, and that its further reformation by Pericles and Ephialtes (a bare three years before the production of this play) left it with little else.

The *Eumenides* theme of Athens's friendship with Argos is also clearly intended by Aeschylus to remind his audience of events in the real world; and he probably wrote the solemn account (in the *Agamemnon*) of death and privation at Troy with one eye upon Athenian sufferings in military campaigns abroad at the middle of the fifth century. In general, and for good reasons, scholars are less eager than they once were to find references to contemporary history in Greek Tragedy.

The image of deadlock recovers its massive simplicity when we cease to believe that it is transcended.[1] And the same is true of the dilemma prefacing the trilogy; this too is ultimate, and appreciation of its cogency waits on our abandoning of the fretful search for an acceptable adult morality against which to interpret Agamemnon's problem and his address to it. To look for a non-existent higher wisdom is to overlook the wisdom which fact and event simply expose; this is the heroic gravity of the Aeschylean "kindness coming from the gods" which brings "understanding even to those who do not want it".[2] Here, within a Greek and altogether alien modesty of expectation, Aeschylus is distinguished by his grateful hailing of the sufferer's compulsion towards understanding of the force that crushes him. We remark again the absence of the outraged individual in the *Oresteia*, and the unabject submissiveness (also very alien) that comes with acknowledgment of a guilt that is coextensive with the generations of a tainted family. The collective conscience surveys Agamemnon's dilemma without protest.

The clarity and rigidity of that dilemma are achieved through Agamemnon the king and general confronting Agamemnon the head of the house of Atreus and father of Iphigeneia; there can be no way out while the one man respects both his obligations. That "while"—all-important to a modern sensibility—holds no dramatic interest for Aeschylus, who would merely obscure the inexorable objectivity of Agamemnon's plight if he were to admit, as it were beneath the status-determined clash of king and father, an accompanying "personal" hesitation between two possible courses of action. (There is no such thing as inaction in Greek Tragedy.) The effect would be to focus attention, through Agamemnon's struggle to do the right thing, upon his final choice (like Orestes killing his mother in the

---

[1] Those who believe that the deadlock is transcended concentrate variously on religion, morals, politics, law and (I am thinking of Professor Thomson) sociology; while Professor Kitto argues for a "progressive" Zeus who begins a savage tyrant and improves during the trilogy: see his *Form and Meaning in Drama*. (A progressive Zeus has often been postulated in the Prometheus trilogy.) Wilamowitz stands a little apart, in *Aischylos. Interpretationen* and elsewhere, because of his preoccupation with the transcending of Apollo's rather than the Furies' position in the *Eumenides* trial.

[2] *Agamemnon*, ll. 180-3.

H

Libation-Bearers and the court acquitting Orestes in the *Eumenides*, Agamemnon decides, he cuts the knot; and in his case as in theirs an utter poverty, imaginative and intellectual, attends the decision itself because it solves nothing) instead of upon the beautiful, wisdom-yielding dilemma in which the trilogy's master-image of deadlock is first seen.

Then all that is required is that Agamemnon shall be at once king and father: if we say "a good king and a good father" we are likely to forget that bad kings and fathers are unkingly and unfatherly, and so to misapprehend the interlocking of status and stage-event which is no other thing than the perfectly clear and rigid figure Aeschylus means us to admire. We ought to distinguish Aeschylean status, while we are observing Agamemnon the king, from status in medieval and renaissance literature where the sense of a world of personal choice lying beneath the status-defined situation may be fully awake and may give rise (as in Shakespeare's *Richard II*) to a sustained tragic counterpoint in which the man and the office are played against each other. With Agamemnon there is no suppression of the second world, the lower or inward world, because the man and the office are not conceived in separation; the eye rests on the typeface of the mask, and follows the king in his kingly ways. Exalted status in Aeschylus determines the quality of the event itself, or (for the converse holds) the great event is indissolubly married to exalted status; it cannot *engage* people of modest station, whereas in neo-classical heroic Tragedy, the Rules being what they are, it is merely unlikely to *involve* them.

And so the rare and remarkable action, the dramatically significant action, entails the actor who (almost literally) measures up to it. And the interlocking of status and event which demands the exalted and therefore the extraordinary dramatic personage also directs the dramatic action in accordance with a ruling canon of ordinariness or normalcy, since consciousness of the human self can only speak through status when the relationship between what a man is and how he acts is believed to be constant, so that the leading distinctions of rank, age and sex will be reflected predictably in conduct. If this were not so, men would cease to apprehend one another through status (as in fact they have largely ceased to do) and adopt some more reliable medium. When status isolates a man, it does so in order to arouse a generic interest in him—an interest in the fulfilment of normal expectations. Isolation of this kind may be emphatic, as with Orestes, and yet leave the generic character of the interest unaffected: the duty to avenge falls on Orestes alone, but the convention of status which isolates the surviving son of the murdered father also predetermines his duty. This picture we pervert into one of a Hamletish young man making up his mind what his duty is in the face of competing external claims upon him, and we do so because the norm of conduct and situation is able to provide ourselves with no more than a frame of reference within which to interpret individual gestures of deviation and compliance. The norm itself seems essentially inert.

Aeschylean status brings to mind the *Poetics* and its requirement of appropriateness, for Aristotle's advice to the dramatist to make his kings kingly, his women womanly, his slaves slavish, betokens to us the very inertia now under discussion. Aristotle and Aeschylus share a Greek regard for the rationality of art— in fact for its fulfilment of normal expectations—which leads them to look upon the unkingly king as an intellectual and aesthetic chaos; but, as Aristotle might have added, explaining himself by a reference to Clytemnestra in the *Oresteia*, the artist may create a local chaos in order to define a total order. Clytemnestra is isolated from the beginning of the trilogy by her abnormality; introducing a woman "manlike in her purposes",[1] Aeschylus breaks the Aristotelian rule in order to throw a premonitory light upon the abnormal individual. This seems an unremarkable procedure to us for whom the errant case defying type-classification is art's main concern, and for whom the bare fact of deviation is morally and religiously unpointed: Alyosha Karamazov and Smerdyakov are equally remote from any norm one might assert; everything turns upon the direction of deviation. But not so for Aeschylus, in whose work the juxtaposing of the asserted norm with actual or threatened rupture of normalcy is morally and religiously—and dramatically—stressful. In the *Oresteia*, as we shall now remark, this specifically Aeschylean stress is seen mainly in Clytemnestra's sexual and ritual non-compliance with the socioreligious norm.

[1] *Agamemnon*, l. 11.

Reading the *Agamemnon*, we find silence in two places where we might expect an erotic motif to be prominent, or at least to be discernible. The first is the meeting of husband and wife after long separation—a moment sufficiently appealing for the commentator to feel inspired to defy his text and, dreaming of absent friends, to pronounce that Agamemnon finally allows Clytemnestra to persuade him to walk upon the tapestries because "when she urges him again, he thinks she loves him, and he yields".[1]

And the second is the introduction of Cassandra, the Trojan princess and seer, who appears before us as Agamemnon's war-prize. What are the relations between them? Aeschylus does not say. Cassandra will enter the household as a slave, and it accords with archaic (though not with fifth-century) convention that she should become his concubine.[2] But the last point is left entirely undeveloped; and it strikes us as an omission of primary human material, particularly since there is trouble afoot between husband and wife, that we are not told whether Agamemnon and Cassandra are lovers. In fact, nobody shows the slightest interest in their sexual affairs—except Clytemnestra, who calls Cassandra Agamemnon's "bedfellow", adding the plainly mendacious sneer that she is also a sailors' prostitute.[3]

There is, then, a pattern of acceptance which Clytemnestra alone stands outside. Her isolation (because of the external link between the abnormal in Aeschylus and modern individualistic humanism) gives her a psychological plausibility and firmness of definition which no other figure in the trilogy commands, and a modern sensibility snatches hungrily at the touches of reckless moral autonomy, of sexual insolence and of blasphemy, which Aeschylus bestows on her. These are the marks of villainy for him as they are for us, the difference between ancient and modern resting in the relation between the vicious individual and the work of art in which she appears. While we drive the issue inward and speak (perhaps) of Clytemnestra's

---

[1] J. T. Sheppard, *Cambridge Ancient History*, vol. V, p. 124.

[2] And even in Homer, Laertes did not sleep with Eurycleia: he "shrank from the anger of his wife" (*Odyssey*, I, 433). But Professor Thomson's assertion that Agamemnon "with unperturbed effrontery asks his wife to extend her welcome to his concubine" (*Aeschylus and Athens*, p. 261) is unwarranted.

[3] *Agamemnon*, ll. 1441-3. "Bedfellow" is certain, but not the rest.

jealousy of Cassandra, or of a study of lust in her self-abandonment to Aegisthus, Aeschylus is concerned to dramatise the
impact made by female sexuality run wild upon the norm of
sexual containment within the *oikos*. His eye is upon the independence of her sexuality, not upon its inwardly perverse
character. Of course Clytemnestra behaves as she does because
her appetites are what they are; the Aeschylean theme may be
translated into a familiar language, though not without re-
versing the intentions of the *Oresteia*. Consider Orestes's words
to his mother, after he has killed Aegisthus:

> Come here; I mean to kill you close beside him. In life you pre-
> ferred him to my father—so sleep with him in death; for he is the
> man you love, and you hate that other whom you were bound
> to love.[1]

When he says that Clytemnestra was bound to love Agamemnon, Orestes does not mean that she should have striven to
arouse a feeling of love in herself, but that she should have
conformed to the love-situation in which she was placed; and
the love-situation is the norm, ruptured by Clytemnestra, of
containment within the *oikos*. We may proceed sociologically
and contrast her extra-marital relationship with the probable
one between Agamemnon and Cassandra which, falling within
the accepted *oikos*-framework, presents no live sexual issue to
the Greek observer. The two may be lovers or they may not—
it does not matter. Normalcy prevails, and, with normalcy,
health and peace and absence of dramatic tension.[2] Nobody
has anything to say, except Clytemnestra, and her accusations
are left by the way, unsupported and unrefuted. Or we may
proceed linguistically and recall the nearness-and-dearness
complex of *philia* in the *Poetics*.[3] When Orestes uses the super-
lative *philtatos* of the mother who hates him and whom he hates,[4]
and when the brothers Eteocles and Polyneices, the mortal

---

[1] *Libation-Bearers*, ll. 904-7.
[2] It is superficial to speak of one sexual morality for men and another,
more rigorous, for women: the root concern is for the shared blood of the
family, which is easily safeguarded against the husband's promiscuity by
rules of legitimacy, but not against the wife's.
[3] See pp. 57-8 above.
[4] *Libation-Bearers*, l. 234.

enemies of the *Seven against Thebes*, are called *philoi*, each in relation to the other,[1] we learn from these loveless uses of love that the state of soul and the psychic impulse, involuntary or partly involuntary, have no determined pre-eminence; and, further, that Aeschylus is capable of ironic word-play in his address to family hatreds. While Orestes is holding one love against another—Clytemnestra's love for Aegisthus against the love she owes her husband—the language and the sociology of the *Oresteia* require us to read the irony objectively: I mean to unsettle our likely pre-established focus on the loving soul and on contrasted qualities of emotion, and to stand with Orestes inside that love-situation from which his mother has escaped, thus allowing him to speak at once for the outraged *oikos* and for the ruptured norm. We must see Clytemnestra's brazen sexuality in terms of the corporate values and of the norm which it challenges. To proceed in the opposite way, to build the work of art round the sexually inflamed,[2] the jealous and prurient wife, is to make the tail wag the dog. The simplest Athenian in Aeschylus's audience will not have made this mistake—indeed he will have been further from error than his more sophisticated fellows—because he lived in a society where women had no public life to live, neither political nor sacerdotal nor military, and where their private self was supposed to find fulfilment and a complete exhaustion of resources in sustaining the larger family life in which it was enveloped.[3] And so his response to the local eroticism of the *Oresteia* will have been a thrill of fear at this assault on group stability and peace, and this threatening of the self-identical blood of the family (which is the psycho-physical essence of kinship) with weakening and defilement.

Orestes confronts his mother at last, and the sexual issue suddenly flares into prominence. At this great moment of the

[1] l. 971.

[2] A fragment of Aeschylus (243) speaks of "the burning gaze of a girl who has tasted man".

[3] I believe it to be true, and remarkable, and relevant to the study of Attic Tragedy, that Athenian women had less independence than the women of other Greek societies which were in most respects less liberal than Athens. But see A. W. Gomme's challenge to the older orthodoxy to which I subscribe: "The Position of Women in Athens in the Fifth and Fourth Centuries B.C." (in his *Essays in Greek History and Literature*).

trilogy the vital and dramatic fact is that sex has escaped from its proper place in the world of women:

OR.: It's you I'm looking for. He [*pointing towards the corpse of Aegisthus whom he has just killed off-stage, or perhaps pointing at it lying visible on the ekkuklēma*] has had enough.

CL.: Alas! Dead then, my brave Aegisthus, my dearest.

OR.: You love the man? Then you shall lie with him in the grave, faithful to him for ever—in death.[1]

The very exceptional erotic sharpness on both sides of the dialogue is the occasion of that thrill of fear which we have distinguished from the horror (Hamletish again) that comes to rest in contemplation of a depraved consciousness. "You love the man?" is awkwardly primitive (these two have been "lovers" for many years) if we suppose Orestes to be peering into his mother's mind, but not if we stand within the norm, with Orestes and the house of Atreus and Aeschylus and the fifth-century audience, denouncing the naked circumstance of aberration. And with the Chorus, whose song at the moment when the plan for the double killing is put into action insists upon the generalising and "impersonal" standpoint from which Clytemnestra is to be observed and judged. The theme of their song is that "inordinate desire, mastering female natures, proves too strong for the established couplings of animals and of human kind"[2]; and they go on to offer the listener "who is not frivolous-minded" three *exempla* from legend.[3]

Broad-based as this indictment is, embracing against Clytemnestra the cause of ordered sexuality through all nature, we should be wrong to confine her challenge to normalcy and health entirely within its terms. (In fact the first *exemplum* does not illustrate sexual passion.) The Chorus, as so often in Aeschylus, let free a shifting cloud-pattern of suggestion and ampler truth in the first words of their song when they mention the "terrible things" and "monsters" of earth and sea.[4] For Clytemnestra is a monster. "What loathsome monster", asks Cassandra, rapt in prophetic vision, "affords me a just comparison with her? An Amphisbaena? Or a Scylla . . .?"[5] She is the female killer of the male as well as the wife possessed of lurking and potent sexual

---

[1] *Libation-Bearers*, ll. 892-5.   [2] *Ibid.*, ll. 599-601.   [3] *Ibid.*, ll. 602-38.
[4] *Ibid.*, ll. 585-8.   [5] *Agamemnon*, ll. 1232-3.

independence. Primarily she is the blasphemer. Her parodying of ritual forms, the baneful twists and inversions which she gives to cult-language, isolate her after the manner of her *oikos*-affronting desire, but more decisively because within a fuller socio-religious context of life's stability and normal working. Her account of her murder of Agamemnon brings out the connection between blasphemy and the life-process very clearly:

> I struck him twice. Twice he cried out, and crumpled up on the spot. When he was down I struck him a third blow in thanks and reverence to the infernal Zeus, saviour of the dead. And lying there he vomited up his life, spurting over me a shower of dark blood-drops; and I was glad just as the crops are glad at the blessing of Zeus-given rain when the sheath is giving birth to the ear.[1]

The passage opens with a hideous translation of the fact of husband-slaying into the language of religious sacrifice,[2] and then expands into a universal topsy-turvydom in which murder is rejoiced in as the bringer of life. Clytemnestra's giving of welcome to the quickening rain of her husband's blood will have struck the keenest tragic fear into a fifth-century audience; beneath the manifest affront to human decency they will have sensed an assault on life itself (their association of water with life was wider and more urgently human than it is for northern men: compare the "rivers that pour their gentle flood through the land and give increase of children, blandishing the soil with their rich waters" in the *Suppliant Women*),[3] and they will have flinched before this great objective blasphemy uttered from within nature, shaking its frame. The modern instinct, as with Clytemnestra's eroticism, is to make the tail wag the dog—to divert the main dramatic energy towards a presentation of the satanic individual. Difficulties then arise. We find ourselves

---

[1] *Ibid.*, ll. 1384-92.

[2] The blasphemy is heightened by the fact that Agamemnon has entered the palace intent on performing the religious offices required of the head of the *oikos*: the sacrificer is sacrificed. It is also possible (ll. 1056-8 have been variously interpreted) that Aeschylus makes play with the ambiguity involved in talk about sacrifice before the murder. There are two sets of sacrificial victims—the animals at the palace altar, and Agamemnon and Cassandra.

[3] ll. 1026-9.

repelled by Aeschylus's text in our most elementary enquiries about Clytemnestra's insincerity and blasphemous intent. We find the "good" people taking part with the "bad" in the sinister deflection of cult-language.[1]

We begin to suspect some initial misconceiving of Aeschylean villainy, and perhaps to reconsider its leading characteristic in the *Oresteia*, which is *tolma*, translated "recklessness", "over-boldness", or "daring". "Such is her daring"[2] says Cassandra of the husband-slayer. Helen, eloping with Paris, "dared a deed that is not to be dared".[3] These momentous transgressions have nothing to do with taking an unjustifiable risk in the familiar subjective sense; they are both condemned because they place the objective order in jeopardy, just as "the all-daring desire of women"[4] presents a threat to the norm of female sexual containment which it defies, while the danger self-incurred by the errant case, by the single lustful nature, is almost unfelt. The punishment of the wicked is the restoring of the shattered norm. And villainy itself, because objective and floating free within the blood-stream of the trilogy, is a transpersonal dramatic reality; while Clytemnestra remains isolated in her terrible life-death inversion, the malaise of blasphemy is shared; while Orestes belongs to the side of good (*mutatis mutandis*, Aeschylus would find this statement meaningful), his killing of Clytemnestra is in his own mouth "this deed of daring".[5]

Therefore the scope and force of Aeschylean *tolma* dictates his reader's standpoint inexorably. Not, of course, that the issue hangs upon a single word; for the religious fear diffused through the trilogy and wearing many linguistic faces (of which *tolma* is perhaps the most memorable) preserves the same compulsion. "I see it a thing of fear for a mortal man to tread upon fine embroidered work"[6]: Agamemnon's words are not easily misunderstood; no commentator, whatever he may say about heroes and villains, can be unaware in his heart of the precious and fragile peace Agamemnon is fearful for. All dramatised humanity is in the same boat; and the coarse justice of this

---

[1] Cassandra and the Chorus in particular. See Professor Fraenkel's notes on *Agamemnon*, ll. 1144 and 1278.

[2] *Agamemnon*, l. 1231.　　　　　[3] *Ibid.*, l. 408.

[4] *Libation-Bearers*, ll. 596-7.　　[5] *Ibid.*, l. 1029.

[6] *Agamemnon*, ll. 923-4.

image unites the corporate theme of the *Oresteia* with the always vulnerable stability which has evoked the critical concept of the norm.

Naturally, since he is a tragic artist, Aeschylus apprehends the norm in and through danger to itself, not directly, as a prose apologist might. The life-movement of the trilogy places under stress the values the poet lives by as much as it creates dramatic tension in the narrower theatrical sense; and those values, the norm itself, are seen only fleetingly in mysterious iceberg shapes, the main bulk of the object being invisible and hard for a modern sensibility to guess at. A warning of its formidable strangeness may be taken from the Chorus of the *Agamemnon*, when they meditate upon the danger inherent in "excessive health". The risk once again is objective, "for disease, the neighbour who shares its party-wall, presses against" this excessive health.[1] The subjective rash-thinking which exceptional health may arouse in its possessor is contained (of course it is never excluded or denied) within the entirely characteristic objective formulation, and we must respect this Aeschylean priority in order to experience the plenitude of the "merely" objective in his work. Beneath the extraordinary idea of excessive health lie the undisclosed and largely irrecoverable resources of the norm, which we are entitled to think of as the dramatist's version of his society's famous Mean. But if we do, we soon discover that the comfort of the more familiar term is superficial. The *Eumenides* Chorus of Furies declare, in complete truth to the Greek spirit as well as to Aeschylus: "God gives the victory to moderation in every form"[2]; and while the idea expressed here is not arrestingly alien like that of excessive health, it becomes emaciated beyond recognition in its transference from their society to ours. (Greekless students are justifiably perplexed by the feeble obviousness of the Mean, by its *meanness*, as it is expounded to them, and equally by quasi-gastronomic renderings of Excess.)

Nevertheless, we hold to the norm because Aeschylus's trilogy articulates tragic stress through aberration rather than through excess: this judgment as to relative emphasis depends on the whole work of art, not merely or primarily on our

[1] ll. 1001-4.   [2] l. 530.

anatomising of villainy through *tolma* and through the fear which *tolma* arouses. The Chorus of the *Agamemnon* compare Paris's action in bringing back Helen to live with him in Troy to that of a man who rears a lion cub in his house—at first a delight to all with its pretty ways, but later the destroyer of those who nursed it.[1] The simile proceeds by leisurely, atmospheric parallelism in which detailed correspondences are not attempted; and as we pause over the magnificent vitality of the cub "held in those human arms like a very little child, its bright eye turned towards the hand, fawning under the compulsion of hunger", a deep anxiety begins to stir. The exploit is dangerously attractive; the cub is pretty, but it is not a human baby; this is an unnatural thing to do. We surrender, no doubt unconsciously, the muted complexities of a post-Romantic response to wild life for a fear and mistrust of what is simply and decisively alien. The lion lies outside the manageable world which Aeschylean man has constructed for himself; introduced into that world it threatens a painfully achieved and always precarious order. And the threat, as always, is objective; that is why the thought of the emergent ferocity of the animal, instinctively dominant for us, is subordinate for Aeschylus (the link between Helen and the pretty cub is at its most tenuous where the cub has grown up and itself destroys its human nurses). With the keepers of the lion, the master-image is that of playing with fire "out there" in the objective scheme of nature. The parallel with the norm-challenging outrage of Helen's abduction is broadly conceived, but it is characteristically radical.

Scholars, some of them distinguished, have found it hard or impossible to believe that Aeschylus wrote of Aegisthus as "a craven lion wallowing in his [Agamemnon's] bed"[2]—despite the flimsiness of linguistic objections to the text. The true source of difficulty is the failure of Aeschylus's phrase to fit the narrow and unvarying image of leonine noble courage which we import into the *Oresteia*. While more supple than this, Aeschylean usage is not without its own rationale. For immedi-

---

[1] ll. 717-49.

[2] *Agamemnon*, l. 1224. Wilamowitz deleted the line and Maas attempted emendation. Many others, while keeping the text, have voiced their doubt about it.

ately after Cassandra has called Aegisthus a craven lion she
turns to speak of Clytemnestra: "an accursed bitch licking his
[Agamemnon's] hand and pricking her ears in a show of gladness"[1]; and here the contrast between the cowardly wild animal
from outside[2] and the treacherous domestic animal touches the
essential difference between his intrustion while the master is
away and her false welcome from within the *oikos*. At the same
time, the lion is unnatural in its cowardice (lion courage was a
Greek commonplace also) and in its entry into the house; so
that the human offence and the straining of nature are dramatically one.

Again, in her inspired vision of Agamemnon's murder while
it is occurring out of sight off-stage, Cassandra speaks of the
husband and wife as bull and cow, and Clytemnestra's double
death-blow becomes a goring of Agamemnon with her "black
horn".[3] This is more than slightly grotesque to us because we
have lost the profoundly felt sexual norm (compare the song in
the *Libation-Bearers* with its theme of the universal destruction
wrought by truant female sexuality) where human marriage
comes to rest alongside the peaceful coupling of animals within
the pale of ordered nature. On another occasion Clytemnestra is
"this two-footed lioness who lies with the wolf when the royal
lion is absent"[4]; and here we find the flexible lion-image turned
more familiarly towards Agamemnon roaming far from home,
while the idea of ruptured normalcy is at work in the monstrous
union of different animal kinds. The modern objection that
now Aegisthus and now Agamemnon is a lion, and that now
Aegisthus is a lion and now he is a wolf, is entirely unAeschylean.

We recall that the action of the *Oresteia* is closely involved
with the goddess Artemis who, ten years earlier, had delayed
the sailing of the Greek expedition against Troy and thus
enforced, in effect, Agamemnon's sacrifice of Iphigeneia. It is
a famous crux and one which (as I have suggested) breaks the
back of personalistic interpretation that Aeschylus gives no

---

[1] *Ibid.*, ll. 1228-9.

[2] Aegisthus's cowardice is repeatedly affirmed. The Chorus address him
"You woman!" (l. 1625), thus sustaining the omnipresent association of
villainy with the abnormal.

[3] *Agamemnon* ll. 1125-8.   [4] *Ibid.*, ll. 1258-9.

reason for Artemis's anger with Agamemnon. He merely states, in the person of Calchas the seer, that Artemis was made angry by the fact that[1] two eagles were seen to devour a pregnant hare at the time the expedition was assembling. Instead of a grievance against Agamemnon we are baldly presented with

> two kingly birds, one black and one white-tailed, near the palace on the spear-hand, perched in full view as they tore the body of a hare big with her unborn young and checked in her last running.[2]

The occurrence is received by all as an omen, and is interpreted as such by the professional seer. Its overall sense is favourable since the birds appeared on the right hand[3] (the "spear-hand"); Troy will finally be captured, but at the same time Artemis "loathes the eagles' feast".[4] Omens were a universal feature of the ancient world, subjected to elaborately formal rules of interpretation and extending to happenings as trivial as a sneeze. It is said that anything in the least unusual might be taken for an omen—a statement of greater consequence than its frequent casual utterance suggests. For the reading of an omen is a proving of nature, an enquiry into its state of health in which abnormality is the criterion of disease. And we do wrong to exclude gods and men from nature, or to give a limited spiritual meaning to health, because any such narrowing of interest leads us in the present case to place Artemis and Agamemnon outside the portentous event, and then to expect the importance of the event to rest in what it is able to tell us about the goddess and the soldier-king. The event retaliates by revealing nothing satisfactory, thus indirectly warning us not to strip the Aeschylean poetic drama of its objective wealth. We are meant to begin by reposing in the

---

[1] It is perhaps impossible to avoid appearing to take sides in the debate as to whether Aeschylus has in mind an event which is the cause of Artemis's anger, or a sign of her anger. Certainly "made angry by the fact that" will not really do.

[2] *Agamemnon*, ll. 115-20.

[3] Throughout the world, the right hand stands to the left as right to wrong, sacred to profane, clean to unclean, auspicious to inauspicious. This socio-religious polarity is examined by Robert Hertz in his *La prééminence de la main droite*.

[4] *Agamemnon*, l. 138.

event's vivid separateness within the first great choral song of
the *Agamemnon*, and in its extraordinariness: Aeschylus's audience will have seen many eagles and many hares, but they are
unlikely to have seen two eagles feeding together on one hare
since this does not happen in the normal course of nature.[1]
Something is wrong, and the nature of the trouble emerges in
the establishment of an evil harmony between the destruction
of the mother with her unborn young, stirring pity and fear in
all and anger in Artemis,[2] and those other offences against life:
Thyestes's dreadful meal, the sacrifice of Iphigeneia, the
blasphemous life-death inversion attending Agamemnon's
murder, the polluted victory of Orestes's achieved revenge.

We still want to know how these things are connected, and
in particular, what the eagles' feast has got to do with Agamemnon. This is the point at which the problem raised by the
declared relevance of the omen as a whole to the fortunes of
Greeks and Trojans chiefly engages us. Now it cannot be denied
that causality is here dormant; so much I tacitly admitted when
I said it was a mistake to abstract Artemis and Agamemnon
from the incident of the eagles' feast in the hope of making it
refer meaningfully to them. They and it go together with the
existential inter-commitment of the strands of the spider's web
whose whole slender frame is set trembling by a touch. Aeschylus,
confident in the fact—it is not a theory—of inter-commitment,
does not bother about the question (a vital one for almost any
modern morality) of where the disturbing touch happens to
occur. And at the same time we have no right to judge him
incapable of rational thought, or to invoke the almost useless
concept of the primitive.[3] Everybody in the world lives much
of his life at a level at which four o'clock means tea and young
lambs bring the Spring; that the *Oresteia* should offer this kind
of sufficient parallelism in its treatment of moral responsibility
is not surprising, or irrational, to the observer who is prepared

---

[1] Professor Fraenkel (vol. II, p. 96, citing D'Arcy Thompson, *A Glossary
of Greek Birds*, 2nd edn., p. 189) points out that the occurrence is, "in the
opinion of experts, 'utterly untrue to nature' ". This fact has been im-
prudently ignored in the critical literature.

[2] Because of her special care for newborn and (by extension) unborn and
pregnant creatures.

[3] Lucien Lévy-Bruhl's influential studies of what he calls pre-logical
mentality do not distinguish clearly enough between capacity and habit.

to accept the working of Aeschylean guilt, if only within the bounds of the trilogy. (But certainly there is savagery, as horrible as other and later savageries, in a world of inherited guilt and pollution.) Aeschylus would be unrealistic if he were to proceed causally in his study of the wrath of Artemis and the punishment of Agamemnon, for guilt does not work like that. The parallels between the eagles' feast and the human situation (the two eagles "are" the two sons of Atreus, and so on—this conforms to the pattern of ancient omen-lore and may be much more detailed in its correspondences than we can now recognise) are out there in nature, observable; whereas modern discussion of the parallelism often states or implies that its rationale is somehow the successful pinning of guilt upon Agamemnon. And thus its objective force, which is its moral solemnity, becomes weakened.

This talk of the spider's-web frame of nature does not fail, I hope, to take account of the religion of the *Oresteia*:

> And if you allow us to perish—us children of him who honoured you with sacrifice and solemn worship, where will you find another hand so liberal in making you rich offerings?[1]

Orestes is urging Zeus to support Electra and himself against their enemies. The surface impression of a primitive man trying to bribe his god veils an anxiety for the sovereign stability of the relationship embracing both the god and his worshippers; for, as Orestes now points out to Zeus, failure to heal the breach in nature caused by the as yet uncorrected subversion of the house of Atreus will disturb not only men's sacrificial gesture towards the god, but also the god's reciprocal communication with men:

> Destroy the eagle's [Agamemnon's] young ones, and you cannot afterwards send tokens men will trust in; nor, if this royal stock be utterly withered, will it tend your altars on the days when oxen are sacrificed.[2]

Zeus and Orestes are both immediately, selfishly concerned that the breach shall not remain unhealed, the norm unrestored. Neither of them can escape the religious consequences of

---

[1] *Libation-Bearers*, ll. 255-7.   [2] *Ibid.*, ll. 258-61.

failure. Then what of monotheism and transcendent deity in
Aeschylus?

> Lord of lords, most happy of the happy one, strongest of strong
> accomplishers, O blessed Zeus, hear us. . . .[1]

The Judaeo-Christian accent is unavoidably misleading, and it
causes trouble when this and other passages in reverent praise
of Zeus are placed alongside the dialogue of the chained
Prometheus with the Chorus of Ocean's daughters:

> PR.: Art is far weaker than Necessity.
> CH.: Then who directs Necessity?
> PR.: The triform Fates and the unforgetting Furies.
> CH.: You mean that Zeus is less strong than they?
> PR.: Yes, in that he cannot escape what is foredoomed.[2]

People accustomed to make up their mind between omnipotent
deity and some kind of secular necessitarianism have been
tempted to force the familiar decision upon Aeschylus, who
was without the concept of omnipotence and whose Necessity
was religious. The earlier liberal orthodoxy was to play down
the limiting statements in his plays (thus Gilbert Murray
postulated a Prometheus who saw the error of his ways in the
lost third play of the trilogy, recanted, and was forgiven by
Zeus) in defence of the advanced religious thinker; whereas the
contemporary trend is towards acceptance of muddle and
crudity. Certainly more honest in its refusal to hush up contradiction, the second view encourages a number of large and
unscientific assumptions about the nature of the primitive,[3] and
it also fails to reflect the Aeschylean emphasis in such thoughts
as that of Zeus's inability to escape "what is foredoomed". It
makes the search for a higher foredooming and quasi-personal
authority loom larger than the motion of unabject prostration
before the law to which gods and men must submit. In the light
of this search Aeschylus appears a babbler about Fates and

[1] *Suppliant Women*, ll. 524-7.   [2] *Prometheus Bound*, ll. 514-18.
[3] I have particularly in mind two assumptions. First, that Aeschylus's
belief in a number of gods and demons establishes a primitive mentality;
second, that the workings of intellect are sufficiently constant through
millennia for us to be able to say that Aeschylus was a great poet but no
"thinker". Both are found in the Introduction to Denniston-Page's edition
of the *Agamemnon*.

Furies, a simple-minded polytheist, and the prostration is scarcely noticed.

Necessity in Aeschylus, and especially in the *Oresteia*, becomes sublimely grave in the compelled man's understanding of his case. What he sees is the world making sense, which is a richer (though not a more merciful) vision than one of compulsion's neat brutality. "But does the Aeschylean world make *civilised* sense?" receives the general answer "Yes and no", no greater precision being possible until the works of art are before us, open for discussion. And then I would suggest that the individual inflection of tone which judgment waits on is most clearly heard at those moments when Aeschylus drives the critic towards an elementary philosophical absurdity. For the critic finds himself arguing both that Aeschylean Necessity is comprehended and that it is ultimate; and he talks like this because of the power over him of those great situational deadlocks of the trilogy where he meets Necessity incarnate. When Agamemnon first expounded his dilemma and then "slipped his neck through the strap of Necessity's yoke" he understood what he had no means to circumvent. And "understood" is the right word here; Agamemnon did not resign himself (he "slipped his neck" because there is no such thing as inaction for him or his creator, not in order to stress the voluntary character of the action) or accept the working of a mystery, and so transcend his suffering. He had to choose, and his understanding illuminated the circumstances of his choice.

These circumstances are religiously and intellectually important, and unpessimistic in conception, because, we say, the Necessity that crushes a man also vindicates the world's sense. The cruelty of the sense is unqualified, but it is not absolute: I mean that we must, without mitigating Agamemnon's pain, honour his fate, being aware that his and the other situational deadlocks have no sense and no life in divorce from the rich concrete objectivity of all life. They too are out there in nature —whence their tragic dignity, which would be lost were they to assume the autonomy of the independent fictional structure and so become traps set for stage humanity.

Aeschylus impresses upon the reader a religio-moral order which is the reverse of narrowly malignant, and he does this through, not in spite of, the dreadful calm clear hopelessness of

I

Agamemnon's plight. Again we experience the sufficiency of the event, the worthiness of what is endured. We see that there are no accidents, for Aeschylus's falling short of guiding omnipotence is exactly balanced by his falling short of rudderless contingency; all life's felt seriousness comes between. The things that happen are the heart-beat of the universe, and it is the closeness and care of his regard to what happens that gives Aeschylus's comment its authority:

> We have a saying, an ancient saying first uttered long ago: when a man's prosperity has reached full growth it does not die without issue, but begets a child; from that man's good fortune there springs up unquenchable suffering for his descendants.
>
> But I think alone, apart from the rest. I say sin begets more sin in true likeness to its own nature.[1]

The debate is conducted at the level of fact. We attend to the poet's voice, carried here on the voices of the Chorus, because his account of what happens in the world impresses us as accurate; he speaks with the *Oresteia* behind him. Therefore there is a certain unbrilliant truth in calling his moral thought advanced, provided the discussion about what actually happens is not converted into one about the merits of rival interpretations of experience, with Aeschylus penetrating the surface of fact in search of its unapparent sense. Much spiritualising and Christian glossing of Aeschylus begins here; his devotional address to his god ("O blessed Zeus, hear us") is wrongly made the validating source of his moral rhetoric, so that we look to Zeus as to one who finally ordains and maintains the universal rhythm in which "the doer shall be done by as he does",[2] when we should be simply observing that this rhythm is perceptible. And by thus falsely exalting Aeschylean divinity we create the pseudo-problem of the civilised morality's savage anti-self: how can the god who is behind the fact—the observed moral rhythm —of accountability for what is done also tempt and encourage men to sin? But the god is more within the rhythm than behind it; and therefore the divine malice of "when a man hastens to his ruin, god helps him on his way"[3] must be placed in the

---

[1] *Agamemnon*, ll. 750-60.
[2] *Agamemnon*, l. 1546; *Libation-Bearers*, l. 313.
[3] *Persians*, l. 742.

transforming context of the tune to which both the god and the man are dancing.

Warning Zeus of the trouble that will assail both of them if the norm is not restored, Orestes grasps a reciprocity which has nothing unserious or impious in it. In Aeschylus, the religious issue may be inspected and defined from either end, and this sometimes gives rise to surprising inversions, as when Eteocles declares: "A city that prospers pays honour to its gods"[1]— which in his mouth is no less reverent than the counter-proposition that those cities which honour their gods find prosperity. Because of this single relational stress we may say that Aeschylus's religious experience falls within the norm, and may retain our monistic image of the spider's-web frame of nature. A single and structural and outward complex—reality's self—is everywhere affirmed. The very prominent legalism of the *Oresteia* requires us to abandon the standpoint of the right which triumphs through the establishment of a duty corresponding to itself (this way of thinking about legal relations is deep-set in the modern layman and has nothing to do with formal instruction in the theory of law), in favour of a vital, jostling outwardness in which right contends with right and the weak go to the wall. "Right shall encounter right"[2] cries Orestes as the time of vengeance draws near; and the Chorus's ecstatic " 'Let word of hate answer word of hate!' shouts Justice aloud as she exacts the debt"[3] shows the congruence of juridical instinct with retributive morality, once again disturbing premature conclusions as to Aeschylus's primitivism. Aegisthus, we recall, has a valid claim against Agamemnon arising from the affairs of the previous generation—a claim which nobody denies. It is a false sophistication that imposes on Aeschylus the argument that Aegisthus has forfeited his right by his adultery with Clytemnestra. His right endures, but it cannot resist Orestes's right and when the time comes it is swept aside "out there", in the stress of conflict. Thus Aeschylus populates his wide, fertile outward with a contradiction of rights whose strengths are proved in mutual strife. Or a right may be asserted and left untested, a teasing loose end to our

[1] *Seven against Thebes*, l. 77.
[2] *Libation-Bearers*, l. 461.
[3] *Ibid.*, ll. 309-11.

understanding, as when Agamemnon is arraigned by the kinsmen of those Greek soldiers who died at Troy "for another
man's wife".[1]

In all these ways the *Oresteia* confronts us with the formidable
sufficiency of its own action. And through its broad and cloudy
effects, through the massing of block-impression against block-
impression and through the extreme logical flexibility, Aeschylus
drives a clear line of stage-event which the eye follows easily,
reporting what happens. The refrain of the first choral song of
the *Agamemnon* runs: "Cry 'Sorrow, sorrow!'—but may the good
prevail!"; and the final lyric dialogue of the *Eumenides* has a
thread of benediction running through it (*chairete, chairete*: "Fare
you well, fare you well") which proclaims that the good has
in full and public fact prevailed. The action of the trilogy
moves in a bold arc between these two extremes, from tragic
disquiet, through death and absence and sterile hatred, to
fulfilment and blessing.

Aeschylus's audience will have looked back from the conclusion of the trilogy, upon a process of healing and of the
norm's restoration; and they will have accorded the *Libation-
Bearers* a very much larger part in this than now seems just or
even possible.

At the end of the *Agamemnon*, with the king newly dead, the
Chorus ask: "Who shall bury him? Who shall sing his dirge?"[2]
—to which Clytemnestra replies that he shall be denied all
"household lamentation"[3] at his burial. Her withholding of the
customary mourning rites must not be received at the level of
insult that is added to injury; it falls within the outrage done
to Agamemnon, is a prominent aspect of Clytemnestra's norm-
challenging aberration and merits the attribution of *tolma,* that
leading trait of villainy, to the "all-daring mother" who "had
the boldness to bury a husband unbewailed".[4] We gain insight
into the seriousness of "unbewailed" through the exchange
between Cassandra and the Chorus immediately before she

[1] *Agamemnon*, l. 448. Agamemnon's guilt is elaborately studied in B.
Daube's *Zu den Rechtsproblemen in Aischylos' Agamemnon.*
[2] *Agamemnon*, l. 1541.
[3] *Ibid.*, l. 1554.
[4] *Libation-Bearers*, ll. 430-3.

enters the palace to meet the death which she, the inspired seer, has foretold:

CA.: Well then, I will go inside the palace to bewail my own and Agamemnon's fate. Enough of life.

Oh, oh, oh, my friends—this dire lament is not raised in fear, like the cry of a bird frightened by a bush, but so that you may bear me witness of this offence when I am dead, in time to come when for my woman's life a woman's life shall be taken, and for the man, ill-wedded Agamemnon, a man shall fall. A stranger here and standing upon death's threshold, I claim this favour of you.

CH.: Poor lady, I pity you the fate you have foretold.

CA.: Yet once more will I speak—or chant my own dirge. To the Sun I pray, facing his light as it shines its last upon me, that those who requite these wrongs may do my enemies to death, encompassing in their act of vengeance the murderers of a slave-woman, an easy prey.[1]

It is important to recognise (what is indeed obvious) that Cassandra's reiterated concern for the death-dirge does not touch self-pity. Its pathos is objective, by which I mean that the ancient consciousness here apprehends the failure of the human individual to realise himself as a social being when there is no public expression of grief at his death. Cassandra is far from home and family and friends. So, in another play, is the Chorus of despairing maidens who have just landed in a strange country with a powerful enemy behind them: "While yet I live, I chant my own dirge."[2] She and they perform the office which will otherwise, they reasonably fear, be neglected, offering to themselves the mourning rite which, in a tradition stretching back through our literary record to the funeral of Patroclus in the *Iliad*, is the last gift of the living to the dead.

These outward qualities of death in Aeschylus, so remote from the extreme singleness and secrecy of our hoping and fearing, illuminate the vital dramatic truth that Clytemnestra's refusal of mourning does not stand to her murder of Agamemnon as exacerbating addition to substantive injury. It is part of "killing" him. Therefore when Orestes returns to Argos at the

---

[1] *Agamemnon*, ll. 1313-26, reading ἀλλ᾽ ὡς θανούσῃ μαρτυρῆτε at 1317 and Ἡλίῳ at 1323. I attempt only a general indication of the sense of the corrupt l. 1325.

[2] *Suppliant Women*, l. 116.

beginning of the *Libation-Bearers*, and he and Electra and the Chorus of domestic slave-women render at Agamemnon's tomb the service denied him by Clytemnestra, we must understand that the slow self-healing of the *oikos* (which is also the restoring of the norm) has at last begun. The great lyric dialogue spanning the first half of the play is an achievement within the world of action, and it blends the restorative motif with the retributive one which becomes dominant in the later vengeance-killing of Clytemnestra.

Observe also, at the objective-pathetic moment when Cassandra sings her own and Agamemnon's dirge, that her first utterance is coupled with a calling of those present to bear witness to the outrage, and her second with a prayer for vengeance. This thickening of the texture of lament, characteristic of ancient practice,[1] is further developed in the *Libation-Bearers* where we find the Chorus declaiming:

> The one who was killed has received his dirge, and the one who did the hurt stands revealed. Lament for fathers and for parents, when raised in justice and vehemently uttered, searches out the facts on every hand.[2]

And they go on to pronounce "The victory is the children's"[3] before Orestes has even expounded to them his plan to kill Clytemnestra and Aegisthus.

No doubt the matter has its social rationale, in that the formal public dirge would serve to rouse the neighbourhood against offenders; but this is merely one aspect of the wider confluence of the ritual form with the world of fact, through which the second play of the trilogy gains an unsuspected mass and forward thrust. Agamemnon gets his lament; in this service to its dead master the solidarity of the *oikos* is beautifully celebrated. The check that comes with Clytemnestra's killing (is Orestes a "saviour" or a "doom"?) leaves a tragic resonance for which that killing is only in part responsible: the young creative effort we have been witnessing, the renaissance, is still unassured.

Sanction and blessing are found at last in the trial verdict of the *Eumenides* where, we recall, nothing is solved but a decision

---

[1] See Professor Fraenkel's discussion at pp. 613-17.
[2] ll. 327-31.
[3] *Libation-Bearers*, l. 379.

is reached. The state tribunal which cuts the knot has to bear
the full weight of affirmation in the trilogy, and Aeschylus
shows himself here at his most mysterious and inaccessible in
an attitude of reverent patriotism which we brush past in our
search for a higher wisdom to be spelt out of the trial proceedings. A profound and simple institutional piety possesses him;
the culmination of the *Oresteia* grows out of Orestes's acquittal
at his trial before Athena and a panel of Athenian judges, in
the presence of the body of citizens. The historical status of the
stage-event[1] touches us only in our awareness of what is irrecoverable, and nothing more than a faint impression of the
final massive (and perhaps characteristic) Aeschylean effect in
the trilogy can survive the total loss of his music and choreography. We are left with an empty choral and processional
shell, and with a text which was not meant, the words being
sung, to possess the consecution of spoken dialogue or narrative.

The shell is nevertheless wonderful. Cheated of their prey by
the verdict for Orestes, the Furies respond with a threat of
hostile action against the city which has shielded him:

> Dishonoured, joyless, dreadful in wrath, I will discharge upon
> this land (and woe betide it) drops of poison, my heart's oozings,
> to blight its soil in requital of my grief. Whence a canker shall
> spread over the land, blasting leaf and child—a just return; and
> it will taint the earth with a pestilence deadly to mankind.[2]

The threatened venom of the Furies is a psycho-physical force
comparable with Clytemnestra's defiling blood; it must not be
spiritualised into pure malignity since it is a real poison as well
as a distillation of hatred. Its double nature (which in Aeschylean conceiving is a single continuous nature) is brought out
by Athena who now begs the Furies to relent:

> Then will you launch forth your dire displeasure upon this land?
> Consider, cease from anger, do not bring barrenness by letting
> fall the ghostly poison-drops, those sharp and merciless devourers
> of new life.[3]

They respond with an exact repetition of their initial out-
burst. She pleads once more, they rage, she pleads again—this
highly stylised exchange spoken on her side and sung on theirs

---

[1] See p. 112 above.   [2] *Eumenides*, ll. 780-7.   [3] *Ibid.*, ll. 800-3.

—until at last the terrible Furies yield to her entreaty that they
shall make their home at Athens and bless the land rather than
curse it. They ask her: "What blessings would you have me
sing over this land?" And she replies:

> Blessings in harmony with a victory that has no evil in it: blessings
> from the earth and from the waters of the sea and from the sky.
> And you must pray that the wind's breath may pass across my
> land in sunlight; that the fruits of the earth and increase of
> grazing beasts, abundant, thriving, may not fail my citizens in
> time to come; and that the seed of man may be kept safe.[1]

Taking their lead from Athena, they sustain and amplify her
theme in far-reaching tenderness of reference that must have
stood out marvellously warm and life-fostering against their
earlier malison:

> And may no hurtful, blighting wind touch the trees (thus I
> declare my grace), nor sear the young buds in its trespassing
> within your country's boundaries; and may no disease visit the
> fruit to kill it; and may Pan give twin lambs to your thriving
> ewes at their time of bringing forth. . . .[2]

A transformation of curse into blessing crowns the *Oresteia*,
natural and prodigious, like a snowfall in the night to the
morrow's wakers. The final opposing of blight and increase is
a guide to intention, and a hint of scale and even of achievement within the trilogy, and it ought not to be ignored. It
breathes dramatic life into the concept of the norm to which
analysis has driven us. And we may discover here the outward
collective self of Aeschylean humanity; also its experience of
existing within nature, of having no separate fortune.

The prayer voiced at the outset, that the good may prevail,
is now answered by a drawing together of divine, human and
natural forces, animate and inanimate, in mutually dependent
wellbeing. We witness a kind of epiphany of the good in this
moving vision of the processes of life fulfilling themselves
quietly, unhindered—a universal onward-thrusting of birth and
growth. Not behind, not refined out of this vision, but within
it, are found a morality and a religion as coarse (and as delicate)
as life's stuff: hence it matters supremely that nothing should

[1] *Ibid.*, ll. 902-9.   [2] *Ibid.*, ll. 937-45.

be lost in the final settlement. The Furies, as Athena points out,[1] were not defeated at the trial; the votes cast by the judges were equal; there is no question of subjection, nor yet of conflict in the sense entertained by those who have held that Aeschylus is advancing the moral superiority of the younger Olympian religion over the older order represented by the ancient chthonic goddesses. Such reasoning obscures the fundamental inclusive urge at work in the *Oresteia*. Expecting two contrasted religious attitudes to appear in conflict and then the more elevated to prevail, we overlook Aeschylus's insistence upon concord lying beneath the immediate quarrel when he assigns to the Furies a lyrical meditation on the nature of piety —perhaps the fullest and finest in his extant work—at the moment when the trial of Orestes is about to begin.[2] We substitute a principle of expulsion for that of inclusion, falsely moralising the Aeschylean Good and confining his "victory which has no evil in it".

[1] *Ibid.*, ll. 795-6.   [2] *Ibid.*, ll. 517-65.

III: SOPHOCLES

SOPHOCLES

1 Sophocles's Electra:
The Orestes Myth Rephrased

SOPHOCLES died in 406 or 405, at the age of ninety or ninety-one. Therefore he was born three or four years after 499—the date at which Aeschylus presented his first play. For twenty years or so he will have been an adult spectator of the older poet's work; indeed we know that they competed against each other at the Great Dionysia festival between 468 (when Sophocles won the first prize at his first appearance, aged twenty-eight) and 456, when Aeschylus died. Nobody doubts that Sophocles knew the Aeschylean drama intimately, or that he was influenced by it.

The *Electra* of Sophocles affords a singular opportunity to examine this relationship since nowhere else in the extant literature do we find him dramatising a mythical narrative already treated by Aeschylus.[1] The story of the *Electra* is that of the second play of the Orestes trilogy, the *Libation-Bearers*; Orestes has grown up in exile and now, some years after his father's murder, he returns home to Argos where he makes himself known to his sister and proceeds, with her help, to kill Clytemnestra and Aegisthus. Beneath this surface similarity of plot very substantial differences are perceptible, which must be related at the outset to the fact that Aeschylus was composing the middle section of a trilogy whereas Sophocles intended his *Electra* to stand on its own. The function of the *Libation-Bearers* is transitional; it picks up the story at the stage of inconclusive and uneasy transfer of authority following the king's murder, and it leaves it with Clytemnestra newly dead and Orestes's

---

[1] Greek dramatists were constantly rehandling the old stories; thus we know of ten or more poets, apart from Sophocles, who wrote Oedipus tragedies. But only seven plays by Aeschylus survive out of rather less than a hundred, and seven by Sophocles out of considerably more than a hundred. That is why no other examples are at hand. In some cases reliable information is available about the plots of lost plays (thus the *Philoctetes* of Sophocles survives, and we have a fairly detailed account of the lost *Philoctetes* of Aeschylus and the lost *Philoctetes* of Euripides by an essayist of the first century A.D., Dio Chrysostom); but this kind of summary is almost worthless for critical purposes.

pursuit by the Furies already under way—an entirely open ending. Aeschylus needs more space than a single play provides in order to deploy the resources of his dramatic universe—to realise the *oikos* of Agamemnon and the hazy envelope of guilt surrounding it, to expose the norm in its socio-religious completeness, through rupture to final restitution. But the action of Sophocles's *Electra* is at once distinguished and contained by an entirely new sharpness of definition. Instead of the tissue of family guilt receding into total obscurity we have a single light but firm reference to the original transgression of a famous ancestor, Pelops, as the source of all the trouble that has happened since.[1] And instead of a mother-slaying which is both a desired end and a prolongation of strife ("I grieve for my mother's deed and for my own requital of it and for our whole family",[2] says the Aeschylean Orestes), the killing of Clytemnestra in the *Electra* is understood and accepted as nothing more than the successful execution by Orestes of the god's command to him. Orestes himself rests confidently on the authority of the oracle,[3] and his mother's death, once accomplished, is in the fullest and simplest sense the play's conclusion. By it, so the Chorus declare in the final lines, the family is "made perfect, coming at last, through suffering, to freedom".[4]

Of course, any dramatist who set about rehandling the plot of the *Libation-Bearers* would recognise, if he knew his job, that he must supply the framework which was missing (because not required) in the middle play of a trilogy. We need to show that Sophocles understood the whole mythical situation very differently from Aeschylus, so that the new framework may be seen to grow naturally out of a new conception. A point of departure is provided, as often happens, by the tragic Chorus. The Chorus of the *Electra* are freeborn women of Argos, Electra's friends and advisers; and thus although they are Argives and natives of the city of Mycenae, they do not live in Agamemnon's palace. We recall the Aeschylean Chorus of domestic slave-women who were inmates of—whose entire humanity was contained within —the *oikos*, and who were united with Electra in corporate and passive defiance: "common is the hatred," they tell her, "which we cherish within the house"[5]; and a profusion of imagery

---

[1] *Electra*, ll. 505-15.   [2] *Libation-Bearers*, l. 1016.   [3] *Electra*, ll. 1424-5.
[4] *Ibid.*, ll. 1508-10.   [5] *Libation-Bearers*, l. 101.

presents the *oikos* itself as a sentient creature languishing in subjection. Sophocles now changes all this; and the Chorus's new independence, their altered relationship to those within the royal household, marks a decisive weakening of the family solidarity which dominated Aeschylus's treatment throughout. The *oikos* has lost its sufficiency. There is nothing in the *Electra* to compare with that enormous lyric dirge in which the parts of Orestes, Electra and the Chorus are intertwined in single corporate utterance—the voice of the suffering, the self-restoring house. The Orestes of the *Electra* is in duty bound, as he was in the *Libation-Bearers*, to cleanse the house with purificatory rites and repair its wasted substance; but the main stress (as we shall see in a moment) falls elsewhere: Sophocles does not conceive a stage-figure who stands in urgent and tragic—the word acquires an Aeschylean precision at this point—relation to the larger life which gave him his own life and which is now threatened with extinction; so that Aeschylus denotes him, in majestic and untranslatable phrase, "its hope of saving seed".[1]

The weakening of family solidarity is a much-studied theme of Greek political and social history. This process, a slow one and by no means perfectly understood, was relatively swift during the fifth century, the threshold of which was marked by a set of radical public reforms designed to substitute a new principle of locality for the traditional one of blood—of kinship in the widest sense—as a basis for the ordering of Athenian society. And we may be sure that these public measures would not have proved successful unless a shift in private sensibility had accompanied them. Thus at the close of the same century we find Sophocles, in his *Oedipus at Colonus* with its Chorus of village elders, investing the tiny community of Colonus (which was in fact his own community under the reforms of Cleisthenes) with a keen and very eloquent feeling for the tie of mere neighbourhood. A local Athenian whom the Theban stranger, Oedipus, meets there, concludes his description of the place:

> Colonus has never been honoured in legend, but it has a kind of greatness in the hearts of those who live here.[2]

[1] *Ibid.*, l. 236.
[2] *Oedipus at Colonus*, ll. 62-3. Locality is also emphasised in the respect paid throughout the play to the peculiar religious customs of Colonus. And locality inspires the choral song in praise of Colonus and Attica: ll. 668-719.

An earlier poet—Pindar or Aeschylus—could only have rendered the greatness of locality through the mythical heroic ancestor who lived there and through the presence of his blood in living members of the group; but Sophocles in his old age understands local pride, quite simply, and reaches the modern reader to move him.

Local pride is irrelevant, however, to his earlier *Electra*. The weakened *oikos* is not compensated by any very impressive strengthening of locality, which means that our findings in connection with family solidarity do not contribute much to the exposure of active dramatic forces in Sophocles's rephrasing of the Orestes myth.

It should be remarked at the outset that the reader who turns away from Aeschylus disappointed in certain dramatic expectations which are born of his sense of human probability, now finds these expectations fulfilled by Sophocles. For example, the Aeschylean Orestes's anxiety about his inheritance seems an unsatisfactory reaction to the horrible crime of his father's murder; the apparent gross materialism of his account of himself "turned brute-savage by the loss of my possessions"[1] has shocked some commentators into perverting the text's meaning towards a false modern spirituality; and there is no doubt that inheritance evoked for Aeschylus a complex of family substance and individual status, and also of community in blood and worship, which we cannot recover. Whereas Sophocles gives us an Orestes who is convincingly and almost solely impelled by the desire to avenge his father. The play opens with his return to Argos accompanied by Pylades, his friend, and by an aged retainer of the family. They pause in front of Agamemnon's palace. "Here," says the old man,

> is the house of Pelops's descendants, the deathful house from which, and from your father's killing, I carried you away all those years ago, as your sister charged me. Thus I saved you and brought you up to manhood, to be the avenger of your murdered father.[2]

And in his answering speech Orestes sustains and elaborates the theme of vengeance thus firmly introduced by his companion:

[1] *Libation-Bearers*, l. 275.
[2] *Electra*, ll. 10-14.

When I went to the Pythian oracle to learn how I might avenge my father on his murderers, Phoebus answered me the words I tell you now: "Go alone—quite alone—and go unarmed; and secure by stealth the vengeance-killing which is yours by right."[1]

Within forty lines of the play's opening the figure of the solitary avenger (note the requirement that Orestes shall proceed single-handed) has emerged to command the stage. And soon we see that Orestes's avenging role has its counterpart in Electra's waiting and watching for his return; her grief is declared with the same narrow intensity as his retributive anger; intelligibly, with plausible psychological definition, she mourns her dead father.[2] Orestes, she says, has promised to come home[3]; in the meantime she must endure privation and insult. And when her patience fails her, or when she despairs of Orestes's return, her thoughts turn to action and she sounds her brother's note of personal vengeance.[4] Finally, when she receives what seems incontrovertible evidence of his death abroad, she discloses to her sister Chrysothemis a desperate plan (desperate indeed when we recall the enclosed and passive life of women in the Athenian society for which Sophocles was writing) that the two daughters shall do the job which should have fallen to Agamemnon's son:

So long as I heard that my brother was alive and well, I went on hoping he would come some day to avenge his father's murder. But I look to you now—now he is dead—not to flinch from helping your sister to kill the man who killed our father—Aegisthus.[5]

The more timid sister will have no part in what she calls "such rash folly",[6] and Electra is left in a calm and bitter solitude which one encounters again and again in the Sophoclean drama: "Well then, I must do this deed with my own hand, and alone."[7]

And so in the place of receding family solidarity we have individuation and (in a vague provisional sense) personalising of consciousness. Revengeful wrath, self-abandonment to grief, an atmosphere of loyalty to Agamemnon's memory—action and sentiment are less remote than in Aeschylus, so that we

[1] *Ibid.*, ll. 32-7. [2] *Ibid.*, ll. 92-5, 129-36, 145-52.
[3] *Ibid.*, l. 319. [4] *Ibid.*, ll. 110-20, 341-50, 399.
[5] *Ibid.*, ll. 951-7. [6] *Ibid.*, l. 995. [7] *Ibid.*, ll. 1019-20.

K

speak of clearer motive, more realistic emotions, stronger logic. A new apprehension of personal relations is awake, now the dramatic individual no longer bends to an *oikos*-determined life-rhythm and scheme of value. Constancy's and grief's personal nature stands revealed by the touchstone of the Chorus; while the domestic slave-women of the *Libation-Bearers* lament the corporate fortune, the independent friends of the Sophoclean Electra question her thus in the first words they utter:

> Electra, ah Electra, child of a most wretched, most guilty mother, why do I see you all the time wasting away in ceaseless lament for one who died long ago, for Agamemnon . . .?[1]

In her *personal* grief, Electra accuses her sister of a *personal* "betrayal"[2] of their dead father, and she leans upon her brother's *personal* promise to come home. Orestes's long delay causes her to lose heart; she fears he has forgotten his duty. He is always sending secret messages of encouragement, but "he never chooses to come".[3] When Orestes returns, alive after all, Electra tells him: "all my joy is a gift from you and not my own"[4]; and we who read these words look inside ourselves and recognise the strange urge towards self-abasement in love, the desire to confess dependence on another human life. This is altogether nearer than the quaint formal talk about "four parts of love"[5] with which the Aeschylean Electra greets her brother. Surely Sophocles means us to remember that Electra had cried out: "Your death is my death, dearest Orestes",[6] when she felt sure he was dead, and had longed for her own life to be done with; "for when you were alive we shared and shared alike, and now I want to die and share your grave".[7] Her acknowledgment of loving dependence on him has its natural counterpart in this earlier response to the news that he had been killed, and both fall within Sophocles's larger dramatic intention to give the bond between brother and sister all the prominence he can. The Aeschylean nurse who recalls her care of the baby Orestes[8] does not appear in the *Electra*. There, Electra herself is the one who nursed Orestes at that distant time:

---

[1] *Ibid.*, ll. 121-5. The Chorus repeat their question at l. 144.
[2] *Ibid.*, l. 368.   [3] *Ibid.*, l. 172.   [4] *Ibid.*, ll. 1302-3.
[5] *Libation-Bearers*, l. 238.   [6] *Electra*, l. 808.   [7] *Ibid.*, ll. 1167-9.
[8] *Libation-Bearers*, ll. 748-63.

Woe to me for my nursing long ago—my care of you, my loving toil, all gone for nothing. For you were never your mother's darling as much as mine; none but I looked after you in that household, and you always called me "sister".[1]

Personal, too, is the hatred felt towards Agamemnon's murderers. Aeschylus and Sophocles both make Electra express indignation against Clytemnestra and Aegisthus for the way they are treating herself, as well as for what they did to her father long ago; but Aeschylus generalises ("despised, reckoned worthless, shut up like a vicious dog"[2]—the image of the domestic animal is distinctively Aeschylean), while Sophocles specifies the insults and brings them home to the suffering girl:

> like some despised foreign woman, I perform humble tasks about this house which was my father's; shamefully dressed, as you see, and standing to eat my meals at a table miserably stocked with food.[3]

Our response to Electra's degradation, and our broader sense of her, shift with his more circumstantial account of her plight, just as the remote Aeschylean rhetoric investing Orestes ("the man mighty with the spear, come to deliver the house"[4]) gives place to the stage-impression of a young man credibly moved against his father's murderers. And similarly with Sophocles's attitude, and our response, to the guilt of Clytemnestra and Aegisthus; for there is nothing in the *Libation-Bearers* to compare with the enumerative precision of Electra's indictment, declared to the Chorus:

> Then think what my life is like, watching Aegisthus sitting on my father's throne, wearing the robes which he wore, pouring libations at the hearth where my father was killed by him. And watching that ultimate outrage: my father's murderer in my father's bed, with my mother beside him—if mother is the right word for this mistress of Aegisthus who is so without shame and scruple that she lives with the polluted man and fears no Fury. On the contrary, she appears to exult in her deed. She has noted

---

[1] *Electra*, ll. 1143-8.   [2] *Libation-Bearers*, ll. 445-6.

[3] *Electra*, ll. 189-92. "Standing" points to the fact that Electra is being treated as a slave. Free members of the household would eat reclining on couches. See Jebb's note.

[4] *Libation-Bearers*, ll. 160-1.

the day on which my father fell to her treachery long ago, and she celebrates it every month with choral dances and sacrifice of sheep to the gods who have kept her safe.[1]

Thus the Hamlet-oriented sensibility finds consolation at last —though not because the Sophoclean stage-figure is more effectively realised than Aeschylus's in any valid objective sense derivable immediately from the new precisions and particularities of the *Electra*; for Aeschylus has his own fullness of realisation, achieved through the marriage of his generalising temper to a wonderfully direct feeling for action and the single movement. He gives us scarcely a word of individualised description of Helen or of her states of mind in the entire *Agamemnon*, and yet in such touches as that of the lion cub with its bright eye turned hungrily towards the hand of the man feeding it, the idea of her grows definite. Nor does he attempt to describe Paris and Helen in their adulterous relationship. But no attempt is needed, because when Aeschylus tells of the wife stepping through the rich curtains of her chamber and the Greeks setting out in pursuit of "the vanished track of oars",[2] his art delivers the two lovers within their act of elopement. We encounter the same hushed generic vitality in the scenes of war and fearful imaginings of war in the *Seven against Thebes*, where the statement, "the empty-handed hails the empty-handed, looking for a partner"[3] proves grandly, royally adequate to the horrors of looting in a captured town.

And in the *Libation-Bearers* Aeschylus is content to visualise Aegisthus within Orestes's threat of vengeance: "if I find that man sitting on my father's throne . . . before ever he can ask 'Whence this stranger?' I'll make a corpse of him"[4]; the truth here being that a single reference to the throne within the palace is all that Aeschylus needs to point his theme, which is the subversion of the royal household. Therefore we ought not to talk of the Aeschylean massive simplicity as if it were a primitive limitation which he would have escaped had he been born a few decades later than he was: conception and execution are at one. No question of Sophocles's superiority arises, but merely of his difference; we are observing him sharpen and narrow the sub-

---

[1] *Electra*, ll. 266-81.
[3] ll. 753-4.
[2] *Agamemnon*, ll. 687-98.
[4] ll. 571-6.

version of the *oikos* into a theme of personal usurpation.
Aegisthus's wearing of Agamemnon's clothes, the sleeping in
his bed and with his wife, are additions to the older version, and
they serve a new idea.

In the course of his rephrasing of the story, Sophocles
heightens and isolates its sexual aspect. What Electra calls (in
the passage just quoted) Aegisthus's ultimate or crowning
"outrage" gains further stress in her long face-to-face arraign-
ment of Clytemnestra during which she tells her mother that
living with Aegisthus and bearing children to him are her
"foulest deeds of all".[1] The Chorus have already asserted,
touchstone fashion, "Lust was Agamemnon's murderer",[2] and
the keenest sexual edge is given to the guilt of both partners
throughout. Now a modern reader is unlikely to give this the
attention it demands because his response to Sophocles's
attempt to direct and define his interest has been rendered dull
by the assumption that the sexual emphasis he finds in the
Electra is somehow to be expected. Of course he cannot come to
the play as an Athenian would have done, sitting in the bright
morning sun while the Chorus danced and sang and the voices
from within the tragic masks boomed in his ears. But he can
attempt to place it within the ancient dramatic tradition; in
particular, he can turn back from Sophocles to the *Oresteia* and
see how Aeschylus handles the sexual theme there.

So marked is the subordination of sex in the *Oresteia* that we
find ourselves in difficulties when we try to impose a crime-and-
punishment logic on the part played by the Furies in the
trilogy.[3] The Greek belief was that the Furies exercised a
general jurisdiction over wrongdoing within the family—over
sexual offences as well as crimes of blood. This is clearly recognised by Sophocles: hence his indicating Clytemnestra's hardened criminality by the fact that she continues to live with
Aegisthus "and fears no Fury". Aeschylus is certainly *aware* of
the same thing; the wrath of the Furies at the adultery of
Thyestes with his brother's wife—an earlier crime in this
family's dreadful history—is driven home unsparingly. Which
makes us ask why the Furies (who pursue Orestes from the

---

[1] *Electra*, l. 586.   [2] *Ibid.*, l. 197.
[3] The facts are conveniently summarised by F. Solmsen, *Hesiod and Aeschylus*, p. 182 ff.

moment he kills his mother) have not been active against Clytemnestra in the long years between Agamemnon's murder and Orestes's return. Again, why does not the god Apollo raise a counter-plea of Clytemnestra's sexual guilt when he speaks in defence of Orestes at the trial? He does urge that Clytemnestra murdered her husband before her son murdered her[1]; but the sexual issue is never mentioned. We also recall that Aeschylus shows no interest in the erotic potentialities of the scene in which Agamemnon and Clytemnestra meet after ten years' separation; and that although we are probably meant to presume a sexual bond between Agamemnon and Cassandra (he calls her "my chosen flower"[2]), nothing is made of it.

Sex is thus subdued in the *Oresteia*; like the revenge motif, it falls within a story of subversion which it is not allowed to distort. (Translations often give Aeschylus's words a limited sexual meaning which he never intended. Thus the sober and accurate Loeb version makes Electra pray: "grant that I may prove in heart more chaste, far more, than my mother",[3] when the Aeschylean *sōphronesteran* conveys a general prudence and moderation which would of course include sexual restraint.) But Aeschylus, as we saw when we examined the upsurge of eroticism in his Clytemnestra, has one very important use for sex. With Clytemnestra the erotic thread in consciousness is brilliantly isolated, and this brings together the Aeschylean and Sophoclean drama for a moment—a moment at which the understanding of both poets requires us to walk delicately. I have tried to bring to life, or at least to drag into the light of

[1] The Furies meet Apollo with the objection that Clytemnestra's murder of Agamemnon does not fall within their jurisdiction since husband and wife are not "of the same blood and kin" (*Eumenides*, l. 212). A number of commentators—not only the old-fashioned modernists—have discussed this point as a mere technicality. I think they are wrong, because while the tone of the arguments on both sides is legalistic (naturally, since Aeschylus is dramatising a trial at law), everybody in the *Oresteia* believes that kinsfolk have the "same" blood in their veins, and that guilt is carried in the blood, simply and inexorably. We must accept the converse of this belief as equally serious and deep-rooted—that where community of blood is lacking, individual guilt is no concern of the guardians of family life.

[2] *Agamemnon*, ll. 954-5. The commentator who stresses that Agamemnon is "an unfaithful husband" (Walter Headlam, *Agamemnon*, p. 34) flies in the face of the text and of what little is known about ancient concubinage.

[3] *Libation-Bearers*, ll. 140-1.

criticism, the idea of a socio-religious norm underlying Aeschylus's unitary trilogy, and to interpret Clytemnestra's singular eroticism from the standpoint of the norm which it challenges; and now a nice but vital distinction must be observed between the erotic bias of his Clytemnestra and that of Sophocles's. The Aeschylean Clytemnestra's eroticism is the singularity of aberration, so that the question, aberration from what norm? is always primary. The Sophoclean Clytemnestra, on the other hand, achieves a singularity which directs us not to the norm (there is no norm in Sophocles, in anything like the Aeschylean sense), but to herself; and this is because her lustful disposition does not exhaust itself dramatically in the bare fact of deviation, but is so presented as to make us enquire, and enquire urgently, why she acts as she does.

We are embarking upon a study of motive analogous to the one already undertaken of Orestes's impulsion to avenge his father, and our point of departure is the long dispute between mother and daughter in which Clytemnestra defends her killing of Agamemnon. Her argument, already familiar from the *Oresteia*, is that Agamemnon deserved to die for sacrificing Iphigeneia: "Justice took his life—not I alone",[1] she maintains. Now Sophocles intends (I feel sure) that these words shall send our thoughts back to the earlier choral judgment, "Lust was Agamemnon's murderer", for the question of Clytemnestra's motive is seized on by Electra in her reply. "I'm going to tell you," she says,

> that there was no justice in your killing of him. The truth is you were drawn on to it by the seduction of that bad man whose mistress you now are.[2]

Clytemnestra's real motive was lust, and her pretext for killing Agamemnon is swept aside. Electra clinches her counter-argument with a single decisive thrust. Will you say, she asks her mother, that living with Aegisthus and bearing children to him—"will you say that this too is retribution for your daughter?"[3]

Sophocles so manages this debate that it becomes inescapably relevant to enquire why Clytemnestra killed her husband. She herself asserts that she was moved to avenge Iphigeneia. Electra challenges this account and advances a different motive as the

---

[1] *Electra*, l. 528.   [2] *Ibid.*, ll. 560-2.   [3] *Ibid.*, ll. 591-2.

true one—it all seems simple and obvious, and (as with the
erotic emphasis throughout the *Electra*) its importance may
easily be missed since some such wrangle as here occurs is
vaguely looked for. Again we may redress the critical balance
by turning to the *Oresteia*, where Clytemnestra offers the same
defence based on Iphigeneia's sacrifice, but where no word is
said regarding her true motive in killing Agamemnon. Aeschylus
can scarcely have been blind to this possible development of the
story, for Pindar had also asked whether Clytemnestra was
moved by love for Aegisthus when she killed Agamemnon,[1] and
the same question was probably raised in other literary sources
known to Aeschylus and lost to us. Nor is the silence explained
by lack of dramatic opportunity, since Clytemnestra states her
case, or has it stated for her, in all three plays of the trilogy.
Particularly striking is Orestes's failure to make this point when
he is face to face with her and she pleads for her life. Commentators have sometimes made good Aeschylus's omission by
urging that while Clytemnestra has a valid claim against
Agamemnon on account of the sacrifice, she is in no position to
enforce it because her own motives are impure. Thus we resolve
the deadlock of conflicting rights in a manner satisfactory to
modern expectations, but at the cost of doing violence to the
Oresteia's own logic. Aeschylus's omission ought not to be made
good; his refusal to let the religio-moral office of the Furies
crystallise into a distinct guardianship of sex ought to be
sufficient warning to us not to try. He says nothing because
there is nothing to say: Clytemnestra's eroticism exhausts itself
(as I put it) in the fact of deviation, and the entire dramatic
energy is bent back upon the ruptured norm.

Sophocles's introduction, through his Chorus and through
Electra, of the simple point, "You really killed your husband
because of your adulterous love for Aegisthus", is, like Aeschylus's omission of the same point, momentous. It runs to the
root of his apprehension of the myth. It explains, for example,
why the Sophoclean Furies are preoccupied with sexual wrongdoing to the point of reacting against marital infidelity as the

---

[1] *Pythian Odes*, XI, 22-5. The date of this Ode is not known, but it is
almost certainly earlier than the *Oresteia*. The sexual motive appears also
in the *Odyssey* (I, 35 ff.), where Clytemnestra is not mentioned. However,
her name is coupled with the murder elsewhere in the *Odyssey*.

sharpest of provocations.[1] Or better, neither dramatic fact explains the other, but they are neighbours within a single imaginative world whose tone they both communicate, supporting each other in the kind of attention they solicit for the work of art. We are meant to ask why Clytemnestra killed her husband, meant to find the problem interesting; and the ensuing enquiry into motives is part of that general development which I have called, provisionally, the personalising of the dramatic individual in Sophocles. We turn to Clytemnestra and note that her disposition is lustful. We observe a brazen insolence which attends her lust and maintains her in her evil ways, fearing no Fury. It is a characteristic touch, absent in Aeschylus, that she could have instituted monthly celebrations to mark the day on which Agamemnon was murdered. While Aeschylus makes Clytemnestra's irreligion rest mainly on her parody or inversion of ritual forms, her Sophoclean counterpart is distinguished by the pressure of individual will thrusting her along her solitary course against the tide of traditional religious restraints. The tremendous impersonal blasphemies of the one must be contrasted with the outfacing of propriety which makes the defiance of the other so different, so keenly "personal", in its nature.

In fact, the objectivity of Aeschylean villainy is here transformed, and with it the wider objectivity of ritual and language. We remarked the flowing together of the ritual form with the world of fact in Aeschylus, and noted the consequence, at first sight extraordinary, that the working towards a desired end, and also the end's achievement, may be attributed to the ritual form itself. "The victory is the children's", so the *Libation-Bearers* Chorus declare—before the work of retribution has been begun. But in the *Electra*, when at the outset they make a drink-offering to Agamemnon's spirit, a difference is apparent. "Before we do anything else," says the old retainer,

> let us try to carry out Apollo's commands by pouring libations to your father. Beginning in this way puts victory within our reach, and gives us mastery in everything we do.[2]

Belief in the efficacy of the ritual act is no less firm, but the achievement of the desired end is referred (naturally, we should

[1] *Electra*, ll. 110-14, 489-94.   [2] *Ibid.*, ll. 82-5.

say) to the human agent. We find a narrower definition of the bounds of selfhood, setting the individual over against his gods and his ritual life. "Why should I take part in the sacred dance," the Sophoclean Chorus ask, "if evil deeds are held in honour?"[1] A question cast in this form would be inconceivable in Aeschylus, in spite of the fact that an anxious, religion-directed probing of the dreadful truths of experience is one of his most characteristic moods. The Aeschylean form of this question is the one adopted by Orestes when he is urging Zeus to support Electra and himself against their enemies: "If you allow us to perish . . . where will you find another hand so liberal in making you rich offerings?" I call this Aeschylean because of the single relational stress, now faded in Sophocles for whom the threat to religious wellbeing becomes a placing in jeopardy of the human attitude of piety. Calamity and unpunished wrongdoing lead the Sophoclean Chorus to wonder whether the sacred ritual dance is worth pursuing, or to fear that "reverence for the gods will vanish from the earth";[2] the older reciprocity and preservation of delicate balance is succeeded by a religious drama which stands watch over the flow of human respect towards the gods. The pious individual conceives his ritual activity in a new way, instrumentally. Orestes arms himself with a drink-offering to Agamemnon before he sets out. Electra refuses to cease from formal lamentation because it is her only offensive weapon: that is why her grief and her stubborn loyalty to her father are so closely bound together. In Aeschylus, when Clytemnestra responds to her bad dream by attempting to appease Agamemnon's spirit with offerings, stress falls upon the objective futility of "seeking too late to make amends for a wrong that cannot be put right"[3]; but in Sophocles, when she does the same thing, Electra takes her stand on the certainty that Agamemnon will find these offerings "from the wife who is his enemy"[4] unacceptable; and Electra and her sister substitute tresses of their own hair for Clytemnestra's gifts. The wife's offerings are tainted with the personality directing and permeating the ritual act, and this marks a loss in objectivity which is also a gain in the kind of subjectivity, the collected and limited selfhood, now before us.

[1] *Oedipus the King*, ll. 895-6.   [2] *Electra*, l. 250.
[3] *Libation-Bearers*, l. 516.   [4] *Electra*, l. 433.

This change has an even wider linguistic aspect. Like all men before the Sophistic movement—and many since—Aeschylus and Sophocles believed in the possibility of a substantial connection between a man's name and his nature or fate; and therefore the etymology of proper names (Pro-metheus = Forethought, and so on) was a serious matter to them, capable of disclosing truths about the world. Sophocles's Ajax cries out: "O misery (*aiai*)! Who could ever have thought that my name [*Aias*] and my fate would fit so perfectly together?"[1] In his commentary, Jebb recalls the second Richard's "Can sick men play so nicely with their names?" in response to Gaunt's "O how that name befits my composition! /Old Gaunt, indeed; and gaunt in being old." And there is justice in the comparison, since Ajax and Gaunt are both wistfully self-conscious in their name-play. But in an Aeschylean context such reference to Shakespeare must always be misleading. Aeschylus deploys his etymologies (which are more numerous than Sophocles's: as well as Prometheus, Polyneices, Clytemnestra, Helen and the god Apollo have their names' "meaning" exposed) with a certain toneless objectivity which divides him from Sophocles and Shakespeare and invites us to apply our initial distinction between objective and instrumental ritual activity within a linguistic frame of reference.[2] Antigone and Oedipus, like the Aeschylean Cassandra, have to sing their own death-dirges, and in their case as in hers a pathetic effect is aimed at and secured; but its plain objective force is deflected in Sophocles by the stage-figure's awareness of *using* the ritual form (which is also the form of words)—in fact by the instrumental sense. Moreover, the instrumental sense distinguishes the Sophoclean poetic sensibility, not merely dramatised consciousness within his plays, and is largely responsible for our impression of his overall sophistication compared with Aeschylus. For Aeschylus is capable, as Sophocles would never be,[3] of seizing upon—probably of coining—a word (*aphertos*) and using it nine times in a single

[1] *Ajax*, ll. 430-1.

[2] I believe that a study of riddling statements (*griphoi*) in Aeschylus and Sophocles would further substantiate our objective/instrumental distinction.

[3] Contrast Sophocles's way of harping on the word *erēmos* in his *Philoctetes*, and on words of wandering in his *Oedipus at Colonus* (noted below on pp. 216-8). This is not entirely unlike such reiterations as "blood" in *Macbeth*, but the Aeschylean practice is.

trilogy, and apparently nowhere else. And this is surely because *aphertos* is not a linguistic usage in the Sophoclean or Shakespearean sense so much as a feature of the *Oresteia's* landscape. It belongs there. It is one of the *Oresteia*-words. The practice wears a naïve look, of course, and leaves us puzzled by our feeling that Aeschylus's language can at the same time be more natural and more artificial than Sophocles's. *Aphertos* is at home in the *Oresteia*, and it is utterly factitious.

Again, and with similar bewilderment, when we think about the persistent antithetical fondling of "word" and "deed" in Sophocles (in assertions like "You have shown yourself good in word but bad in deed"), we conclude that his language/action rendering of the appearance/reality tension shared by the tragic literature of the West is at once nearer to ourselves and less immediate than the Aeschylean warrior's bare, direct gesture of determination "not to seem the bravest, but to be".[1]

Our broad contrasting of the *Electra* and the *Libation-Bearers* has revealed the stage-figure in Sophocles appropriating psychic vitality to himself with greatly increased definiteness and consistency. The good and the bad people are equally involved in this development; Orestes's circumspect piety places him in clearcut opposition to his mother, but he and she are at one in their articulate awareness of the distinct attitudes which they maintain in conflict with each other, and which they hold to as their own *vis-à-vis* divinities and other human beings. In fact, we may widen the discussion to include all that the term *character* has been made to mean.

Sir Richard Jebb was not generalising to very much purpose when he distinguished Sophocles from Aeschylus thus: "With Sophocles the interest depends primarily on the portraiture of human character"[2]; but already enough has been said to make his judgment intelligible. Those contrasts which we have attempted between the two Electras, the two Oresteses, the two Clytemnestras, might understandably (though dangerously) be transposed into a remarking of the growth of human interest in Sophocles, of his introduction of natural touches. Consider the maternal feeling of the Sophoclean Clytemnestra. When she receives apparently reliable news of Orestes's death, a self-

_____
[1] *Seven against Thebes*, l. 592.   [2] *Electra*: Introduction.

division is at once evident between her relief at being finally
safe from reprisal and her grief for her child. Conscious of this
double response in herself, she broods over the "strange power
that rests in motherhood"[1]—power she has already felt and
displayed over the death of another of her children, Iphigeneia.
Jebb translates (Clytemnestra is engaged in her long debate
with Electra):

> this father of thine, whom thou art ever lamenting, was the
> one man of the Greeks who had the heart to sacrifice thy sister to
> the gods—he, the father, who had not shared the mother's pangs.[2]

"The one man . . . who had the heart"[3] brings out very well
the personal bitterness of Clytemnestra's counter-charge, and
it recalls the Aeschylean situation in which the mother's claim
and the father's duty to lead the Greeks against Troy are
opposed with extreme objective baldness. There, Agamemnon's
duty being status-determined, the fact that he is king and
commander in chief is enough to impress its absolute nature
with all necessary force. He has nothing—no physical hindrance
—to prevent him disbanding the army and sending the soldiers
home; the point is simply that this action is impossible for one
in his position (position, we have seen, is inherent in the man;
it is not added to the man), and this is the sense in which
Iphigeneia's sacrifice is forced on him. But when Sophocles
recounts the same incident he manages it differently. Instead
of leaving Artemis's anger with Agamemnon unexplained, he
prefaces her withholding of a favourable wind with a hunting
adventure in which Agamemnon annoys the goddess by shoot-
ing a stag in a grove sacred to herself, and then boasting of his
marksmanship.[4] This little episode has none of the prominence

---

[1] *Ibid.*, l. 770. Jebb cites two Aeschylean phrases (*Prometheus Bound*, l. 39;
Seven against Thebes, l. 1031) to illustrate the sense of "a mysterious power"
for the Greek *deinon*. It is noteworthy that both are concerned with the
generic tie of kinship, not (as here) with a specific relationship such as that
of mother and child.

[2] *Ibid.*, ll. 530-3.

[3] The Greek is a verb form of our old friend *tolma*, and this passage has
an exact counterpart in *Agamemnon*, l. 224, where the same word appears,
but where it would be misleading to translate "had the heart"—if my view
of Aeschylean *tolma* is correct.

[4] *Electra*, ll. 563-72.

or splendour of the killing of the pregnant hare by the two eagles—the portent of Artemis's wrath and also, within the Aeschylean dramatic universe, its sufficient cause—but it procures for the independent Tragedy a trimness of effect that was absent before. Secondly, the consequences of Artemis's displeasure are altered by Sophocles.

> And so it came about that she was sacrificed, there being no other means of getting the fleet under way—either homeward or to Troy. That was why he killed her, entirely against his will, cruelly constrained. . . .[1]

The detail of the expedition's immovability is most suggestive. It gives the plight of the commander and his men a wholly new aspect, with the result that Agamemnon's status is no longer called upon to bear the full weight of his dilemma. He cannot disband his army, even if he wants to.

I do not conclude from this introduction of a supporting factor that the status-defined possibilities and impossibilities of conduct are weakly felt in Sophocles, but rather that the dramatic factor which we provisionally call personal has grown so importunate (the *Electra* is a late play) that he acknowledges the need to reinforce the Aeschylean account of Agamemnon's compulsion to act as he did. A new physical helplessness is called upon to oppose Clytemnestra's new accusing particularity, her thrusting home of the issue by way of the assertion that the only Greek who had the heart to go through with the sacrifice was the human victim's father.

Being aimed at Agamemnon's lack of pity, her challenge has special force; again and again we shall observe Sophoclean pity transform those cruel stories which he takes from the common tragic stock, touching them with healing generosity of vision and an uncanny tonal sweetness, hard to speak of. Venturing from within the *Electra* a final contrast with Aeschylus's *Libation-Bearers*, we turn to the scene in which Orestes surprises his mother and she pleads with him not to kill her. "Have pity" is the rendering given by some translators for her appeal to Orestes in both plays,[2] and "have pity on your mother" is precisely what the Sophoclean *oiktire tēn tekousan* means. He is talking about the human feeling we call pity—the feeling

---

[1] *Ibid.*, ll. 573-6.   [2] *Libation-Bearers*, l. 896; *Electra*, l. 1411.

pathetically exposed when Electra tells her brother whom she has not yet recognised but who has shown kindness to her, "You are the only one that ever pitied me."[1] But the Aeschylean Clytemnestra says *aidesai*, which means something like "show respect for"; so that here the sense of pity is more than a little Pickwickian. And while the distinction between *oiktire* and *aidesai* is elementary and very well recognised, most of the further, would-be critical distinctions that are built upon it, between the religious poet and the poet of humanity, are altogether too coarse to do more than encourage facile thinking both about religion and about the dramatic presentation of human beings.

2 *Sophocles and the* Poetics

The movement, then, is from restoration to revenge, from the house's self-healing to the young adventurer and his single-handed exploit, from lamenting of the corporate troubles to the girl grief-stricken for her father, from subversion to usurpation, from aberrant eroticism to the lustful soul. These are of course mere tendencies; to indicate them does not add up to a review, even the sketchiest, of Sophoclean Tragedy; and they introduce the difficult subject of naturalism.

Obviously we have no right to suggest that any absolute standard exists whereby the people in Sophocles may be judged more naturalistic, closer to the appearances of life, than those in Aeschylus. (The opposite may have been the conviction of many older spectators, sharing the Aeschylean predispositions at the time when the two dramatists were competing against each other.) We may only say that Sophocles's rehandling of the Orestes myth causes group consciousness to be weakened, collective vitalities to be splintered, the objective parallelism of ritual and linguistic form with fact and event in the world to be lost or intermittently forsaken; and that, by a compensating development, more energy is generated by (and therefore more attention is focussed upon) the dramatic individual.

While no absolute standard exists, there are as many relative standards as human beings to apply them, and the fourth-

[1] *Electra*, l. 1200.

century context of Aristotle's life and thought will certainly have led him to think that the Sophoclean people were in fact closer to nature than the Aeschylean. It is also undeniable that Aristotle was holding Sophocles before him as his model when he wrote the *Poetics*, rather than any other of the great practitioners of Tragedy; and this invites the question: how is Sophoclean humanity to be reconciled with that reverence for dramatic action which impelled Aristotle to pronounce that Tragedy is not an imitation of human beings?

In fact this question does not get asked—partly because the comfortable diplomatic valuation commonly given to the *Poetics* has removed all urgency from the intellectual scene, and partly because the prevailing tendency of Sophoclean criticism is to ignore Aristotle altogether. Jebb, followed by a number of lesser men, adopted a sort of compromise: Aristotle was right (of course) to admire Sophocles, but he did so for the wrong reasons; his respect for *Oedipus the King* was plainly enormous— he used it in the *Poetics* as a standard of achievement; and yet "the points for which he commends it concern general analysis of form, not the essence of its distinctive excellence".[1] Jebb's honesty is welcome in acknowledging a gross discrepancy between the modern feeling for Sophocles and our received account of the *Poetics*. But as a solution, if solution be the right word, it is not happy. Beneath the surface of Jebb's estimate lies the immemorial confusion of the two Aristotelian levels of stage-event and visionary action, of *muthos* and *praxis*; while the chill phrase "general analysis of form" marks a separation, wider than the most radical misreading of Aristotle could account for, from ancient sensibility and ancient art.[2] Even if we reject Aristotle and ask what Sophocles's "distinctive excellence" may be, we are left with the impenetrable formula, "portraiture of human character". And the truth is that light-hearted rejecting of Aristotle (Jebb, like many others, does not *argue* against him) ought not to be indulged.

The Aristotelian Sophocles is obscured by notions about literary history which have become entangled with tragic

---

[1] *Oedipus the King*: Introduction.
[2] Needless to say, "general analysis of form" exactly describes Aristotle's intention and achievement. The words only require to be understood.

speculation in the *Poetics*, so as to influence it profoundly though not always obviously. Aristotle repeatedly says or suggests that a work of art is like a living creature in the organic unity of its action, and he applies a similar idea upon the generic plane, tracing the birth and slow growth towards maturity of the poetic art. But here a remarkable limitation appears. He fails to persevere with his organic metaphor beyond the stage of maturity, so that we look in vain for a discussion of the ways in which, or the reasons for which, an art form declines and dies.

Had Aristotle held firmly to the organic metaphor, I suppose he would have abandoned the *Poetics*, for it must have struck him that to teach the art of fifth-century Tragedy to students of the late fourth century was a futile exercise. Fortunately he did not think like this; he was saved by a view of history remote from our own—surprisingly remote on first consideration since the evolutionary sense was strong in him, and this, together with our contemporary stress on the biological foundations of Aristotle's thought (for which Werner Jaeger is primarily responsible), creates the illusion of a familiar nineteenth-century historicism. For Aristotle there was no natural dying away from the fullness of achievement. Nor did he recognise even the most general dependence of art upon the changing society which produces art; literary history in the *Poetics* is an autonomous study. Moreover, it is curiously unilinear in that he had no respect for the distinct virtues and capacities of the different poetic genres, but went on, once he had distinguished poetry from the rest of literature, to decide which of the poetic kinds is the mature one—which, in fact, is fully poetry. Hence his long, tedious discussion of the relative merits of Tragedy and Epic: Aristotle is holding a brief for Tragedy against the other kinds (Lyric is not an opponent he feels he need reckon with) in order to show that in concentrating attention upon Tragedy he has been confining himself to what is essential. And the relevance for us of this part of his treatise lies in the fact that Epic's necessary inferiority to Tragedy is demonstrated in terms of Aristotelian *praxis*. In brief, the nature of Epic is to present a number of actions loosely strung together, while Tragedy nurses a single action into one harmonious form co-extensive with itself. And the epic poets are unable to counter Aristotle's argument by presenting a single action, because "if they take

L

what is really a single story, it seems truncated when briefly told, and spun out and watery when of the normal epic length''.[1]

Now when Aristotle surveyed the classical dramatic literature with a vision thus coloured, certain discriminations will have been inevitable. At once Aeschylus's preference for the form of the connected trilogy will have given him pause; an obvious contrast with Sophocles's equally marked preference for the independent play will have presented itself; and, overshadowing those technical innovations and advances of Sophocles which he notes in the *Poetics*, he must have recognised what his own theory of Tragedy compelled him to recognise—that by inclining towards the single play for his dramatic unit Sophocles had transformed a sort of quasi-epic into the mature tragic form. Not that Aristotle ever calls the connected trilogy quasi-epic; in fact he ignores the point which we are now raising, and, if pressed to state his opinion, would probably have said that each of the three plays in a connected trilogy ought to imitate a single and distinct action. We have only to glance at the *Oresteia*, our one surviving trilogy, to be aware of a formidable gap between this doctrine of the single distinct action and the dramatic fact; and it is incredible that Aristotle, whose ideal was one of tight, boxlike self-containment—witness his joy in *Oedipus the King's* construction—I say incredible that Aristotle was unconscious of so wide a gap.

There is therefore a strong underground connection between Aristotle's master-concept of *praxis* and the Sophoclean drama. The thematic independence of the single play is only one strand. The overall crispness of definition and clarity of inner causal relations, which became evident when we placed his *Electra* alongside the *Libation-Bearers*, is another. And more important than either of these is the way action proceeds in Sophocles, its distinguishable idiom. His *Philoctetes* will supply an illustration. The story of that play concerns the Greek warrior Philoctetes who is supporting a lonely, painful life on the Aegean island of Lemnos. Some years earlier he called there on his way to Troy with other Greek leaders, and chanced to be bitten by a snake. An ulcerous wound then developed in his poisoned foot, so foul and offensive and causing such ill-omened cries of pain that the others marooned Philoctetes on the island

[1] *Poetics*, 62b5-7.

and sailed off to the Trojan war without him. He was not entirely helpless, however, for he kept with him his bow of supernatural qualities, a present from the demi-god Heracles; and he would no doubt have ended his days on Lemnos, reliant on his unerring bow for food, nursing his wounded foot always, had not the Greeks at Troy learned by oracle that they would never win the war without the help of this famous bow. Therefore they sent two of their number, Odysseus and Neoptolemus, to find Philoctetes and bring him and his bow to Troy. Guile was clearly needed since in his bitterness at his ill usage he would never have gone to Troy willingly or helped the Greeks in any way. And so by a series of pretences—Philoctetes is made to think that he will be taken home to the Greek mainland—they secure his compliance, and the three of them are on the point of embarking when Neoptolemus (who has been the half-unwilling accomplice of Odysseus throughout) confesses the truth, tells the deceived man that their destination is Troy; whereupon Philoctetes asks for his bow which he has in the meantime surrendered. After much wavering Neoptolemus is about to hand it back when Odysseus steps forward and prevents him. Philoctetes has now lost his bow as well as his hope of return, and he cries out:

> I will not come.
> ODYSSEUS: But I say you shall—and I command obedience.
> PH.: Plain in my misery I see that I was born to live a slave's life.
> OD.: Not so. You were born to be the equal of our bravest, and with them are destined to capture Troy and raze it to the ground.
> PH.: Never, I say; anything rather than that. Never—while the island's sheer and rugged cliff is beneath me.
> OD.: What do you mean to do?
> PH.: Throw myself down this moment and shatter my head upon the rock below.
> OD. [*to two of his men*]: Seize him, both of you! Don't let him take that way out.
> PH. [*overpowered*]: O hands of mine, Odysseus's close prisoners, how ill you fare for lack of your loved bowstring![1]

The Sophoclean idiom is distinguished first and foremost by extreme lucidity in the execution of the action's detail. Execu-

[1] *Philoctetes*, ll. 994-1005.

tion seems the best word to use here because it pays respect to
the formalism which suspends the dramatic event, here the
violent event, as in a medium of limpid, intense, unbroken
calm. We are witnessing—the visual imagination is busy while
we read Sophocles—an attempted suicide, but the dialogue's
development robs the attempt of all life-begotten urgency; its
drama (in the vulgar sense) is removed by Odysseus's question
following Philoctetes's vague threat and itself followed by a clear
statement of intention which forewarns the enemies of the
helpless man and leads at once to his arrest. That question,
"What do you mean to do?", is the detail on which to concentrate. It draws forward the suicide resolve so that it can
realise itself in a world of action, or (viewing the scene his-
trionically) of stylised gesture and counter-gesture. We must
not narrow this question into a request for information; at once,
if we do that, we are floundering in a morass of psychological
irrelevancies: asking ourselves why, if he is seriously bent on
suicide, Philoctetes advertises his intentions; concluding, perhaps, that he is something of a self-deceiver or that his nerve
has temporarily failed him; losing ourselves (certainly) in
admiration for Sophocles's character-drawing. The simple
directness of "what do you mean to do?" is likely to mislead
the reader who associates straightforward address of this kind
with naturalistic art. Indeed, Sophoclean lucidity in its various
aspects is mainly responsible for the idea that an objective
standard exists by which he may be proved more naturalistic
than Aeschylus; whereas the worthwhile enterprise is to distinguish one from the other in their kinds of non-naturalism.

When the Aeschylean Orestes asks questions about Clytemnestra's dream,[1] we cannot suppose we are within a convention
where the spectator or reader is meant to conceive of the question being asked in a spirit of simple enquiry, and of information
being supplied in order to satisfy the questioner's curiosity.
Neither in Aeschylus nor in Sophocles is the question really, in
its full dramatic nature, a request for information; its function
is expository, and the difference between the two writers falls
in the object thus exposed. Aeschylus is coaxing into the open
those features of the dream which he wants to render visible;
his basic attitude is narrative, whereas Sophocles in the *Philoc-*

[1] See p. 102 above.

tetes is executing a detail of his play's action. And so we return to our distinction between quasi-epic and true drama, this time along the path followed by Aristotle when he surveyed the then large extant literature and defined Tragedy—mature Tragedy —as the imitation of an action. The Sophoclean grasp of action is caught in the very characteristic little sequence: "What do you mean to do?"; "I mean to commit suicide"; "Stop him, both of you". This cuts deeper than plot-construction and reveals a serene aloofness of presentation less like drama, we might say, than like the dance. And in truth we find the dialogue working choreographically to transmute life's activity into the action of the stage, in such a way that Aristotle's association of dramatic action with the *schēmata* of the dance gains suddenly in force, while his intellectualist account of Tragedy, his reading of the fluid patterns that combine, when the play ends, to make a single distinct action, loses the academically remote flavour it had before.

Once Aristotle's position is reconstructed, the problem of reconciling Sophoclean humanity with the exalted place of action in the *Poetics* almost solves itself. Ultimately, as our survey of the internal economy of the *Poetics* and of Aristotelian psychology was intended to establish, the antithesis of humanity and action is false; humanity serves action rather as colour serves the finished portrait in Aristotle's own simile; humanity does not vie with action. And a preliminary glance at the *Philoctetes* suggests, I hope, how in Sophoclean dramatic fact this is so. Philoctetes's touchingly "human" resolve to end his ruined life does not vie with the dancelike movement towards self-destruction and the counter-movement of arrest. It colours that movement. The dramatist who brings his stage-figure close to nature (in the Sophoclean sense of close) is not diverting Tragedy from its proper end.

"The Sophoclean sense" is a necessary qualification since Aristotle's ideal is suspended between immature quasi-epic and the Euripidean manner which prevailed in later times. Aristotle virtually ignores the former because his primary concern is not with history and he has little room for secondary issues in his astringent thesis. When he lectured to his pupils he may have amplified in all sorts of ways the text which has come down to us, but it is unlikely that the development from an unfolding of a dramatic narrative to an imitation of an action was at all prominent. For this was mere history, an affair of Tragedy's immaturity and so over and done with. But the Euripidean question was not historical; the demand that the contemporary dramatist should refrain from imitating human beings was made in the face of an enemy felt to be very much alive. One result of Aristotle's truncated historicism (recall that he abandons the organic metaphor at the stage of maturity) is that he regards the vicious fourth-century trend in Tragedy not as decadence but as deviation from the true abiding principle which he sets out in the *Poetics* to defend.

3 Men and Mutability

"Avoid excess" and "observe the Mean" are the rules which we spell out of the Greek religious drama—both ridiculous in separation from what Henry James called the felt life concerned in producing a work of art. "Observe the Mean" inclines towards Aeschylus; we render it "Preserve the norm", and follow the norm into a region where respect for mediocrity has no place at all. "Avoid excess" is more Sophoclean, finding its tragic voice in the admonition, "Remember you are a human being". Again, living humanly has nothing to do with living less than fully, and nothing to do with asceticism; poverty, for example, allied with impiety, destroys a man's life,[1] and Sophocles's frequent coupling of wealth and *hubris* is directed not against wealth but against the man who has grown so much more prosperous than his neighbours that he is in danger of forgetting he is human too.

That man is ignoble, slavish, stupid (and "stupidity is the sister of wickedness"[2]), who does not strive to excel. And yet if he is led on in the rivalries of life to think thoughts "too great for a man",[3] the gods will crush him. Here is the home field of Sophoclean Tragedy; but to state the matter thus trimly is misleading in that the apparently fine and focal distinction between living to the human limit and going too far arouses no

---

[1] This thought is explicit in Fragment 944. For the perverting effect of poverty alone, see Pearson's note.

[2] Fragment 925.　　　　　　　　　　　　　　[3] *Ajax*, l. 777.

answering discriminatory effort within the plays; and this lack of intellectual edge in Sophocles becomes the critic's back door into his art. He creates situations and then lets them ride. He expounds dilemmas confronting individuals, and the wide haunting ambiguities at the wellspring of all experience, but he does not treat them. His strangely undestroying scepticism allows him a kind of open salutation where others would recognise a problem and lay siege to it. In fact, his lack of intellectual edge is a grace in him and a mark of his genius's magnanimity.

We are talking too much at large, for several of the very great writers of the world have the confident creative strength to make one feel that there are no problems, there is only life. It is the remembering and forgetting one's humanity, this theme's exposure, its acted-out quality and its lyric timbre in choral meditation, that points at Sophocles. Which thoughts are too great for a man is not a problem for him because he cannot pose the question without knowing the answer; the proposition "nobody is wicked on purpose" which comes to the fore in Plato's early work is an intellectualised refinement of the common Greek inclination, simple and strong in Sophocles, to discover a failure of ordinary intelligence in the condition which we, distinguishing the operation of the will, would isolate as one of moral depravity. Stupidity is in very truth the sister of wickedness, and when the Sophoclean drama imputes frenzy and numbing, half-mad recklessness to its overreachers, the association must be granted literal force. These people have grown unable to ask whether they are thinking thoughts and doing deeds too great for a man; they blunder past a limit which the sane and sober are bound not only to recognise but to respect, since effective possession of the human faculties entails their proper use.

The picture becomes less abstract, perhaps, when we consider the case of the blind man in Sophocles. Blindness fascinated him, and there is reason to think that the interest which is very evident in the extant plays was also present in a number of the lost ones.[1] The second Oedipus play, from our surviving record, is constructed round a Sophoclean Everyman, the blind

[1] See Jebb-Pearson, *Fragments*, Vol. I, pp. 176-84; Vol. II, pp. 8-13, 311-20.

old king; and the blind prophet Teiresias is a figure of potent suggestion far beyond the apparent size and function of his parts in the first Oedipus play and the *Antigone*. The blind man explores the way in front of him with tentative movements of his stick, like the sparring gestures of a boxer.[1] He thinks of the people round him as distinct "voices" carried to him on the air,[2] while his own utterance is "swept abroad" into the dark void.[3] He apprehends external objects by his ears ("in sound is my sight"[4]) and defines the limits of his own physical being in terms of the sunlight which his body "feels".[5] Fenced in by his blindness, he acknowledges that "blind men need a guide to help them when they come and go"[6]; and in his obvious measure of incapacity and equally obvious dependence on those who can see, he affords a paradigm of Sophoclean humanity in its natural wanderings and in relation to its gods. All men (the godlike seer is a partial exception) are teleologically blind. All life moves within a shell-like containment of final ignorance and impotence. To act or think in self-founded certainty of what tomorrow will bring is to ape the poor blind madman who throws away his stick, shakes off the guiding hand and plunges forward alone. Humanity's stick is its ritual life, especially its seer-craft. The guiding hand is lent by its gods.

This analogy rests chiefly upon a certain obviousness regarding the facts of the human condition, and upon the postulate of a race of gods who share the world with men and are looked to for guidance through it. The Sophoclean stress falls (as it does in his presentation of the blind man) on human limits rather than on human weakness: this is one reason why his drama, heavy though it is with mistake, failure and calamity, strikes not at all pessimistic; for wonderful things are done and suffered within the due limits—and also beyond, when a god leads. Moreover, the theme of remembering one's humanity, which is the theme of piety, is often given a spatial representation, as when blind Oedipus says to Antigone, his daughter and guide:

> Lead me, child, to a spot where, within piety's bounds, I may speak and hear others speak; and let us not oppose necessity.[7]

---

[1] *Oedipus the King*, ll. 454-6.
[2] *Oedipus at Colonus*, ll. 863, 1177.
[3] *Oedipus the King*, l. 1310.
[4] *Oedipus at Colonus*, l. 138.
[5] *Ibid.*, l. 1550.
[6] *Antigone*, ll. 989-90.
[7] *Oedipus at Colonus*, ll. 188-91.

There is a subtle doubleness in the first part of his appeal in that the figurative sense of piety's limits is blended with the literal circumstance that Oedipus is at this moment retiring from sacred ground on which he has been forbidden to tread. So too in the second part, with its reference to necessity. Oedipus is admitting his helplessness in the face of the Chorus of village elders, anxious for the local sanctities of Colonus, who can force him to move if he refuses. This is his immediate meaning. But a second, universal application is also intended: necessity is at the same time Necessity, lightly personified, and all men must bow to her. Thus the king's blindness and his humanity are at one.

Another Sophoclean trait to be noted in Oedipus's short address is that the stage-figure should conclude a statement, sometimes a long speech, with the observation that Necessity or Fate or Destiny is irresistible, or that for a man to attempt resistance is wrong. A coda of this sort appears cold and inconsequential—irrelevant to the dramatic issue at hand—if we regard Necessity and the others as more or less unified transcendent forces bearing down on men from above. But if we hold fast to the analogy of physical blindness and recall the almost palpable enclosure of the blind man's world, Sophoclean Necessity becomes a kind of shorthand designation of human limits, not formulated in an abstract way but progressively experienced, acquiring its concrete filling, in the business of life consciously lived. Thus the fact of death is inescapable, and death is the agent of wonderfully varied illumination and surprise in Sophocles. Very different from that single climactic effect which the modern West learned from Christianity and Seneca, death surrounds Sophoclean humanity like a sea, inscrutably responsive to every contradiction of mood, from terror to joyous hope, from abhorrence to desire; and this rich confusion is enfolded within the single certitude of the unknown neighbour whom we shall all meet; of that which, in the chances of life, is equidistant from all. This last is an important consideration (and easily lost sight of in an age of life insurance statistics), for the evenness of pressure which death exerts in Sophocles depends on it. Men would be less than men if they became insensitive to this fringe to their lives; they would lose a faculty similar to that which enabled the blind king in the play to feel the sunlight falling on his body, declaring its limits. The thought here is not a sad one; at least not one the sadness of which can be isolated without damage to the tender and unwearying delicacy of Sophocles's acknowledgment of the "debt that all of us must pay".[1]

The naturalness of death, the inescapable adventure which is harshly obvious and also precious to contemplate, provides the religious drama with a means of reminding its audience of what it cannot fail to see. In the plays death, like (I guess) the Wittgensteinian mystical, shows itself. You must keep in mind, the Chorus urge Electra, that you are the child of a mortal father, and that your brother Orestes was mortal too; therefore do not lament too much, for all of us must die.[2] That very Sophoclean "therefore" catches the tragic imagination in mid stride. If Electra really does "keep in mind" (*phronei*) these plain mortal facts, she will gain a wisdom (*phronēsis*) which will enable her to see for herself the wrongness of too much grieving. This wisdom is prominent in Aeschylus, who says that Zeus forces it on men even against their will, and who calls it a divine blessing that the mere process of living and suffering should make men wise.[3] And the final lines of Sophocles's *Antigone* celebrate a similar blessed compulsion towards wisdom:

> Wisdom is the crown of happiness; we men must reverence the gods. Great talk is always greatly punished, and the proud learn to be wise in their old age.[4]

A modern reader might protest that no amount of wisdom could have solved Agamemnon's problem for him, or Antigone's for her. Such a response would expose the gulf between our drama of outraged individuality and the tragic wisdom of the Greeks. In both Aeschylus and Sophocles, the moment when a man perceives the operation of the powers that are destroying him is one of solemn religio-tragic exaltation—not because the individual is "saved" thereby, but because Necessity and Fate and the ways of Zeus have been exposed for human consciousness in a flash of perfect clarity: a demonstration which is also a sufficient vindication. Aeschylus broods with evident intellectual passion upon the thought that the final working out

---

[1] *Electra*, l. 1173.   [2] *Ibid.*, ll. 1171-2.
[3] See p. 113 above.   [4] ll. 1347-53.

of things could not be otherwise than as it is. Sophocles's experience of Necessity is more scattered and fluid, as his supple response to death has indicated; and old age is scarcely less prominent than death in its proving of human limits. Of course, age and death are intimately linked in the thought that "a slight alteration of nature's balance brings the aged to their rest",[1] and for this reason the old man is a living refutation of the *hubris* of the society which contains him. But the quiet decline of physical powers is also a profoundly admonitory spectacle for a people who place athletic virtue on a plane with intellectual and spiritual, as the Greeks did. And as with death and old age, so with the common perils of life. When a man is out at sea in a small open boat, "driving his path beneath the weltering wave-crests that threaten to engulf him",[2] or caught far from shore on a starless night[3]; or when, in a zestful passage, the cowardly voyager hides from the storm in the bottom of his boat ("he covered himself with his cloak and allowed the whole crew to trample on him at will"[4])—at such times as these Necessity is a felt presence, whether or not she is named. We have no reason to think that Sophocles was a great war poet, as Aeschylus certainly was, but he brings danger home to the solitary fluttering heart in a way which the huge block-impressions of terror in the *Persians* and the *Seven against Thebes* do not attempt.

The second point of the analogy between physical blindness and the condition of Sophoclean man is the need for, and the fact of, guidance by the gods. This makes us ask how the gods are related to that circumambient Necessity we have been considering. Are they above it, or are they too bound by it? Sophocles's answer is an easy, almost casual "Yes" to both alternatives. I think we should have to say that Aeschylus also replies with two mutually contradictory affirmatives, but an awareness of the existence of a problem robs his voice of the Sophoclean simple blandness. Far too much has been made of the trend toward monotheism and transcendent deity in Aeschylus; in fact the discussion seems to have been largely misdirected, and one of the false clues, assiduously followed, has

---

[1] *Oedipus the King*, l. 961.   [2] *Antigone*, ll. 336-7.   [3] Fragment 143.
[4] *Ajax*, ll. 1145-6. Jebb found this passage "wholly repugnant to a modern taste" (Introduction, xliv).

been the tension, the faintly hinted threat of an intellectual showdown, that sometimes emerges when Zeus, Fate and Necessity rub shoulders in his work. Nevertheless it is a just observation that the tonal difference between the two dramatists becomes here most marked, Sophocles's lack of intellectual edge once again distinguishing him. In his world, Fate, Necessity, Zeus and the other gods co-exist in calm unanalysed confusion, and life is a single enterprise which they share with men. We have said that humanity is teleologically blind. The gods can see, however, and so are able to guide men about the world; but they cannot see everything; they are powerful but not omnipotent. By calling the war god Ares "the right-hand trace-horse"[1] for his part in the battle to defend Thebes, the Chorus of the *Antigone* indicate the most important aspect of mankind's relation to its gods. The defence of Thebes was undertaken by the Theban citizens and Ares together; Ares was stronger than they and did most of the work (just as the right-hand horse did most of the work in the race run anti-clockwise round the turning-posts at each end of the ancient hippodrome, so that the best horse of the team was placed in this position); but the citizens worked hard too, and it would be absurd and no part of pious modesty to deny that the successful defence was a joint achievement of the men and their god.

Sophoclean divinity's chief role is that of strong helper. Athena stands beside Odysseus throughout the *Ajax*, Apollo beside Orestes throughout the *Electra*, and a man's coupling of his divine ally with himself is always perfectly natural and unpointed, as when Oedipus prays to the Furies, "Do not show yourselves ungracious to Apollo nor yet to me"[2]—incidentally exposing a further confusion in his fear of conflict between the Olympian god and the chthonic goddesses. The chaos is cheerfully borne. Of course Sophocles feels a difference in majesty and power, and in the corresponding human duty of reverence, between Zeus and the other gods, but this does not materially alter the situation here described or lessen the folly of attempting to construct a coherent theology on the basis of the poet's welcoming acceptance of Zeus "who sees and orders all things".[3]

For Zeus does not see and order everything, no matter that the mood of devout abandon accords him omnipotence and

---

[1] l. 140.   [2] *Oedipus at Colonus*, l. 86.   [3] *Electra*, l. 175.

omniscience. The forces that vex and uplift and subjugate men
—love, for example—are also felt by Zeus and the other gods[1]:
this is a consequence of the fundamental Sophoclean fact of a
single world which gods and men share. Between the erotic
feeling which assails a god and that which assails a man there
is no difference of kind; they are the same blend of physical itch
and more exalted elements. On the other hand there is a very
significant difference of degree: the gods live and feel on the
grand scale, and the passion which impelled Zeus to his many
sexual exploits in Greek mythology, or caused Apollo to
attempt the rape of Cassandra, the human prophetess, would
no doubt destroy a mortal man in its intensity. And what makes
this difference significant is Sophocles's radical confusion of
moral and physical categories. Thus when Orestes's body is
described as "gigantic",[2] we are meant to think that this figure
from the heroic age was altogether finer, brighter (a favourite
word of Sophocles's), truer to the human ideal than the men
of today; not merely that he was bigger and stronger than ourselves. Conversely, the belief that gods may be relied on to fulfil
their obligations, whereas men may not, is continuous with the
belief that they have greater material power and keener eye-
sight than we have. Sophocles inherits the general tendency of
the Greek mind to blur quality-quantity distinctions—an important subject with a bearing on questions as remote from our
present study as the scientific limitations of the Greeks.

These confusions, or large simplicities, persist unaffected by
the developments noted in our comparative study of the *Electra*
and the *Libation-Bearers*. They work to maintain the race of gods
at once inside and outside nature, free of old age and death but
ineradicably mundane, above Necessity and bound by her. For
Sophocles is not sensitive to these dualisms, or not so sensitive
as to loosen his hold on the easy interpenetration of human and
divine.

We have encountered a roughly similar imaginative monism

[1] "What god can wrestle with Love without taking three falls? If it be
lawful for me to say it—and lawful it is to speak the truth—Love plays
tyrant over the heart of Zeus, needing no spear or sword. Thus does Love
guillotine all the counsels of gods and men" (Fragment 941). See also
Women of Trachis, ll. 441-4; Fragment 684.

[2] *Electra*, l. 758.

in Aeschylus, where the totality of things maintains its equilibrium by a process of unceasing self-correction. For both poets life's health is a balancing of inner relations, and they both articulate tragic stress through the disturbing of balance. They differ from each other primarily in the way this balance is felt and stated; Sophocles's greater mobility and suppleness, and those contrasts with Aeschylus which his rephrasing of the Orestes myth has revealed, lead us to abandon the static image of the norm for the dynamic one of mutability. We approached Sophoclean mutability when insisting, with regard to Necessity and his proving of human limits, that death and old age and danger are double-faced—that they do not serve a pessimistic art. While death is terrible, it is also Deliverer and Healer. Old age was earnestly dreaded in antiquity, if only because there could be scarcely any mitigation of its pains and disabilities; but its bitterness is countered in Sophocles by the thought that the aged are patient and satisfied with very little,[1] that "old age and time's chafing movement teach us all things",[2] that *hubris* fades together with the man himself.[3] Even the common dangers of life at sea are answered by the peaceful joy of landfall—

> of reaching land and then, safe indoors, falling asleep to the sound of raindrops pattering on the roof outside.[4]

Contemplating this two-sidedness, we must not allow the language of balance to slip into that of compensation, for thus we should reintroduce a banished world of problems and solutions—banished because unSophoclean—by falsely emphasising the counter-thought of deliverance and patient insight and joy in safety, as if this were a golden echo or true response to death and old age and daily peril. Life's darkness and its light are not opposed as negation to affirmation within the Sophoclean experience; indeed, the entire antithetical sense is drowned in a vision of self-poise:

> Grief and joy come round to all, as the Bear comes round in his circling paths on high.
> This I say since starry night does not abide with men, nor does

---

[1] *Oedipus at Colonus*, ll. 5-8.   [2] Fragment 664.
[3] Fragment 786.   [4] Fragment 636.

calamity, nor wealth. In a moment they have left us, and someone else has his turn of joy, and of joy's loss.[1]

All ancient Greeks, back to Homer, saw the Great Bear
perform a ceaseless cosmic rondeau about the fixed point of the
Pole. For them this was the constellation which never disappears beneath the horizon: always visible, always in its place;
and its enduring cyclical movement issuing from an ultimate
fixity makes it the just figure of Sophoclean mutability, and
of his moral imagination's obvious and strong confidence.
Sophocles's unforced catching up of the human here-and-now
into the Bear's tune separates this from the familiar stellar
image of transcendence—Shakespeare's ever-fixed mark and
Keats's bright star and Mr Eliot's boar and boarhound reconciled; while we distinguish the turning Bear from the late-
classical Wheel of Fortune by the latter's essential triviality
(the wheel is a mere diagram of the prosperity-adversity rhythm
observed in human affairs), and by the fact that the wheel's
movement is on a perpendicular axis: prosperity at the top is
antithetically opposed to adversity at the bottom—hence the
wheel's long and close association with the Fall of Princes
tradition in tragic theory and practice. The Bear, by contrast,
is a deep-toned reality, up there for all to see, a living power as
were all stars to the Greeks, active in bringing the seasons and
not merely coming and going with them; and therefore the
constellation impinges on us, it has no need to come to humanity cap in hand to borrow tragic interest. Sophocles in any case
knew no vitally conceived "beyond" (in the Platonic, Christian, Kantian, or any other sense) to which the stars might
stand as symbol. For the monistic imagination, they were the
thing itself; and in Sophoclean Tragedy the single tribulation-
and-wealth, gladness-and-bereavement tune which is the Bear's
movement, relates prosperity symphonically to adversity, making neighbours of these opposites.

The movement of stars evokes a peace which seems at first
to have nothing in common with the painful happenings in the
plays. I hope our examination of how action works in Sophocles
will support the conclusion that here at any rate appearances
are liars—and liars not because his violent images of mutability

[1] *Women of Trachis*, ll. 129-35.

will be brought in to contradict or even to supplement his
peaceful ones (thus the Bear is immediately preceded by a
picture of Heracles struggling on through his life like a swimmer
in the stormy Cretan sea, now lifted up to success and honour,
now buffeted to defeat),[1] but because of the overall tragic
impact. In my experience of Sophocles, the Cretan Sea is no
less peaceful than the Bear; and the local circumstance that the
Chorus singing of the Bear are "merely" telling Deianeira not
to fret, and the final event in which Deianeira has every reason
to fret, are both gathered into perfect calm by the way (by the
form of the single distinct action) in which disaster arrives—as
the divine oracle coming to fulfilment, at the right time, surely
(*kai tad' orthōs empeda katourizei*).[2]

It seems strange, moreover, that the poet who could imagine
the sailor lying happily in bed ashore, listening to the rain on
the roof, should realise his tragic vision in the Bear's unindi-
vidualised round from joy to sorrow to joy again. But this is the
truth, the first truth about Sophocles. It reminds us yet once
more of Aristotelian action and the anatomising of action by
means of the concept of reversal (*peripeteia*). Aristotle's reversal,
we recall, is a double movement, from bad fortune to good as
well as the other way. Its relevance to Sophoclean mutability
(which is very obvious) has been obscured for us by systematic
misdirection of the discussion away from the idea and dramatic
fact of action, towards an image of the human self which
neither Sophocles nor Aristotle would have acknowledged; and
the doubleness common to reversal and mutability has been
sacrificed to the academic dogmas of Tragedy, that pseudo-
subject. So deep are the preconceptions about downfall, retribution, the tale of woe, so-called tragic form (no less deep for
being vague and confused), that the eye grows blind to what it
does not expect to see:

> The strength of the earth decays, and the strength of the body;
> faith dies, distrust is born, and the same spirit is not constant
> between a man and his friends or between city and city; soon for
> some, late for others, delight turns to bitterness, and then once
> more to love.[3]

And the sudden Sophoclean lift of "and then once more to
love" is lost in the expectation of Greek Tragedy's heavy down-

---

[1] ll. 114-19.   [2] l. 826.   [3] *Oedipus at Colonus*, ll. 610-15.

hill trudge from Hubris to Nemesis. Lost too are those blazing moments in play after play, when a man is marvellously saved —"beyond my best hope" he will say, dazed with joy as he sees the sky ripped open for him.[1] Or if not lost, they are placed in Wheel-of-Fortune antithesis to the moments of disaster. And then the tune of the circling Bear is never heard, which is the symphonic double movement of Sophoclean action and the reversals of a single day: "For a day can bring low all human things, and a day can lift them up."[2]

4 Ajax

Seven of the plays survive. External information about them is meagre and seldom trustworthy, but the very credible statement that the *Antigone* was Sophocles's thirty-second play,[3] together with the probability that it was produced in 442 or 441, provides a reliable date round which to arrange the surviving seven. In 441 Sophocles was fifty-five. He wrote about 120 plays in all. And so not much less than three-quarters of his output must be attributed to his late middle and old age. This would be a surprising and even suspicious conclusion were it not certain that two of our handful of plays belong to his extreme old age (the *Philoctetes* produced in 409 and the *Oedipus at Colonus* eight years later, in 401), and that both reveal prodigious vigour in conception and execution; while a third play, the *Electra*, is almost certainly also late.[4] To this instance

[1] For example: *Ajax*, l. 1382; *Electra*, l. 1262; *Philoctetes*, l. 1463; *Oedipus at Colonus*, ll. 1105, 1120. The Guard in the *Antigone* reflects that "no pleasure is as great as the joy that is above and beyond what we hope for" (ll. 392-3).

[2] *Ajax*, ll. 131-2. And again, the Chorus of the *Oedipus at Colonus* on "Time, overthrowing some fortunes, and on the morrow lifting others, again, to honour" (ll. 1454-5, in Jebb's translation). The first verb ($\sigma\tau\rho\acute{\epsilon}\phi\omega\nu$) is a conjecture—as it is at *Women of Trachis*, l. 116—but a very probable one.

[3] This information is contained in a prose Argument or summary of the *Antigone* attributed to Aristophanes of Byzantium. The date of the play is an inference, but a reasonable one, from an observation in the Argument about Sophocles's career.

[4] The question largely turns on the disputed relation of this play to Euripides's *Electra*. The latter was probably produced in 413, and many have held—in my judgment rightly—that Sophocles's play is the later of the two. (But see Denniston's edition of the Euripidean *Electra*, xxxv n.)

M

of invention running at full flood in a man's ninth decade, Verdi's music affords the only parallel in our civilisation.

Thus the *Antigone* is by no means a young man's work, and yet more than thirty years separate it from the two latest plays we have. The four others, with one exception, are held on strong grounds to be later than the *Antigone*. That exception is the *Ajax*. The seven survivors fall, therefore, into three groups: the *Ajax* and the *Antigone* are relatively early; the *Women of Trachis, Oedipus the King*, and the *Electra* come next, with the *Electra* inclining towards the third group; and the *Philoctetes* and the *Oedipus at Colonus* are very late.

While I bracket the *Ajax* with the *Antigone* in this rough chronology, the inward signs suggest to me that it is altogether less mature. Its story is based on an incident in the Trojan epic cycle. Ajax, whose soldiership is second only to that of Achilles in the Greek army, has insulted the goddess Athena by boasting that he can do without her help in battle. She bides her time to punish him, until after the death of Achilles when the Greek leaders confer the honour of inheriting the dead warrior's arms not on Ajax, who in his own estimation (which appears to be the just estimation) deserves it, but on Odysseus. Ajax now resolves to be avenged on the Greek chiefs and sets out at night, alone, to murder them. As he reaches their tents Athena afflicts him with temporary madness; he turns aside to butcher some oxen and sheep, the as yet undivided spoil of war, in the belief that these are his human enemies. The play's action begins here. When he regains his wits and understands what he has done, disgrace and misery lead him haltingly to suicide; and the last four hundred lines—more than a quarter of the whole— are occupied in debating whether Ajax's body shall be denied burial because of his traitorous attempt against the leaders. Ultimately mercy prevails, and his friends are setting to work to bury him at the play's close.

Most remarkable is the fact that Ajax responds to his situation always in terms of shame and never of guilt. He has been exposed before the whole Greek army as murderer and traitor to the full extent of criminal intention, and certainly he would have done the deed had not the goddess intervened to prevent him. It is as clear a case of guilt as a dramatist could devise. But Ajax neither admits guilt nor denies guilt nor extenuates guilt (as he might do by urging the unjust award of Achilles's arms); nor does he give any sign that he feels guilt. When he thinks of his foiled plan to murder the Greek leaders, it is with rage and chagrin that "those men laugh exultingly in their escape—never intended for them by me",[1] but by Athena. Of course, their award of the arms to Odysseus is Ajax's reason for attempting to murder them, but he does not make this his excuse. Shame possesses him entirely. He is ashamed of having killed the oxen and sheep, not because this reveals a guilty intent, but for the deed itself:

> Do you see the brave, the stout-hearted warrior, the one who never flinched before the enemy in battle—do you see how I have proved my courage upon beasts that feared no harm? Oh the mockery! What shame is mine![2]

The great soldier feels irredeemably disgraced because the goddess has beguiled him into using his sword against sheep and oxen. This attitude, which is shared by the Chorus of Ajax's sailor-followers,[3] and by his wife,[4] is almost as alien to the moral atmosphere of the Sophoclean age as it is to our own; but it accords very precisely with the aristocratic military culture depicted by Homer. Homer's people live by the standard of honour—live in the literal sense that the forces sustaining life, the deepest kind of self-vindication, depends on being seen and judged to satisfy that standard. And shame is honour's polar opposite, so that when a Homeric warrior incurs shame, a sudden and complete disintegration of personality ensues. On the other hand, he has no sense of guilt, and in this respect the honour-shame polarity of Homeric civilisation presents so striking a contrast with the situation reflected in the later literature of the Greek mainland (the cheerful boasting of Homer's men disappears, and a gingerly, circumspect address inspired by

---

[1] ll. 454-5. [2] ll. 364-7.

[3] Their choral song and subsequent dialogue with Tecmessa, Ajax's wife, show a divided concern for his madness and for the disgrace that will overwhelm him if he is proved to have killed the cattle (ll. 134-355). They fear that reprisals against Ajax will involve themselves, but their failure to engage with the question of his guilt is complete.

[4] Her response to his plight is shame-focussed throughout. Ajax has been brought so low that he utters words "which once he would never have deigned to speak" (l. 411).

fear of *hubris* takes its place[1]; psycho-physical pollution and techniques of ritual cleansing come to the fore; Orphic and Pythagorean teachings about the pure soul's road to immortality gain many hearers and some converts), that the sociological terms of art, Shame Culture and Guilt Culture, have been responsibly applied to these two phases of Greek history.[2]

That the Sophoclean Ajax lives by honour and dies by shame is in every way extraordinary. There is nobody like him in extant Tragedy. He is a solitary shame-culture figure thrown up by a literature of guilt, and his shame is coupled with an equally Homeric blandness of self-assessment ("the brave, the stout-hearted") and with a surrender of life through contact with shame which, outside the epic context, would be quite inadequately motivated. In fact, Sophocles makes Ajax build this context round himself when he defines the dilemma which is driving him to suicide. He cannot go home:

> What countenance shall I present to my father Telamon when I get there? How will he bear to look at me standing honourless before him—with nothing achieved to bring me back, like him in his day, glory-crowned? That I cannot face.[3]

And he cannot stay where he is and meet death gloriously in single-handed assault on the Trojan defences, since that would be a service to the Greek leaders whom he hates.[4] He has no third way, other than suicide.

The consequent epic neatness and clarity investing Ajax may have been evident in some of those plays, now all lost, which Sophocles was writing in the first half of his long life. This may form a link between the surviving play and what has disappeared, and it ought to make us suspect that the very ancient critical tradition designating Sophocles the most Homeric of the Tragedians had more to it than now meets the eye. At the

---

[1] Theseus in the *Oedipus at Colonus* is the type of valiant and devout soldier-king. His assurances of help to Oedipus are characteristically qualified: "Unless I die first, I will not rest until I restore your children to you" (ll. 1040-1); "I have no wish to boast, but you should know that your life is safe so long as any god saves mine" (ll. 1209-10). Such careful avoidance of *hubris* is essential to his piety.

[2] By E. R. Dodds, in Chapter Two of his book *The Greeks and the Irrational*: "From Shame-Culture to Guilt-Culture".

[3] ll. 462-6.   [4] ll. 466-70.

same time, his *Electra* is sufficient warning that a pronounced epic bent is not by itself a trustworthy sign of relatively early composition. The Homericisms of that play (among which the silence regarding Orestes's pollution through mother-slaying is the most impressive) suggest that Sophocles could be self-consciously epic when occasion demanded; could use Homer to remove himself from Aeschylus. They also provoke deeper reflection upon something individual to the Sophoclean temperament and manifested throughout his work: a serenity of religio-moral attitude which makes the Shame Culture/Guilt Culture distinction apply uncomfortably to him. There is a natural as well as a sophisticated aspect to his Homeric inclining, and it follows that reference to the epic values of the *Ajax* must be wary.

In particular, one should stress that the *Ajax* is being judged immature not because epic values are discernible but because they cause a damaging incoherence. Which is this, that up to the moment of Ajax's suicide the dramatic and moral logic is determined by his lost honour, and from then on by his guilt—the established murderous intent—in its bearing on his right to burial. Commentators have sometimes argued that Sophocles allows Ajax to die too soon, with the result that the long posthumous debate about burial falls into anti-climax; and while this diagnosis is falsely framed (the tragic hero and a modern conception of stage-death are working mischief here), the disease itself is genuine. The mad slaughter of the sheep and oxen had been projected from the beginning of the play as a calamity "terrible as death"[1]; in the choric judgment "Ajax will die"[2] if the killing be proved against him, for by that action he will be seen to have destroyed his own fair fame along with his victims.[3] And so it turns out as he sits alone in his tent, sane at last and despairing, that "the great brave deeds which once his hands did are fallen, fallen . . .".[4]

The mad killing is at once the substance of his shame and the focus of dramatic interest. But when Menelaus, the Spartan king and Agamemnon's brother, enter bent on denying burial to the body, he brings a change of climate with him. I forbid Ajax burial, he says, because

[1] l. 215.
[2] ll. 229-30.
[3] ll. 405-9. The text is unsatisfactory.
[4] ll. 616-20.

when we brought him here from Greece we hoped he would prove an ally and friend to us. On trial, we found him a worse enemy than the Trojans; he struck against the whole army with a murderous plot, setting out, spear at the ready, in a night attack upon us chiefs; and if some god had not smothered this attempt, our fate would have been his: we would be stretched out, ignobly killed, and he would be living still. But in the event a god deflected his *hubris*, so that it fell on sheep and cattle.[1]

At once Menelaus overlays shame with guilt. This development happens to coincide with Ajax's death, but the widely shared feeling that the play is broken-backed derives from confused intention in the artist (fumbling execution does not appear to be in question), rather than from any supposed mistiming of the hero's suicide. The guilt, moreover, which we are suddenly confronted with, is precisely tragic guilt; Ajax's *hubris* is here named by Menelaus who proceeds immediately to expose its working in the presumption and insubordination that led Ajax to challenge the award of Achilles's arms to another man.[2]

The trouble with this very familiar Sophoclean theme of overreaching, of thinking thoughts too great for a man, is that it fails to engage with what has gone before; it offers the fruit of latter-day religious experience to Homeric innocence. And when we touch Ajax's guilt at a second point—at his original affront to Athena—a similar inconsequence appears. His insulting boast that he can do without divine help in battle is grafted on to the action most clumsily, by way of explanatory flash-back in which a cumulative effect is aimed at through recounting together two separate hubristic utterances.[3] The cause of Athena's terrible and extended punishment of him is too important to be introduced like this: contrast Agamemnon's peripheral boast about the stag in the *Electra*, where the flash-back device proves entirely adequate. A more serious criticism springs from our experience of confusion when the strenuous epic world of vaunting and taunting, of honour and shame, collides

---

[1] ll. 1052-61.   [2] ll. 1071-90.
[3] ll. 762-77. Late in the day my eye falls on a sentence in Richmond Lattimore's *The Poetry of Greek Tragedy*: "Sophocles sometimes writes as if he had been reading the handbooks of Attic tragedy and suddenly realized that he had left something out, namely, the theory of *hamartia*, or of pride and punishment, or of *hybris*, or what you will" (p. 73).

fortuitously—inartistically that is—with a *hubris*-dominated
morality. Ajax, turning to thoughts of suicide, addresses the
the Trojan river Scamander: "You shall see Ajax no more—
Ajax whose equal (I will now speak a proud word) Troy has
never known, not in all the warlike host that sailed here from
Greece"[1]; and the reader catches a microcosmic reflection of
the general disturbance in this parenthetical intrusion of near-
apology into the plain epic boast. Character-consistency is of
course not in issue, but we may fairly glance forward from the
Ajax in order to remark that Sophocles habitually attains
identity of moral atmosphere as nice as Jane Austen's.

If the *Ajax* betrays unsure command, a failure of fingertip
delicacy in controlling emphasis within the tiny dramatic ambit
of fifteen hundred lines, it is also very obviously Sophoclean;
and just as an overreaching *hubris* cuts across the theme of lost
honour, so other signs of his mature presence come and go
bewilderingly. Sometimes the voice of Sophoclean pity is heard
above the jeering and bragging of Homeric chieftains, never so
clearly as at its first utterance. The play is still young. Athena
has been telling Odysseus, her favourite among the Greek
leaders, how she made Ajax mad during the night now past and
turned him against the sheep and oxen. She calls Ajax out from
his tent in order to demonstrate to Odysseus her continuing
power over him. Ajax appears. He has brought some of the
animals alive to his tent in the belief that they are his human
enemies. Odysseus, he says, has been singled out for further
torture; he intends to tie him up and flay his back crimson.
"O no!" replies Athena in mock dismay, herself playing horribly
with Ajax, "do not torture the wretch so cruelly."[2] But he
insists, and then, letting him go with her blessing, she turns to
Odysseus:

> Do you see, Odysseus, how great is the power of the gods? Could
> you have found a man with more foresight than Ajax? Who was
> better at doing the sane and sensible thing at the right moment?[3]

Odysseus answers:

> I know none. And yet I pity him in his mad distress, for all that
> he is my enemy, because of the hideous fate which is inescapably

---

[1] ll. 421-6.　　　　[2] l. 111.　　　　[3] ll. 118-20.

his. In this I am thinking of myself no less than of him, for I see
that we are phantom shapes, every living one of us, and shadows
without substance.[1]

This unexpected calling halt to horror is impressive in itself,
and it grows in power to move us when its decisive role in the
debate over burial becomes apparent. Menelaus, the opponent
of burial, has demanded that Ajax's body "shall be thrown out
somewhere on the yellow sand, for the gulls to eat"[2]; and now
he says to Teucer, Ajax's half-brother who wishes to honour
the body:

And I warn you not to bury him. If you do, you may come to
need a grave yourself.[3]

The phrasing of this threat is well considered. Sophocles is
thinking forward to the dialogue with Agamemnon, the supreme
commander, in which Odysseus finally wins the day for mercy:

AG.: So you want me to grant burial to the body?
OD.: Yes. For I too shall come to that need.
AG.: It's plain everyone works for himself in everything.
OD.: And for whom should I work rather than myself?
AG.: Then let this be called your doing—not mine.
OD.: Either way you will earn high praise.[4]

It is a characteristic reversal in miniature that the thought
which now impels Odysseus to ask for burial on behalf of his
enemy should be the one whereby Menelaus had sought to
frighten the friends of Ajax into surrendering his claim. More
important, Odysseus makes us turn back over nearly the whole
length of the play, towards his exclamation to Athena of pity
for Ajax. His attitude draws together the primary Sophoclean
elements: death—the debt we all must pay—exerting its even
pressure upon life; the sudden alleviating shaft of pity; the
morality (not yet examined) of visionary, selfless selfishness;
mutability's full circle. In so far as it can be isolated, this is the
mature and altogether worthy segment of the play, and in its
working out of human fortunes it gives dramatic body to the

[1] ll. 121-6.
[2] ll. 1064-5. The controlled *legato* phrase distinguishes this great writer:
ἀλλ᾽ ἀμφὶ χλωρὰν ψάμαθον ἐκβεβλημένος
ὄρνισι φορβὴ παραλίοις γενήσεται.
[3] ll. 1089-90.   [4] ll. 1364-9.

statement of universal flux which appears here as it does in everything of Sophocles's that has survived:

> The snow-bound days of winter yield to summer's fruitfulness; night ceases her long patrol to give day's white horses place to shine; the fearful gale-blast eases and allows repose to the groaning sea; and, like these others, sleep sets free the man he has bound, holding no one captive for ever.[1]

Once again, as in the movement of the circling Bear, mutability overwhelms antithesis in a great symphonic voice which is also a kind of silence—as if the poet held the world's heart beating in his hand. Some insight into this high mystery is afforded by Odysseus's reply to Athena, already quoted. There he makes three points: he pities Ajax; in feeling pity he has his own human state in mind as well as Ajax's; all men are ghosts and shadows. The third point has a closer and more sustained connection with the other two than at first seems possible, because where we should isolate the temporal character of mutability within the "here today, gone tomorrow" range of sentiments, the Sophoclean view embraces potency together with duration. This is why his account of life's progress towards death escapes so impressively from the unilinear forward movement which we might expect to find dominant:

> What joy is there in day following day, now edging us forward upon the verge of death, now drawing us back?[2]

The ebb and flow imaged here is that of life's ground-rhythm —of time at its most potent, of "Great Time",[3] as Sophocles calls it. So that when Odysseus is stirred by Ajax's fate to think of all men as shadows without weight and substance his meaning is not simply that we are gone tomorrow. He is also positioning individual existences in relation to this firm central pulse and noting how comparatively weak they are. There is less reality-stuff in them. They must all meet death, of course; but the leading Sophoclean thought is rather that none of them can embody more than a morsel of life. For the society which produced Sophocles, death is an experience which the life of the group comprehends; it is only the human self at its most solitary that affirms "Death is not an event of life. Death is not

---

[1] ll. 670-6.   [2] ll. 475-6.   [3] l. 713.

lived through.''[1] And for Sophocles himself, death is not so
much the end of each life's journey as it is all life's constant
fringe.

With our perception of time and death thus changed and
perhaps made richer, the self-poise of Sophoclean mutability
ceases to be altogether strange. The solemn peace at its heart
grows out of such darkness as the monistic imagination of Ajax
conceives—darkness at once deathful and life-begetting, from
which "the long and countless years draw all things to the light,
then bury them once more".[2] And since time is power (sometimes figured as an adamantine substance wearing away men
and things by its action, causing them to "wither"),[3] we must
be careful to catch the accent of temporal frailty proper to
Odysseus's "shadows without substance". It is an accent which
advertises Sophocles's traditional cast of mind as well as his
individual idiom, since by stating the mortal theme in the
words "men are shadows" he gives it an entirely Greek turn.
The connections between the shadow-life of tragic humanity
and the shadow-life of the epic dead, and between both of these
and the pervasive substance-and-shadow dialectic of Greek
speculation, are many and vital, for all that they run irrecover-
ably deep.

Odysseus's expression of pity for Ajax raises a second traditional issue in the selfishness of its form. "I am thinking of
myself no less than of him", he tells Athena, and the self-
regarding bent of his solicitude is further exposed in the dialogue with Agamemnon:

> OD.: Yes [I want you to grant Ajax burial]. For I too shall come
> to that need.
> AG.: It's plain everyone works for himself in everything.
> OD.: And for whom should I work rather than myself?

Sophocles takes care that Odysseus's decisive action in supporting the claim of Ajax shall rest, and shall be seen to rest, on
consideration of his own advantage. The stress is inescapable;
but it is one which the reader educated in a morality of altruism
may be expected to interpret precisely wrong: I mean he may

---

[1] Ludwig Wittgenstein, *Tractatus Logico-Philosophicus*, 6.4311.
[2] ll. 646-7.
[3] l. 713. The *Ajax* Chorus are "worn by time" (l. 605).

take for worldly-wise acknowledgment of the selfishness that
sustains generous action what Sophocles intends as a kind of
homage to enlightened self-love—as a demonstration of its
moral efficacy. The standpoint from which to regard Odysseus
is that of the old blind Oedipus at Colonus. Oedipus is awaiting
the arrival of Theseus, king of Athens, who (Oedipus hopes)
will come forward to befriend and protect him. And this is a
rational hope because Oedipus is able to show that various
benefits will accrue to Athens if the people there receive him
kindly—benefits promised by Apollo's oracle. When he hears
about them Theseus will surely prove gracious; "for what good
man," so Oedipus concludes, "is not his own friend?"[1]

Now Theseus is very evidently a good man—the type of the
just and brave soldier-king in ancient tradition, almost the
founder of Attic virtues; and the action of the *Oedipus at Colonus*
declares him his own friend both through anxiety for his city's
welfare and in a personal way:

> I would never turn aside from a stranger, coming as you do now,
> or deny him help in trouble. For I know that I am a man, and
> that the day comes when my portion is no greater than yours.[2]

We observe his course running parallel to that of Odysseus who
grew merciful in the thought that he would come to need a
grave himself, one day. The connection, moreover, between
concern for self and remembering that one is a man (which was
implicit in the *Ajax*) comes into the open in the late play, and
points the difference between the vulgar selfishness of average
unheroic humanity—the selfishness of the guard in the *Antigone*
who expresses regret that he can only escape punishment himself by incriminating Antigone, but concludes: "all these things
matter less to me than my own safety"[3]—and the self-love of
the good man who is his own friend.

Odysseus of the *Ajax*, then, is another such good man, and
the moral tone and prominence of his statement to Athena, and
of his dialogue with Agamemnon, are very materially affected
by this consideration. The local naturalness of Sophoclean
dialogue is an agent of confusion here, as often happens; it
appears to solicit a rueful or cynical inflection for Agamemnon's
"It's plain everyone works for himself in everything", and a

---

[1] *Oedipus at Colonus*, l. 309. [2] *Ibid.*, ll. 565-8. [3] ll. 439-40.

corresponding narrow defensiveness for Odysseus's "For whom should I work rather than myself?"—the exchange between them amounting to no more than a skirmish with the ignoble theme of selfishness, but perfectly adequate to that modest end. It ceases to be adequate when the end ceases to be modest— when the self-love of the good man receives its due scope and force in the play's economy. In fact, the obvious and "human" interpretation of the dialogue collapses when the altruistic ideal of the modern reader is laid aside. This will have imposed no strain on Sophocles's first audience who, unlike ourselves, had never assumed that ideal. For them a self-regarding bent in moral discourse was inevitable. Their habit was to ask where a man's true interest lies, and they did so without (of course) any sense of a slightly comic inversion of civilised procedure such as assails ourselves when we encounter this habit in Sophoclean Tragedy or Socratic Dialogue or Thucydidean History or Aristotle, or elsewhere. A conviction, usually un-reasoned, that the individual's just appraisal of his advantage is the stuff of corporate moral health runs through Greek human-ism and helps to establish its characteristic buoyancy of mood.

Then banish those rounded Sophoclean characters, Odysseus and Agamemnon, dandling between them lightly, with Sopho-clean irony, the thought that selfishness begets its opposite; and admit the type-faces of the tragic masks, turned inward, certainly, in the subtle contact of line-by-line dialogue—supply-ing ethical colour to the action, as Aristotle says; but turned outward also; facing the world; expounding, acting out, doing again the religio-legendary triumph of Odysseus's self-love. This great moment when Odysseus secures burial for his enemy is one the public import of which contains the private: the mercy shown to the dead man falls within the establishment of the hero's cult. For to Sophocles and his audience Ajax was a hero in the technical public and religious sense of one whose spirit, while not divine, was the recipient of sacred honours. Moreover, the focus of the Greek heroic cult was the tomb where offerings were made, so that any defect or omission in funeral obsequies would touch the object of contemporary worship adversely, while to refuse him a tomb was almost to deny his subsequent cult altogether.

It is therefore not surprising that the *Ajax* should be built round the hero's burial rather than his death. The play is about the winning of a tomb for one who was revered at Athens in later times, and when it is regarded in this way the inner connection between private charity to the helpless dead and the successful inauguration of the public cult needs no stressing. In this closely worked segment of the play we see very clearly that the action which is the object of tragic imitation is Ajax's entry upon heroic status.

The moral impulse of Odysseus's self-love brings first to mind, from the large cognate tradition, Aristotelian pity-and-fear, the tragic emotions which we hyphenate because there can be no pity for Aristotle where there is not also fear. The correspondence with Sophocles runs deeper than the general disposition to link pity for another with fear for self, and to found both upon the self-regarding instinct; Aristotle is reconstructing, in the language of spectator-psychology, the experience that falls within the Sophoclean play. Responding with pity-and-fear emotions to the reversals taking place on the stage, responding ultimately (as the *Poetics* would have it) to the action's universal tendency of change (*metabolē*), the fourth-century audience stand where Odysseus stands, and King Theseus, and, with interesting modification, Queen Deianeira in the *Women of Trachis*.[1] In fact pity-and-fear are specifically tragic emotions

[1] Deianeira's pity for Iole, the captive princess and newly acquired concubine of her husband Heracles, is stated thus: "When I set eyes on her I pitied her most earnestly, because her beauty has wrecked her life" (463-5). The wording recalls Deianeira's own feelings of long ago, when Heracles fought with a monstrous river-god, his rival in love, to make her his wife: "I sat there, overcome with terror lest my beauty should finally bring me pain" (24-5). Her present feeling of pity is disinterested in that her own initial experience of the sad conjunction of beauty and pain lies in the past —and I think this affords one clue to Deianeira's elusive modernity. But that experience of hers is a continuing one; the play principally concerns her immediate and justified fears for her marriage with Heracles, and her unsuccessful attempt to save it. The pity-and-fear complex is preserved in the community of interest and experience between herself and Iole, and it is sustained in poetic continuity by the Chorus who follow her declaration of pity with a flash-back narrative of the fight between Heracles and the river-god, raging long and loud while "she, the tender girl with the beautiful eyes, sat on a distant hillside, waiting for the one who would be her husband" (523-5)—an example of dramatic purposefulness lurking within the ornamental choral lyric.

because they grow out of the root-situation of Tragedy at its full maturity; and while the abruptness of Aristotle's text makes the selection of these two emotions appear arbitrary, all the available evidence requires that we understand 'mature' to mean 'Sophoclean'. There is no need to labour the commendations of Sophocles scattered through the *Poetics*, or the singling out of *Oedipus the King* for special praise; Aristotle's whole attitude to Tragedy—its premises, its system, its purposes—proves sufficiently compelling. And we may pause, while noting the interpenetration of Aristotelian critical concept and Sophoclean dramatic fact, at the point where fear on the one hand (or the hidden resources of fear) engages with the self-love of the good man who is his own friend on the other. For the self-regarding instinct common to the *Poetics* and the Sophoclean *œuvre* presents a fruitful paradox in the fact that its issue is a kind of selflessness. Thus Odysseus moves easily, with no sense of hiatus, from his self-interested argument ("I too will come to need a grave") to the statement that the burial of Ajax will be in itself a good and generous act. Selfishness seems to spend itself in determining the deed, which can then be contemplated in its objective rightness. The essence of this movement is a self-externalising process, already encountered in visions of mutability:

> This I say since starry night does not abide with men, nor does calamity, nor wealth. In a moment they have left us, and someone else has his turn of joy, and of joy's loss. Therefore I bid you—you our Queen—hold fast this truth in expectancy; for Zeus always looks after his children.[1]

Such tragic peace depends on the ability not merely to see the self out there, caught up in the mutability rhythm, but to realise this affectually. And what seems to call for moral heroism —without reservation to lay the self alongside other selves, to accept the touch of joy and pain, on me, on him and him and him, on me again, for consummation and cosmic sufficiency —reveals in Sophocles, apparently, a natural inclination to think and feel thus; self-surrender of this kind is almost ordinary.[2] We are at grips with that most extraordinary problem,

[1] *Women of Trachis*, ll. 131-40.
[2] Remember that this utterly Sophoclean Mutability grows out of a shared Greek Mutability which is a consolatory commonplace of their literature.

the absence of problem in Sophoclean Tragedy. His Chorus of Trachinian women, so far from thinking that the will must be educated to the acceptance of the passing touch of joy and pain, tell Deianeira to embrace the fact of mutability so that she may remind herself of Zeus's care for his son Heracles. It is not simply a case of the harsh disconnection which is here presented to a Christian understanding (and to others) being tolerable to the Sophoclean Chorus. The disconnection does not exist for them at all. This is partly explained by the absence, for nearly all important purposes, of the infinite: there is a limited stock of joy and pain under Zeus's rule, and he ensures fair shares. And partly by the strength of the collective consciousness. But nothing must obscure the ease with which the dramatic figure realises his projection into universal flux. This is not felt to be an achievement, not an end toilfully gained. The expected overtone of visionary resignation is missing, and so are the splendid prematurities of individual resentment and outrage—everything that falls before the resolving moment of Hamlet's "Let be". It follows that not many of the received ideas about tragic experience and its fruit are worth retaining: they distract the modern eye from the ancient dramatic object, and especi-ally from its enfolding, upon a single level of experience, of indulgent self-nursing in debate and statement of motive together with the letting go of self now before us.

The issuing of selfishness into selflessness recalls that principle of self-spending which exerts its hidden but very powerful influence upon the *Poetics*. We contrasted self-spending with the counter-principle of self-conservation in an attempt to dis-lodge various misconceptions, and chief among these was the taking of a single and inward focus of being for the universal type of achieved selfhood.[1] We had to supplant this image by one of discrete and centrifugal selfhood in order to make sense of Aristotle; and we have now to repeat the process when we encounter the Sophoclean stage-figure moving unanxiously outward in self-subjection to the rule of change, and declaring Zeus's care for his children as he does so. When we wonder why he does not attend his god in his own heart's solitude—in that pure extreme of self-identity—we have only to remember that he does not look for himself there either.

[1] See p. 32 ff.

5 *Action and Actors:*
Antigone *and* Oedipus The King

Our comparison of Sophocles's *Electra* with the *Libation-Bearers* of Aeschylus disclosed a development in what we guardedly called personalising of consciousness. The reason for caution was partly fear of seeming to make unwarranted assumptions about Sophoclean naturalism, and partly the need to keep all initial reference to this new interest provisional. But we indicated the direction which further enquiry must take when we observed of Sophocles's introduction and vigorous working up of the theme of Clytemnestra's motive in killing Agamemnon, that these make it dramatically relevant to ask why she acted as she did. The instinct which directs our curiosity towards her deed is one to respect and explore. It matters not the least that the distinction between "why does Clytemnestra act as she does?" (which is our question) and "what sort of a person is Clytemnestra?" is in other connections empty; here, the distinction is one of substance and a determinant of principle in critical procedure. Nor is it in point that our question is ambiguously framed. The Chorus's conclusion in this matter is also ambiguous: "Guile planned the deed, lust did the killing"[1]; they may be talking either about the character of the planner and killer or about the character (ethical colour) of the planning and killing. But we do not hesitate before deciding where the Chorus stand.

While this ambiguity is merely formal, it does embarrass any critical attempt to prevail upon the very common state of mind which will not advance, except under compulsion, beyond the thought that since the action is Clytemnestra's which we and the Chorus are contemplating, we may as well speak of her as of it. For the language of characterful action may nearly always be translated into that of Character—of the stable, unitary centre of consciousness—without reducing the text to obvious nonsense. Where the crudest sort of proof is wanting we have to rely on such sequences as that in the *Philoctetes*—

> *What do you intend to do?*
> *Kill myself.*
> *Stop him!*—

[1] *Electra,* l. 197.

in order to remark the troubles that ensue if we allow dramatised humanity first to escape into independence of the action,
and then to turn the tables on the latter so that it is only felt to
be interesting for what it has to tell us about the actors.

A more general and impressive consideration, a stimulant to
the torpid reader, is Sophocles's failure to deal consistently with
his people, even in matters of first importance.

Antigone is the most sharply individualised and the richest
in human probability of Sophoclean stage-figures. Her tragedy
stems (in the traditional language of commentary) from her
being placed in a situation where there is only one course open
to a woman of her noble heart and single mind—to defy King
Creon's edict forbidding all citizens of Thebes to bury the
soldier Polyneices, Antigone's brother, who has been killed
leading an unsuccessful assault against the city. To bury him,
Antigone risks the prescribed penalty of death, and in doing so
she gives voice and body to the conflict between the lower law
of Creon's edict and the higher law of heaven—for the Greeks
regarded burying their dead as a most solemn religious duty.
Antigone recognises this conflict; her path towards death grows
magnificent and also credible through Sophocles's crossing of
her gentle courage and resolution with backward glances at
the life under the warm sun which she is leaving.

The essential feature of this situation, as I have outlined it,
is its adequacy for the Romantic imagination. Antigone has
from the time of Goethe been the subject of a "stainless soul"
school of commentary, which allows room to those momentary
falterings and gestures of anguish in which the humanity of
Sophoclean portraiture is displayed; but not to anything else.
Anything else is not merely superfluous but an affront, and one
which is most keenly felt where it affects the central theme of
Polyneices's burial. It is essential to this view of the play that
Antigone's action (in which she is detected and for which she
dies) should be impelled by the single heroic motive of duty to
her dead brother. Which is why the following passage has
proved very embarrassing:

> Had it been a child of mine or a husband who lay dead and
> rotting, I would never have defied the city in taking upon myself
> the task of burial. And my reason (for you may ask what warrant
> I have for this declaration) is that I might have found another

N

husband after I had lost the first, and he might have fathered a child to replace the dead first-born. But, with my father and mother dead, I could never hope to have another brother.[1]

How can Antigone's soul be called stainless once she has betrayed herself with these ignoble admissions: first, that she would not have defied Creon's edict if the relative lying un-buried had been a husband or child instead of a brother; second, that Polyneices's singular claim rests in the fact that he is her only surviving brother and, unlike husband or child, irreplaceable? Within the received critical framework only one solution strikes as deep as the problem it is meant to solve, and that is to declare the passage spurious. This has been done, and often, but not without misgivings as to the frailty of the technical linguistic argument against Sophocles's authorship, and not without discomfiture at the certainty that the inter-polation—assuming there is interpolation—must have occurred at a very early date since we know that Aristotle's text of Sophocles contained the offending passage. It may fairly be urged that no general outcry would have been raised against these words of Antigone if their drift had been found un-exceptionable.

But as things are, and although Goethe's hope that the passage would one day be proved spurious has not been ful-filled, the advantage, at least in numbers, is with those who cannot believe that Sophocles gave this passage to Antigone. If we allow her to distinguish between one dead relation and another, the absolute character of the duty to bury is denied; and then, in the same instant, the rationale of the play dis-appears and Antigone's clear sight of what is inescapable becomes overwhelmed in a grimy fog of picking and choosing. Two considerations stand between us and acceptance of her words: the single dilemma which is the play's backbone, and the exalted nature of the heroine.[2] Fundamental to both is the absolute duty to bury.

We pause parenthetically at "absolute" because it conceals

[1] ll. 905-12.

[2] Commentators have also argued that the sentiment which is false to Antigone's nature appears much more appropriate in the corresponding passage of Herodotus (3.119). Hence a further reason for rejecting it in Sophocles's play.

an unwarranted assumption of correspondence between the
ancient and modern mind. Through Antigone's response to the
edict and by other means, Sophocles has placed the conflict of
the lower human law with the higher divine law at the heart of
his play. So far so good. The next stage, which appears to be
determined by universal human processes of reason and
common sense, is the beginning of error. We suppose that the
conflict of royal edict and religious duty presents Sophocles—
and Antigone—with a rigid choice from which the play's action
flows. Our reason for thinking so is the full articulation of the
conflict by the playwright and its recognition by his dramatic
personae; a collision has been arranged, and its purpose, we
should say, is a certain decisiveness of effect. And here a false
emphasis is introduced by our importing a sense of qualitative
difference between divine and human which there is every
reason to believe Sophocles did not possess. The god is man's
stronger partner in the enterprise of life, he is "the right-hand
trace-horse"; but he enjoys no absolute power and is owed no
absolute duty. The monistic imagination enfolds religious experience within the one seamless garment of nature, and the
result, for Christian and other dualisms, is a puzzling taint of
relativism in the pious individual's acknowledgment of religious
obligation. It is a distinctive feature of Greek Tragedy, and
especially of Sophocles, that the presentation of the tragic fact,
the *donnée* of the situation, should have an almost intolerable
clarity about it, but that its treatment (I mean its manipulation
from within the play, through the apprehensions and responses
of dramatised consciousness) should appear blurred and contradictory. So it is with Antigone and her address to the duty
of burying Polyneices; an expected exclusiveness and con-
clusiveness are missing. The religious demand upon her takes
its chance within a single life-complex of stress and counter-
stress, of contingent buffetings.

Therefore the local problem of Antigone should be studied
within the wider one of Greek Tragedy's very alien expression
of value. At the same time it compels attention to the particular
and (for us) central question of the human self in Sophocles by
its exceptionally clear display of contradiction, or doubleness,
within the individual mind; for Antigone tells Creon, "I did
not reckon your decrees strong enough to justify mortal trans-

gression of the unwritten and unalterable laws of heaven",[1] and she also says that she would not have buried Polyneices had he not been her only brother, and irreplaceable. The fact that for her the man-god relationship is not absolute (in a broadly Kierkegaardian sense) has a general relevance, as we have argued, but it does not explain how she can both affirm and deny the higher law. Higher continues to mean higher, within the one scheme of nature as well as outside. Sophoclean relativism is not mental chaos.

Our impression of impasse at this point grows out of our manner of referring the issue of burial to Antigone. We picture an inward debate, perhaps protracted and painful, which is determined in favour of burial and which results in a victory for the divine law being registered at the abiding seat of consciousness. This is our image; and it now requires us, when the question arises as to what Antigone would have done if Polyneices had not been her last brother, to answer that she would have looked within, would have recognised her achieved solution to this problem, would have been true to herself and would have buried him. Our reading of the case is not concerned to note that Antigone was not in fact faced with the burial of anyone other than her last brother—understandably, since her response to the hypothetical circumstances must have been the same as to the actual. Nevertheless, the omission is crucial in that the presupposition which renders vain the distinction between actual and hypothetical circumstances is entirely unSophoclean—the presupposition of that abiding seat of consciousness where, in the mere process of living and maintaining self-identity, the once-acknowledged superiority of the divine law must always claim respect. Here are exposed the ultimate inflexibilities of modern psychologising commentary: the vision of the heroine's enduring loyalty to principle, and the refusal to believe that Sophocles gave her these words of self-betrayal and senseless self-contradiction. And so the text is impugned.[2] But the trouble lies elsewhere, in the ignored

---

[1] ll. 453-5.

[2] There have been a few psychologising defences of the received text, but to my mind they are not impressive. "She is moved by an intense love for her brother. . . . So she explains herself in this unsophisticated, even primitive way" (C. M. Bowra, *Sophoclean Tragedy*, p. 95); "here she has suffered

distinction between what happened and what might have happened, and in our failure to make contact with a Sophoclean Antigone whose apprehension of self in absent circumstances is so shifting and feeble that she projects in debate an *alter ego* who can subordinate the religious duty to the royal edict. In short, she knows no adequate modern "you" which would give an adequate modern sense to the question: "What would you do if it were a husband or child lying unburied?"

To speak of psychologising commentary as modern was a little old-fashioned. Contemporary scholarship tends increasingly, when treating passages and problems like the present, to stress the forensic element in Sophoclean Tragedy. The argument is one of diminished naturalism, of receding human probability, at moments when the dramatic character assumes the quasi-legal mode, so that we must conceive of Antigone retreating from the *engagement* of her living plight in order to offer an alternative formal defence of her conduct, as if she were pleading in a court of law. This approach has the obvious attraction that it withholds seriousness from Antigone's statement of how she would have behaved in other circumstances (and also mitigates the offending contradiction since there is no need for alternative pleas to be mutually consistent); but it buys its advantage too dearly, at the cost of Sophocles's art. For we are now being asked to accept the kind of heterogeneity that afflicts the dramatic medium in its infancy (the analogy of the Tudor history play comes to mind) or at the hands of gross incompetents; and while it is true that the older critical tradition underestimated the importance of forensic rhetoric and manners in Tragedy, it is also plainly irresponsible to let fall the unexamined inference that the operation of quasi-legal argument in these mature plays of Sophocles is intrusive. Indeed, if we allow that Sophocles was artist enough to digest his material, the problem of Antigone grows keener with this shift towards a legalistic interpretation, calling attention as it

a momentary loss of certainty about the wisdom of what she has done" (G. M. Kirkwood, *A Study of Sophoclean Drama*, p. 164); "Antigone is neither a philosopher nor a *dévote*, but a passionate impulsive girl, and we need not expect consistency from one such, when for doing what to her was her manifest duty she is about to be buried alive, without a gleam of understanding from anybody" (H. D. F. Kitto, *Form and Meaning in Drama*, pp. 170-1).

does to something which one would have expected the drama-
tiser of consciousness to find singularly intractable.

Surrender of prejudice, followed by a new flexibility in
contemplating Sophocles's version of the human self, enables
us to see that Antigone's quasi-legal argument is not grafted
on to a *psyche* which is in other respects like our own, but rather
that it mirrors faithfully the near-indeterminacy of hypothetical
selfhood: hence the significance of the distinction between the
present and the absent circumstance—between the brother who
was buried and those others who might or might not have been
buried, leading back to our initial psychological premise of the
self's realisation in action, and to the corresponding habit in the
dramatist to find sufficiency of character in the things men do.
The *Antigone* is about the burying of Polyneices: this is the
single distinct action which, in the Aristotelian analysis, the
tragedy imitates. Antigone and Creon are the play's principal
figures because the one performs burial and the other forbids
and then punishes burial. Their conflict is dramatised in and
through the deed of burying. If we forget this last truth and
look for the direct and fresh mentality, for the actuality of
contact, which an immediate opposing of the two individuals
ought to disclose, we shall be disappointed. Creon and Antigone
find each other within the forbidden and performed deed; this
is the sense in which the masks face outward towards their
audience and the world as they carry the action, and a corresponding faintness of inward contact ensues.

Antigone is not the familiar steadfast heroine with eyes fixed
intently on her adversary. She regards the deed; her heroism
and her solitude rest in her appropriation of the deed: in her
exclusion of her sister from any share in it ("you did not consent
to the deed, and I refused your help"),[1] and in her claiming it
for herself when she is brought before Creon:

> CR.: You there—you with your eyes on the ground—do you
>   admit or do you deny this deed?
> AN.: I admit it. I do not deny it.[2]

And throughout her examining of the conditions under which
she would have left a blood-relation unburied, we must imagine
her facing the audience with the deed between her hands, con-

---

[1] l. 539.   [2] ll. 441-3.

templating possibilities and an unrealised self, her apprehension of Creon correspondingly mediate and muffled.

Creon on his side undergoes a revulsion of feeling during the play without achieving at any time the expected direct contact with Antigone. He moves from formal prohibition of the deed to condemnation and punishment of the doer, to a change of heart after the blind seer Teiresias has declared the impiety of his edict forbidding burial, to final ruin and a kind of penitence when Antigone's suicide (she is entombed alive at Creon's command and hangs herself rather than die slowly) is followed by that of Creon's son, who is betrothed to her, and that of his wife. The generic irrelevancies of Creon's utterance are incompatible with a developed awareness of the will and intelligence opposed to his own; he is much concerned that men should not be overruled by women in any circumstances,[1] and he makes the mere fact of Antigone's deviation a reproach against her ("Are you not ashamed to adopt a view of your own, apart from these citizens?"[2]) with only dim regard to the specific considerations and turn of argument by which her position is sustained. Indeed, his assessment of her singular case extends not far beyond this fact of deviation, manifested in her act of solitary defiance of his edict.

Later, when Antigone is dead, it becomes increasingly clear that Creon's eyes are upon the deed of burial no less fixedly than hers were. The triple suicide answers broadly to the name of tragic *dénouement*, and the last hundred lines of the play are mainly taken up with Creon's lamenting this disaster and his repeated admissions of responsibility for it. A distinction must be drawn, however, between the suicides of his wife and son and that of Antigone, because his expressions of guilt embrace their deaths but not hers. Haemon's (his son's) death was the result, says Creon, of his own royal folly[3], and responsibility for that of Euridice, his wife, "can never be fixed on any man"[4] but himself; he is the "unwitting murderer"[5] of them both. But no word of Antigone. It is not surprising that Creon should spend his grief on the two near relatives; what deserves attention (his contrition being bitter and complete) is the failure to mention that he has caused the death of Antigone.

[1] ll. 484-5; 525; 677-80; 746; 756.　　[2] l. 510.　　[3] ll. 1268-9.
[4] ll. 1317-18.　　[5] l. 1340.

In fact Creon is not regarding Antigone at this time, or rather, his wide confession of "folly"[1] and his use of the common Sophoclean image of "some god" leaping on him from above and thrusting his conduct towards impious recklessness,[2] comprehend the dead girl sufficiently. We have here one of those instances where the converting of the language of characterful action into that of Character can be shown to work decisive nonsense, and in order to avoid this nonsense our ordinary notions of dramatic figures standing *vis-à-vis* each other must be enormously dulled. Creon's failure, after the conflict has been resolved against him, to say "She was right and I was wrong", or "I am guilty of her death", forces us to understand that he is finding his adversary, experiencing her, within the forbidden and performed action of burial. It is precisely because his guilt in relation to her is singularly conclusive and immediate —the other two suicides flow less directly from the original culpable edict—that it is felt to be sufficiently acknowledged in Creon's general admission that his attitude to the burial of Polyneices has been refuted.

This is the manner in which the conflict at the heart of the *Antigone* is projected into the single, faceted action of Polyneices's burial, and is not referred back to the two opposed consciousnesses of the principal stage-figures. Thus two cardinal affirmations of the *Poetics* (the object of tragic imitation is a single distinct action, not human beings; Character is included for the sake of the action) find their warrant in the text of Sophocles. The theoretical discussion of action has its practical counterpart in Sophocles's unwearying preoccupation with what men do. Prominent among our memories of learning Greek is the glad recognition with which the eye fell upon *oimoi ti drasō*—"Alas, what shall I do?": the aboriginal tragic cry, found three times in the *Ajax* in this very form[3] and echoing through the whole Sophoclean drama. There is no sitting and doing nothing; there is only action and action's anti-self, suffering, and these are the rude stuff from which the dramatic form emerges.

It is much easier to state, even to state convincingly, that the *Antigone* concerns a burying than to make effective contact with

[1] l. 1269.   [2] l. 1272-5.   [3] ll. 809; 920; 1024.

the work of art; for the discipline which we must consciously invoke in order to resist our instinctive adjectiving of action—making action qualify and reveal interesting truths about the individuals who promote it—is itself hostile to the relaxed and penetrable attentiveness which art demands. *Oedipus the King* is more accessible than the *Antigone*, and this is principally because the single action which it imitates (the self-discovery of Oedipus) is able to command the modern imagination as the burying of Polyneices cannot. It has been said that *Oedipus the King* possesses the merits of a good detective story. The point of the comparison is not merely the piecemeal disclosure of hidden facts, nor the process of investigation, but a kind of mental innocence; Sophocles unfolds a cat-and-mouse situation of great horror while leaving the obvious psychological resources of anguish and dread and recurring false hopes strangely unexploited. This suggests such highly stylised modern forms as the detective story and the cowboy film where, because of a withdrawal of human interest which leaves the action naked, we witness death and pain lightheartedly.

But the comparison ends there, on the threshold of the Sophoclean play's seriousness. This seriousness is hard to experience since action's proper wealth of meaning for the fifth-century Greek is virtually irrecoverable: to say that *Oedipus the King* is like a good detective story is to suggest that the cat-and-mouse horrors are not there at all, when in fact they rest in the action: the interrogations by which Oedipus exposes the truth about himself have a sublime impersonal malignity such as a series of forced moves at chess would impart if the game possessed tragic relevance to life. Furthermore, to say that *Oedipus the King* is like a good detective story is to ignore the differentiation of action and plot upon which the *Poetics* depends. Aristotle's intellectualist vision of the lucid form which the artist coaxes out of rough circumstance must not be directly imposed on Sophocles, of course; but still a general correspondence exists between the Aristotelian form and that life-situation from myth which Sophocles's play defines and re-defines, compresses, reduces, renders essentially, epitomoses. "He shall be found"—so the blind seer Teiresias declares—"at once brother and father to the children of his house, son and husband to the woman who bore him, murderer of his father and suc-

cessor to his father's bed."[1] Teiresias is a prophet; he speaks for
the god and his words disclose the hard bedrock truth of the
situation. The vulgar notion of prophecy as the power to predict
future events must be absorbed within a wider and juster
conception of god-inspired exposure of the myth's essentials;
otherwise we fail to give due prominence to the fact (vital to
the religious ambience of *Oedipus the King*) that the stage-figures
groping forward in the play's action are brought sharply up
against something that was there before.

As the dreadful truth unfolds, the people in the play recall
the terms of Teiresias's prophecy—with very striking iteration,
but without pointed reference to the seer himself; they are
falling upon the truth, only in a very secondary sense confirming
a prediction, and we should place their mortal encounter with
this adamantine quasi-substance in a context of the "Great
Time" investing Sophoclean humanity, and of life's cruel
margin which is called Necessity. And so they nurse the essential
facts with strange unmorbid concentration. A messenger describes how Queen Jocasta, on the point of suicide, "bewailed
the marriage in which, unhappy lady, she had borne a twofold
race—husband by husband, children by her child"[2]; and how
Oedipus burst into the palace, asking "where he should find
the wife that was no wife, but a mother who had borne his
children and himself".[3]

The same concentration is maintained by the newly blind
Oedipus:

> Those three roads, that secret valley, that wood and narrow
> passage where the roads met and where I spilt—for the dust to
> drink up—my father's blood, and mine. . . . That marriage which
> gave me life, then gave life to other children from my seed; and
> created an incestuous kindred of fathers, brothers, sons, brides,
> wives, mothers. . . .[4]

He summons his young daughters to him:

> Where are you, my children? Come here—come to your brother's
> hands . . . which are the hands of a man who, seeing nothing,
> understanding nothing, became you father by her that bore him.[5]

---

[1] ll. 457-60.   [2] ll. 1249-50.   [3] ll. 1256-7.
[4] ll. 1398-1407.   [5] ll. 1480-5.

He contemplates the wretched life in store for them:

> What misery is lacking? Your father killed his father and got children by his mother, and you two are the fruit of the womb which once held him—[1]

this series of declarations culminating in the demonstrative choral gesture ("Behold, citizens of Thebes—this is Oedipus"[2]) with which the play ends, and which the Chorus have themselves anticipated:

> Alas, renowned Oedipus! The one ample haven enfolded son and father; coming to your bride you found your own beginning. How was it, unhappy one, that the furrow which had received your father's seed received yours also without mark of protest, all this time?[3]

Such definitional fondling of the truth, so far from being morbid, is the means to restoration, and almost an act of peace. When Sophocles's text has been given a fair hearing we respond to the co-operative endeavour of the outward-turning masks in their advance towards full discovery of Oedipus. Our experience is of something decisively accomplished.

The play opens with the city of Thebes prostrate in a passion of despair because of a mysterious pestilence or blight which is destroying its citizens and all living things there. A group of suppliants has assembled to ask Oedipus to save the city. They approach him not merely because he is their king but also because he saved Thebes once before, when the monstrous Sphinx was oppressing her, and they naturally turn to him now. Great stress is laid on Oedipus's fame and proven virtuosity as a problem-solver[4]; his finding the answer to the Sphinx's riddle after all others had failed is repeatedly cited as a reason for believing that he will again rescue the city. His task is to find out what has angered heaven to the point of visiting Thebes

---

[1] ll. 1496-9.   [2] l. 1524.

[3] ll. 1207-12. I believe it has not been remarked that the Freudian insight of this passage, especially in the image of the ample haven (μέγας λιμὴν), deserves to be compared with that of Jocasta's famous assurance to Oedipus: "Many a man has slept with his mother in his dreams" (981-2).

[4] ll. 31-9; 132; 391-8; 503-11; 689-96: 1197-1203.

with pestilence, and then to make amends; and this task he successfully performs. This last point (which has been almost totally ignored) is very relevant to the final sense of accomplishment. Thebes is put right with her gods, and the religious institutions of oracle and prophecy are vindicated.

Oedipus's first step towards saving his city is to send Creon, his wife's brother, to consult the oracle of Apollo. On his carefully staged return Creon's first words are that he brings good news[1]; the god declares that their troubles will end when they detect and punish the murderer of Laius, who was king of Thebes before Oedipus and died at the hand of an unknown assailant when on his way to Delphi. Their present sufferings are due to the defilement they have incurred by unwittingly harbouring the murderer.

And so the search begins. Of course, there is irony in the long struggle to reach the truth, and especially in the successful outcome; but it is an irony whose force and tone will be misapprehended so long as all judgment of the play is required to come to terms with the hero's tragic fate, making the play's meaning and message primarily those which it has for him, or even in relation to him as an independent dramatic *exemplum*. Oedipus's solitary eminence, which is undeniably dominant and impressive always, may be rendered in the critical language of Character and psychological individuation (isolating Oedipus by way of the pains and problems that assault the hero's consciousness), or of action: in the latter case we say that Oedipus stands alone because of the extent—unique in Greek drama— to which he carries the action single-handed. The true Sophoclean standpoint is suggested by a glancing reference in the *Antigone* to Oedipus's "sins brought to light by his own search"[2]; Oedipus does the work in this success-story, and *Oedipus the King* maintains throughout an extraordinary intimacy between the substantive sins themselves—their religio-moral quality, the subjective innocence of the wrongdoing and adjacent themes— and the sinner's action in laying them bare. A kind of godly faithfulness is lent to Oedipus's exertions by the fact that his progressive self-exposure is suspended in a mesh of oracle and prophecy; in fact it *is* the movement of these god-inspired pronouncements towards fulfilment, and its accomplishment *is*

1 l. 87.   2 l. 51.

their final vindication. The process and its completion matter supremely.

We have noted Teiresias's words and the answer with which Creon returned from Delphi. Another and deeper oracular layer is exposed by the Chorus:

> I will go no more to Apollo's inviolate shrine at the navel of the world, nor to the temple at Abae, nor to Olympia, if these oracles fail in fulfilment so that each man's finger points at them. . . . The old prophecies about Laius are losing their power; already men are dismissing them from mind, and Apollo is nowhere glorified with honours. Religion is dying.[1]

They are referring to an earlier oracle or oracles which Laius received from Apollo's ministers at Delphi. Jocasta has already stated their content[2] which was that Laius would one day be killed by the child of his marriage with herself. The reason for the Chorus's dismay is that these oracles appear to be utterly discredited; Jocasta's baby died at birth (as everyone supposes), and when Laius finally came to be murdered the accepted story was that "foreign robbers"[3] were responsible. When Sophocles makes his Chorus of Theban elders declare that "religion is dying" because of the apparent non-fulfilment of the oracles, we should allow them to mean what they say. This is the Chorus which indicated their religious despair by asking (and we used the question in order to distinguish Sophocles's piety from Aeschylus's): "Why should I take part in the sacred dance?" Theirs is the voice of Theban religious practice; they lend the present crisis a full and obvious urgency.

It is therefore an ultimately fortunate thing that the parricide and incest should be established, and that the construction of events now prevailing, the humanly more comfortable but religion-wasting construction, should be refuted. The outcome of the play is a dreadful necessity, paradoxically divine and also embracing Oedipus's individual fate since yet another oracle has pronounced, this time in answer to Oedipus himself, that (as he reports)

> I must live in incest with my mother, and bring before my fellow men a family they will not bear to look upon, and kill the father who begat me.[4]

[1] ll. 897-910. [2] ll. 711-14. [3] ll. 715-16. [4] ll. 791-3.

By exposing the full horror of the situation Oedipus demonstrates that things have come out right; nature follows the
divine plan, experience is sanctified. And the long search which
achieves this is his own: we are defining the sense in which the
role of Oedipus is heroic.

If these facts within the Sophoclean play have not received
attention, it is largely because of the presupposition that dramatic action is bound to be crude and dull and mechanical when
it is determined from above—in the present case by oracle and
prophecy. The outraged individual of Romantic criticism is
again to the fore, in consideration of Oedipus's sins; not only
did he proceed in ignorance that the old man whom he
attacked (after extreme provocation) was his father, and that
the woman whom he subsequently married was his mother,
but he was fated to do these things. The question of acting in
ignorance need not detain us, since for Sophocles in this play,
as for Aeschylus, psycho-physical defilement follows the deed
without regard to intention. But the divine binding of Oedipus
to his fate has a daunting and detailed rigidity which the inherited curse and prophecy seem never to impart in Aeschylus.[1]
It suggests the determined movement of the stars which is a
leading image of Sophoclean mutability. And indeed the stage
downfall of Oedipus is the acting out of that lyrically foreshadowed mutability—but only in part, since the circling Bear
is used by Sophocles to present a single cyclical movement
bringing sorrow to one and joy to another. Romantic concentration on the figure of the king blinds us to the plight of Thebes
and its final remedy; the city's terrible sickness, which over-
shadows everything else at the beginning of the play, is the
result of harbouring a defilement, and it is cured by that single
process of self-discovery leading to expulsion from the city which
we incline to think of solely as Oedipus's tragedy.

The final impression of acomplishment is at one with the
doubleness characterising Sophoclean mutability; the Chorus's

[1] The human situation of the *Oresteia* is mysteriously fluid and "free"
beneath the inexorable curse. Aeschylus also wrote an *Oedipus*; his play was
the second part of a connected trilogy of which only the third part, the
Seven against Thebes, survives. In this trilogy, as in the *Oresteia*, the working
of a family curse is traced in the affairs of a later generation, and the
influence of the Furies is powerful. Parricide and incest are almost certainly
less prominent than in Sophocles's play.

vision of Oedipus "with his life reversed"[1]—the thematic strand
which criticism has gathered up gratefully—issues from a corporate consciousness occupied with divine fulfilment and the
city's health; and the play comes to rest in a conclusion
adequate to their anxieties. We return to our earlier insistence
that the relationship of prosperity and adversity within the
mutability-rhythm is symphonic rather than antithetical, its
application at this moment being that the image of Oedipus
falling as Thebes rises must be judged insufficient—insufficient
and also misleading in that a number of false conclusions flow
from it. In particular, it is impossible to invoke the late-classical
Wheel of Fortune (or anything like it) without reducing
Oedipus's downfall, and the saving of Thebes together with her
religion, to complete aesthetic penury: we then have a mechanical and determinist scheme of no interest, both on the
universal plane of mutability—the Bear's course is fixed—and
in the plot of *Oedipus the King* which simply follows the course
laid down for it in Apollo's oracle.

That Sophocles is not at all like this is a mystery experienced
at the outset in the bright lyrical freedom investing his images
of mutability; and the fullest human reflection of this mystery,
we have already observed, is the binding of Oedipus to his fate.
One or two considerations are relevant. Oedipus's dramatic
solitude—the solitude of the single-handed sustainer of the
action—co-exists with a high measure of social integration. His
relation to the people of Thebes is quasi-paternal; he calls them
"my children" in the first words of the play; he insists that he
is carrying the sorrows of the whole city on his shoulders.[2] And
it follows that our symphonic apprehension of opposite fortunes
must be pursued within his single destiny: the sense in which
his downfall means his city's salvation is immediate and intimate. It is true that Oedipus does not console himself, when
disaster strikes him down, with the thought that his ruin is
inextricably bound up with his city's deliverance from the
killing plague. But the genius of this play is not compensatory.
In any case, the spectator's point of view is not his. And when
we do examine his own attitude, something of interest emerges.

Oedipus surveys his sins in two different ways. On the one hand
he laments the pollution into which he has blundered. He has

a lot to say about his ignorance of the true circumstances, but his motive in this is not to deny or even to mitigate culpability. He is exposing a might-have-been (or rather, a would-not-have-been: the analogy suggests itself of Antigone declaring the circumstances in which she would have left a relative unburied); he is saying that he would not have killed Laius or married Jocasta if he had known who they were. This situation-rooted simplicity is fundamental, it must not be perverted into false moral sophistication.

On the other hand Oedipus has an attitude to his sins which is narrowly institutional. Early in the play, when he is setting out to solve the mystery of Laius's death, he pronounces a solemn religious curse upon the unknown murderer,[1] and this curse is treated as a fixed point of religio-moral reference as the story unfolds. Therefore *Oedipus the King* accommodates the formal curse on the sinner alongside the fact of his sin. The seer Teiresias, who is the first to state the truth, proceeds by way of directly accusing Oedipus of the polluting deeds, and at the same time charges him to "abide by the decree of your own mouth".[2] Later, when it begins to dawn on Oedipus himself that the old man whom he killed long ago was none other than Laius, he cries out: "Unhappy me! It seems I have just been placing myself under a dreadful curse—and never knew".[3] And later again:

> Suppose this stranger had any blood-connection with Laius—then who is now more miserable than the man before you, who more loathed of heaven? Neither stranger nor citizen is allowed to receive him; no one may speak to him; all must repel him from their homes. And it was my mouth and nobody else's that laid this—this curse—upon me.[4]

He also refers his final expulsion, when it occurs, to this initial curse (which was coupled with a command to the people of Thebes not to shelter or have social or religious communication with the murderer): "noblest of Thebans, I have doomed myself to banishment by my command that all should thrust out the man of sin . . ."[5]; and a messenger describes how Oedipus shouted out for somebody to unbar the palace gates,

---

[1] ll. 246-8.   [2] ll. 350-1.   [3] ll. 744-5.
[4] ll. 813-20.   [5] ll. 1379-82.

"purposing to expel himself from the land—at once, so as not to bring the house under his own curse".[1]

Thus a double representation of Oedipus's sins persists throughout; the curse and the discovered acts of pollution are two ways of stating the single fact of his guilt, and so far from the curse being absorbed within the parricide and incest (when these are established), it continues to the end, undiminished. It is plain from Oedipus's manner of shifting between "I was fated" and "I have doomed myself" that he regards both representations as adequate to his case, and we should surely be mistaken in supposing that he manipulates them advisedly. They are nothing more than modes of statement lying at hand, probably not even conceived as alternatives. The importance for us of this double representation resides in the sins themselves; the whole colour of unwitting guilt is changed when we observe the guilty sufferer apprehending himself as heaven's victim and, at the same time and indifferently, as self-doomed. The individual is no longer simply set upon from above, and a crude unilinear determinism gives place to something not entirely unlike the complex of human freedom and divine omnipotence in ordinary Christian belief—something that mystifies the observer from afar, an apparently pointless binocular agility.

Further, Oedipus's representation "I have doomed myself" does not indicate his surrender to a kind of trick, as though he had set a trap and then fallen into it himself; for the curse is a trap (if we are to save this analogy) in which only the guilty man can be caught. Moreover, it is a trap created and maintained by an expressive act of self-realisation within the play —by the king's utterance of a formal religious curse, and for this reason the language of self-doom cannot be pressed too literally. Our tendency to be repelled by what seems mechanical and unfeeling is due in part to a falsely limited understanding of the ritual act's externality; underestimating the principle of the self's presence in the "mere" deed, we resent the spectacle of his self-uttered doom bearing down on the human agent senselessly, inhumanly, from behind and beyond him.[2]

---

[1] ll. 1290-1.

[2] Our brief mention of ritual behaviour in the *Electra* (pp. 153-4 above) is relevant to the present discussion. Oedipus's curse is instrumental in the

O

These are points of substance for the entire unitary action of *Oedipus the King*, as well as for Oedipus's conception of his guilt; given due prominence they modify our experience of discontinuity between the world of human affairs and the dense tissue of oracle and prophecy controlling (but not only controlling) that world. And so the corporate consciousness surprises us, as Oedipus's does, by its enfolding within acknowledgment of responsibility the alien, the superhuman and the uncontrollable. When Oedipus warns Teiresias to mind his words since he is too weak to save himself from punishment, the seer twice answers that he is strong in the truth which he holds[1]; he indicates what has already been noted—that prophecy is present possession of the invincible truth, and he invites its general application to Thebes and her troubles: disclosure of what lies ahead is secondary to exposure of what lies within, and contemplation of what lies within evokes in the diseased community, as in its king, the double response of a helpless victim and of one who is blameworthy. The Chorus carry the play's omnipresent doubleness upon a corporate voice of timorous, oscillatory conjecture.

In this manner, as it seems to me, the single distinct action in which Oedipus lays bare his own sins and discovers who he is escapes from critical entanglement with a false humanity, and floats free into a Sophoclean independence and self-poise. Humanity is not banished; it colours the action in precisely the fashion of the great central irony of Oedipus's ignorance of what he is doing: this fulfils the apparently artless function (in relation to the automatic guilt of pollution) of keeping alive awareness of a situational might-have-been; of suffusing the parricide and incest in solemn religious contemplation of that mere absence of knowledge in the human individual but for which these horrors would never have been perpetrated. Ironical this surely is, and altogether Sophoclean; and to Sophoclean irony we must join the even more popular subject of *hubris*. "I

---

sense indicated there, and we should now add to our earlier distinguishing of Aeschylus and Sophocles the rider that the instrument falls unfamiliarly —when viewed from an Aeschylean standpoint—within the self that wields it.

[1] ll. 356, 369.

will start afresh," says Oedipus at the beginning of his search,
"and once again bring dark things to the light".[1] How are we
to take this reference to his solution of the Sphinx's riddle, and
this promise to repeat his success? The usual procedure (vaguely
devised and executed) has been to assemble his two or three
assertions of this kind and to inflate them, along with his remarks
about the fallibility of human prophecy, into a hubristic cor-
relative of the ruin that overtakes him. But this is patently
unacceptable—not because the fault is incommensurate with
the punishment,[2] but because it bears no relation to the actions
from which guilt and suffering flow. It is futile to think in
terms of a peremptory, self-confident autocrat who stumbles in
his pride, when Sophocles takes pains to show us that Oedipus
received Apollo's oracle with pious seriousness and left his home
and family in an attempt to escape its fulfilment; the intelligible
connection which we observe, for example, between Macbeth's
half-stifled ambition and his crimes and tormented conscience,
is simply not to be found, nor anything like it.

That this entire method is misconceived becomes plain from
a moment's consideration of the underlying necessity that the
god's word shall prevail. Then why (it may be asked) does
Sophocles bother to create Oedipus peremptory and self-
confident? The broad Aristotelian answer is the correct one: a
multi-coloured portrait is more interesting than a portrait in
monochrome. In other words, a hubristic colouring to Oedipus's
search for the murderer is what Sophocles is aiming at; the
moral import of his proud confidence is carried in the *laying
bare* of his sins; it is not supposed to throw light on, or be in
some way adequate to, the sins themselves. In this respect we
must approach the play with modest expectations. Oedipus's
solution of the Sphinx's riddle, that feat which is stressed
throughout, has only the limited significance that it places him
on a high eminence of achievement and reputation as a mystery-
solver. He is in a position which Greek Tragedy habitually

[1] l. 132.
[2] This objection was favoured by Augustan upholders of the tragic ideal
of poetic justice, but of course its *a priori* application to this or any other
play is futile. Indeed distinguished criticism has been founded on its discredit—Bradley's chink-in-the-armour view of the Shakespearean hero, for
example.

surrounds in an atmosphere of religious dread, because it is very difficult, so the Greeks believed, to excel and still to avoid *hubris*.

Oedipus fails to avoid *hubris*: he is confident of his own success, he is quick to accuse Teiresias and Creon of plotting against his royal person and station, he remarks with near-contempt the fallibility of the god's human ministers (while retaining an entirely respectful attitude towards the god himself); and it is a sufficient indication of the gulf dividing Sophocles from ourselves that the hubristic taint to Oedipus's search affords the dramatist and his audience a satisfying commentary on the action. A second and almost equally alien function of Oedipus's lonely eminence is to initiate the double reversal in which he and Teiresias, and he and Creon, are involved. Oedipus first appears as a man of paranormal vision, able to discern that which is obscure to others; at the end, the teleological blindness of his common humanity has been declared through his blundering against the hard and hidden truth, and is paralleled in his self-inflicted physical blindness. Teiresias is introduced in the helplessness of blind old age; he is taunted by Oedipus for his want of eyes; he utters the prophecy that Oedipus shall end his days "a blind man, who now has sight".[1] Oedipus cries out when he begins to suspect the truth: "I dread the seer can see",[2] and it is part of the final vindication of the divine order that all are brought to realise that Teiresias can see indeed.

Hence the double reversal in which Oedipus moves from sight to blindness and Teiresias from blindness to sight.[3] The relationship between these two individuals elaborates the primary double reversal in the fortunes of the city and its king. So does that between Oedipus and Creon. After Oedipus has publicly accused him of treachery, Creon declares: "It is not right to pronounce bad men good at random, or good men bad."[4] His words point to the end of the play where, in the

---

[1] l. 454.

[2] l. 747.

[3] We have already remarked that it is scarcely possible to exaggerate Sophocles's interest in visionary blindness, and his delight in such paradoxes as "I close my eyes and see" (Fragment 774).

[4] ll. 609-10.

moment of full revelation, Oedipus discovers himself "most vile" (*kakistos*) and Creon, in immediate juxtaposition, "most noble" (*aristos*).[1] The seeming traitor becomes the city's upright king (Creon succeeds Oedipus with an instant demonstration of just authority) while the king falls to the level of blind exiled beggar, the proven source of corporate pollution.

This festooning of quasi-mathematical symmetries is germane to dramatic intention and effect throughout *Oedipus the King*, working at the level of overall oppositions and transverse movements, and evident also in details of phrasing. We recognise Creon's "Don't judge bad men good or good men bad" for a characteristic Sophoclean turn, and one which we do not readily respond to; the utterance seems irrelevant in its first part (since Creon is here merely defending himself—saying that he is a good man who is being judged bad) and woodenly sententious in its entirety. But "Don't judge bad men good" has a hidden reference, which an audience familiar with the myth will have seized on, to Oedipus's as yet unexposed sins: the symmetry is fast maturing on the stage, and what strikes us as sententious and generalised will have gratified imaginations that were in love with structural proportion. So pervasive is this quasi-mathematical mode of Sophoclean Tragedy that it sometimes produces a paralysis of taste and intelligence in the professional classical scholar, so that in Jebb's very literate (if dated) translation of *Oedipus the King* we come across grotesque contortions like "a solitary man could not be held the same with that band"[2] and "how can my sire be level with him who is as nought to me?".[3] It is a pleasant irony that the scholars who are busy impressing on us the continuities of our cultural tradition should so clearly refute themselves in their instinctive vestigial honesty towards the strange texts they are rendering.

Like the quasi-legal mode which occupied us earlier, over the *Antigone*, this endless contrasting and comparing (to which Aristotle extends a due dynamism in his concepts of Discovery and Reversal) springs from Tragedy's contact with fifth-century democratic institutions and with the fast developing art of prose. And again we must insist that the issue of this contact falls within the tragic idea; it is no mere accretion. We have

[1] l. 1433.   [2] l. 845.   [3] l. 1019.

invoked the language of symphonic mutability and of fearless outwardness in the conception and dramatic deployment of action, in order to suggest how this was so.

6 Oedipus at Colonus

The traditional title of Sophocles's last play is happy in that it divides attention between the king and the place, and this is the best way to begin.

Oedipus, here in extreme old age, is the last of a line of solitaries to be found in each of the surviving plays and distinguished primarily by the quality of their solitude. That of Ajax follows his mad act of violence against the cattle; he is left alone in his shame. Antigone's solitude is also religio-moral, but with the important difference that she determines it herself; while Ajax is isolated by the automatic operation of the shame-culture values of Greek Epic in which the play is enveloped, Antigone chooses to isolate herself through her preferring of the religious law to the royal edict. She heightens her solitude by stressing the unbridgeable gulf between Creon and herself,[1] by refusing to allow Ismene to share her punishment,[2] and by insisting that she and her sister are really on opposite sides: "One world approved your wisdom, another mine."[3] But Antigone knows that the world of Creon and his edict exists; it is an alternative upon which she turns her back.

In the first Oedipus play the king's isolation is at the outset specifically dramaturgical, resting in the extent to which he is required to carry the action single-handed. And this expands into a most impressive total solitude when his curse excluding the murderer from ritual and social fellowship within Thebes falls on himself, and he sets out from the city as if to accomplish that mortal exposure of his person which had been bungled at birth.[4] The *Women of Trachis* is close to *Oedipus the King* in its

[1] ll. 499-501.   [2] ll. 538-9.

[3] l. 557. Antigone's clear sense of the distinction between the higher law of heaven and the lower human law has made this play almost a founding text for the jurisprudential literature of Natural Law.

[4] Laius had caused the baby Oedipus to be exposed on Mount Cithaeron in an attempt to prevent fulfilment of the oracle from which he had learned that he was fated to die at the hand of his child. Laius also had an iron pin

concern with the blindness of the human condition. In place of
the single groping king, Sophocles constructs a triple and interlocking confusion of purposes. The demi-god Heracles has been
told (again by oracle) that "he shall have peace from now on,
for the rest of his days",[1] if he successfully concludes his present
task—a war against the people of Euboea. Heracles wins the
war and looks for an undisturbed life, only to discover that he
has been tricked by a diabolical ambiguity in the oracle's
wording: "I looked for prosperity, but it seems the meaning
was only that I should die. Dead men have indeed completed
their life's toil,"[2] Deianeira, his wife, is anxious to keep his love
when he returns from the war, and she sends him what she
believes to be a love charm. In fact it is a poison, and causes his
death. "I win understanding of this too late," she says, "when
it avails no more."[3] And Hyllus, the son of Heracles and
Deianeira, concludes that she has poisoned her husband on
purpose, and his reproaches drive her to suicide. But later,
seeing Deianeira dead, "her son uttered a great cry, for the
unhappy boy knew that in his anger he had driven her to this
deed. He had learned too late from the people in the house that
she had acted without knowledge. . . ."[4] Thus for all three of
them. As in *Oedipus the King*, the ground-movement of human
planning and acting is towards a catastropic stumble against
the hidden truth; the catastrophe is also a revelation, these two
being complements (as Aristotle probably conceived his Reversal and Discovery); and, again as in *Oedipus the King*, a
strange religious half-welcome is extended to the direful events
in which the god's word "is brought home without fail, and in
due time".[5] There is no dominant solitary at all comparable
with Oedipus; the play's single distinct action—itself a process
of exposure similar to that in *Oedipus the King*—is a divided
burden. But in the group of captive women whom Heracles has

---

driven through the baby's feet. A rationalising explanation of Laius's action,
no doubt very ancient, is that this maiming would further reduce the child's
chance of survival; while Jebb holds (Introduction, xix, and his view
has been endorsed by distinguished specialists) that "the incident of the
pierced feet was evidently invented to explain the name Οἰδίπους
('Swellfoot', as Shelley renders it)". But the episode strikes me as original
to the myth, perhaps importing the nailing of a monster.

[1] ll. 80-1. [2] ll. 1171-3. [3] ll. 710-11.
[4] ll. 932-5. [5] ll. 826-7. See also ll. 1159-63.

sent home ahead of him as war prize, one is seen to stand apart. Sensing her separateness, Deianeira singles her out for pity and friendly concern because "she alone shows a proper understanding of her position".[1]

This is Iole; she is distinguished by her bearing from the other captives; a stage-aura surrounds her, and her solitude thus determined strikes us as familiarly dramatic. Iole's personal distinction draws attention to herself, and our interest is heightened when we learn that Heracles is secretly her lover; a situation of high Romantic promise has been created between the wife of fading beauty and her young rival. Sophocles is both aware of the possibilities here and plainly able to exploit them: witness his delicate management of Deianeira's attempt to sustain her initial generous impulse of pity in the face of the superadded fear—a lyrical and tender fear, for all its physical directness—that henceforth she will be wife only in name and that Heracles will not make love to her any more. She tries to accept the passion of Heracles and Iole as "no shame to them and no wrong to me".[2] But then the thought of lying "under the one blanket"[3] with Iole overwhelms her; men are so made that "they turn away from the old".[4] She asks, "what woman could bear that?"[5]

The Deianeira-Iole relationship is drenched in pity, the cardinal Sophoclean emotion, and those who can arouse no serious interest in action are left wondering why this most accessible achievement of the *Women of Trachis* is allowed to melt away into the silly tragi-comical device of the love charm. Iole leaves an impression—even upon the reader—so strong and individual that one easily forgets she has not a single word to speak; the mere presence of this tragic mute is a major contribution to the play, and the first instance of that projection of the human individual which we have just now called familiarly dramatic.

More obvious examples are furnished by the three remaining plays. Electra waits within the house, enemies all round her, while Orestes plans the entry and killing which the god enjoins shall be single-handed: we watch their two solitudes converge. In the *Philoctetes*, solitude (coupled with pain) must not be

[1] l. 313. [2] l. 448. [3] ll. 539-40.
[4] l. 549. [5] ll. 545-6.

reckoned less than the given substance of the myth, the initial and enduring *status quo* from which escape is in sight at the play's end. This is a theme easily misunderstood if we endow the ancient castaway with Robinson Crusoe's individualistic self-sufficiency, for the main consequence of Philoctetes's physical isolation is not loneliness and its attendent miseries—evils to be challenged in buoyancy of spirit—but a kind of social death. Philoctetes is alone (*monos*) and he is also deserted (*erēmos*); the word *erēmos* tolls like a bell through this play,[1] and gives his solitude its due social stress; it is not, as translations are almost bound to suggest, a mere rhetorical intensive of *monos*. *Erēmos* is the second of three adjectives which Philoctetes applies to himself: "friendless, desolate, of no city—a dead man among the living".[2] The idea of social death is here explicit; Philoctetes calls himself dead because he is cut off from the larger life of the human group by which other individuals are sustained[3]; he is "a corpse, a kind of vaporous shadow, a mere ghost",[4] and the play's Chorus of visiting sailors express amazement, when they find him on his island, that he did not simply lie down and die—let slip of life entirely—in that state in which he was "neighbour to himself alone".[5] They also give the pain from his festering heel a social stress, thinking with Sophoclean pity of Philoctetes "having nobody near him while he suffered".[6] Philoctetes has just told Neoptolemus: "I want you beside me in my sickness",[7] and it is no accident that he names "the counsel of friends"[8] among the agents of his ultimate rescue and restoration, the others being Zeus and Fate. The presence of

---

[1] At ll. 228; 265; 269; 471; 487; 1018. See also l. 195.

[2] l. 1018.

[3] In his *Nuer Religion*, pp. 152-3, Professor E. E. Evans-Pritchard describes a sort of converse of the Philoctetes situation. "There was living in a village there an unhappy-looking man of unkempt appearance, called Gatbuogh. This man had some years before gone on a distant journey and had not been heard of for a long time. Then there came to his village news of his death and in course of time the mortuary ceremony was held for him. He later returned home and was living in the village at the time of my visit. He was described as *joagh in tegh*, the living ghost. . . . His soul, the essential part of him, had gone and with it his social personality."

[4] ll. 946-7.   [5] l. 691.

[6] l. 692.   [7] ll. 674-5.

[8] l. 1467.

friends marks the full reversal of the opening situation in which
the island was "untrodden by men, uninhabited".[1]

This deep and almost impenetrable solitude of Philoctetes is
shared by the blind homeless beggar who had once been a king
in Sophocles's last play, *Oedipus at Colonus*. Oedipus, like Philoctetes, has suffered social death. He too is a man "of no city",[2]
and he calls himself a "ghost".[3] Words of wandering haunt this
play as *erēmos* does the other[4]; hereby the beggar is distinguished
from the castaway while being united with him in his exclusion
from Society. But Philoctetes offers an inadequate comparison
since all our preliminary and provisional categories of solitude
—religio-moral, dramaturgical, familiar-dramatic, social—now
cohere in the one man. Oedipus has isolated himself by a
self-pronounced curse, and is automatically isolated through his
defilement. His carrying of the action is less obvious and sustained than it was in the first Oedipus play, but it is also more
decisive; instead of exposing the truth in search and questioning he acts out the truth by going forward visionary-blind to
meet Death in an absolutely strange and benign form, reserved
for him alone. For the play's action is the raising up of one
whom the gods formerly cast down, and this action vindicates
the divine order, as always happens in Sophocles, because the
final raising up of Oedipus has been promised in oracles and
prophecies "declared long ago".[5] Finally, Oedipus is blind:
isolated in his physical helplessness and, more conclusively and
very beautifully, in the rich concentrated individuation, aural
and tactile in its definitions, of his mind's life.

And what makes for solitude also makes for dramatic prominence: Oedipus's envelope of blindness illuminates as it isolates
him. Moreover, this solitary prominence is pursued into the
smallest histrionic detail; in the *Oedipus at Colonus* Sophocles is
often found pointing successive dispositions of the stage-figure
in a way which may appear to us commonplace at first, but
which is quite uncharacteristic of the other dramatists and of

---

[1] l. 2. Aeschylus and Euripides both wrote a *Philoctetes* in which Lemnos
was inhabited. Sophocles is also departing from the epic tradition in which
the island was "that well-built city" (*Odyssey*, VIII, 283).

[2] l. 1357.   [3] l. 110.

[4] See ll. 3; 50; 99; 123-4; 166; 347; 444; 746; 949; 1363.   [5] l. 454.

himself elsewhere—and which the fifteen-hundred-line scale of
Greek Tragedy would seem virtually to prohibit. Thus the few
seconds that it takes Oedipus to obey the Chorus's command—
they are village elders of Colonus—that he shall leave the
sacred grove where he has taken refuge, are brought forward
to us in a kind of action close-up:

OED.: Still further?
CH.: Yes, further
OED.: Further?
CH. [to Antigone, Oedipus's daughter and attendant]: You lead him,
    lady, for you can see how far we mean.

* * *

CH.: Stop there: don't go beyond that slab of living rock.
OED.: Here?
CH.: That's far enough.
OED.: Shall I sit down?
CH.: Yes. There's a rocky ledge beside you. Crouch down on that.
ANT.: I'll help you, father. Gently, now—
OED.: Ah me!
ANT.: Keep step with me. Lean on my arm.[1]

and obviously it will not do to gesture towards Sophocles's
naturalistic rendering of the blind state at such moments. Our
business is with the numinous feel of the action's detail in this
play, concerning which it may not be idle to repeat that
Oedipus is acting out the strong truth of the god's promise to
him, and that the title of the play does well to divide attention
between the king and Colonus: the local circumstances—the
slab of rock, the ledge, the precise distances—matter greatly,
religiously.

The essence of the matter is a kind of interdependence of
man and place, the study of which leads us to observe that
Sophocles's surviving plays fall into two contrasted groups. In
the Antigone, the Women of Trachis and Oedipus the King (and
also, substantially, in the Ajax),[2] the sense of locality, of the
setting of the action, is weak and vague; while in the Electra, the
Philoctetes, and the Oedipus at Colonus it is always strong, and
grows progressively stronger. Conversely, the action in this

---

[1] ll. 178-201.
[2] See pp. 270-1 below. The fleeting strength of locality in this play is
bound up with its change of scene.

second group of late plays loses some of the tightness and symmetry that dominate Sophocles's middle period,[1] and *Oedipus the King* in particular.

The connection is obvious between the sovereign claim of the single distinct action in the *Poetics* and Aristotle's admiration for the first Oedipus play, and he is likely to have reckoned Sophocles's bending of his art towards the action's physical context a poor compensation for slackened rigour in his treatment of the action itself. Be that as it may, when we turn to the *Electra* fresh from the *Women of Trachis* and *Oedipus the King*, the importunate vitality of the murdered Agamemnon's palace is at once apparent. The opening lines embrace Orestes's joy in his homecoming together with a businesslike awareness that the house is now tenanted by enemies; he and his old companion stand before the gates in the early morning, hungrily scanning the familiar scene—and hastily, for they know that plans must be made "before anyone comes out from the house".[2] The blend of home and danger is forceful and sustained; we believe, simply, in the palace stirring to life at sunrise, and we are jolted back to consciousness of it repeatedly, as Electra is when she speaks too loud and long in her reckless joy at finding Orestes alive,[3] and as she and Orestes both are by the old schoolmaster-slave, Orestes's attendant, who finds them laughing and chattering on the threshold, blind for a moment to the menace of the building's closed door[4].

This is quite unlike the impassive, inert, universal palace-fronts before which the *Antigone* and the *Women of Trachis* and *Oedipus the King* are played. So is the cave of Philoctetes, his home for ten years on the desert island of Lemnos; and the art with which Sophocles achieves the effective presence of the cave has not had its due. Odysseus and Neoptolemus, two Greek leaders, have landed on the island in search of Philoctetes and his supernatural bow. We must imagine them in the opening lines standing on the beach, their backs to the sea, looking up at the steep rocky cliff and seeking to identify Philoctetes's cave by reference to a spring "a little below, on the left—if it has not

---

[1] Talk of middle and late is necessarily imprecise; we can only establish a general trend.
[2] l. 20.   [3] ll. 1238; 1259; 1322-3.
[4] ll. 1326-38.

failed".[1] They separate, and Neoptolemus soon calls out that he can see a cave-mouth which looks like the right one. Odysseus asks: "Above or below you? I can't see it." "Here, high up",[2] Neoptolemus replies, so that in the ensuing dialogue Neoptolemus is placed above Odysseus on the cliff-face, passing information down to him. (The fifth-century audience will have had to use their imaginations almost as much as we have to; any stage-representation of these circumstances will have been of the very simplest.) Odysseus calls up to Neoptolemus to be careful; Philoctetes may be inside the cave, perhaps asleep. Neoptolemus peers inside, finds the cave empty. He reports that he can see a heap of leaves, pressed down—a makeshift bed. Also a cup roughly hacked out of wood, some tinder-stuff for a fire and a bundle of pus-smeared rag bandages drying in the sun.

Interspersed with questions from Odysseus, these few details successfully lay the foundations of locality. Their strange level-voiced authority is partly explained by a disinterested love of fact common to all three Greek tragedians, and particularly Sophoclean, which we respond to more readily in the comic mode, as when Mr P. G. Wodehouse's young man is caught by the girl's father and kicked fifteen feet seven inches—a record for the midland counties. But important also is the confirmation these details receive in retrospect, when we look back across the completed play and see what has been built on these foundations. From the moment when Odysseus and Neoptolemus find the cave and mount guard over it against Philoctetes's return until his final farewell to the "rocky sleeping-place"[3] where he has lived for the past ten years, through the intervening false farewell when he has been tricked into believing he is about to leave the island, and through his renewed greeting of the cave after he has discovered the truth and resigns himself to ending his days there, a shared experience is unfolding of which the love-hate oscillation in Philoctetes's address to the comfortless shelter which was none the less a shelter—his "homeless home"[4] in fact—is only one aspect. The cave with a fire inside to warm it gives Philoctetes, as he says, "all I want—except release from

---

[1] ll. 20-1. Note the unobtrusive hint of the passage of time.
[2] ll. 28-9.   [3] l. 160.
[5] l. 534.

pain"[1]; but his sufficiency must be set against the death in life he endures there, and this setting-against is not so much a function of the protagonist's divided consciousness in relation to the object as it is an assurance of dramatic life in the object itself[2]—of dramatic life apprehended primarily through such neutral media as the Chorus and Neoptolemus and Odysseus, the last-named being the first to communicate the cave's grateful anti-self with his account of its double entrance 'offering a sunny seat at one point or the other, in cold weather, while in summer a breeze blows through the rocky tunnel and a man can sleep".[3]

The full interdependence of man and place in late Sophocles —in the *Philoctetes* and the *Oedipus at Colonus*—extends beyond that intimacy with the human which a scene of action sometimes achieves in nearer literatures. (I am thinking of Raskolnikov's bedroom, and Desdemona's.) In the *Oedipus at Colonus* this interdependence is primarily religious; the oracle has declared that Oedipus, now for many years a homeless wandering beggar and helpless in his blindness, shall in the end find rest at "a sanctuary of the holy goddesses"[4] where some sign—"earthquake or thunder or the lightning of Zeus"[5]—shall greet him to confirm that he has reached his goal.

The action is therefore poised on the brink of fulfilment by

[1] l. 299.

[2] To say that Sophocles's concern with individual psychology has been exaggerated and misunderstood is not to deny the local importance of states of mind. After Philoctetes has set out from his cave for the beach, to be taken home as he supposes, a spasm of pain from his foot suddenly seizes him. He cries out to Neoptolemus:

Up there, up there—me—at once!

NE: Where do you mean?

PH: Up, up.

NE: What new madness is this? Why are you gazing up at the sky?

(ll. 814-15)

The two of them are halted on the steep path leading down from the cave to the beach. In his extremity Philoctetes turns towards the "homeless home" where he has found the means to endure many attacks like the present one. Neoptolemus fails to understand him, simply notes his frantic upward gaze. And while state of mind matters, it is in order that the cave shall be further impressed.

[3] ll. 17-19.   [4] ll. 89-90. The goddesses are the Furies.   [5] l. 95.

Oedipus's arrival at Colonus in the opening lines. He sits down to rest. Antigone, his daughter and guide, can identify Athens in the distance but not the grove of olive, laurel, and vine immediately before them. She is setting off to discover the name of the place when a stranger appears and tells them they are on sacred ground; the whole locality is dedicate to the Furies. This, cries Oedipus in Jebb's rendering, is "the watchword of my fate"[1]—a phrase to clinch his long-delayed entry upon peace. The meaning of peace is clear throughout; indeed it is a mark of this play's simple directness (contrast the reversal which Heracles's understanding of the promised "release from toil" suffers in the *Women of Trachis*) that the rest which Oedipus hopes for and in piety expects is nothing other than the favoured death which comes to him. His dying is made difficult—a mild irony of the extreme old age shared by Oedipus and his creator—by the exigencies of Theban politics[2]; but the separate inruptions of Creon and Polyneices, both bent on luring or compelling him from Colonus, make little difference to this essential simplicity: Oedipus comes to Colonus and dies there.

All care is taken to impress the local sanctities. Immediately upon his entry, the stranger interrupts Oedipus's questioning to tell him: "Leave your seat; this place is sacred"[3]; and after the stranger has gone away again and Antigone has told her father that the two of them are alone, the old man falls on his knees and prays to the Furies to show grace towards Apollo, the author of the oracle of his release, and towards himself.[4] His prayer is followed at once by the entry of the Chorus. Rumour has reached them of Oedipus's arrival, and they dart to and fro in a dance of eager, angry search, singing:

[1] l. 46.
[2] The events of the first Oedipus play were followed by Oedipus's banishment from Thebes. Thereafter his brother-in-law, Creon, became regent. Later, Oedipus's two sons, Polyneices and Eteocles, moved to win the throne for themselves, and finally they fell out with each other in a struggle for sole power. That side will prevail (so it has been prophesied) which Oedipus can be persuaded to join, and a second and vaguer prophecy is to the effect that Thebes depends on Oedipus, alive or dead, for her welfare. Hence the courting of Oedipus at Colonus.
[3] ll. 36-7.
[4] ll. 84-110.

Look about! Who was he? Where is he now? Where has he
gone. . . ? A wanderer! The old man must be a wanderer: nobody
from here would have invaded this grove. . . .[1]

The Chorus have mistakenly concluded that Oedipus set
foot within the sacred grove in a spirit of calculated outrage.
Concentration upon the Oedipus-Colonus relationship is thus
maintained, in a juxtaposing of its false impious appearance and
its devout reality, and the moment is brought to ripeness for a
timid stage-by-stage withdrawal by Oedipus from the shelter
of the sanctuary—a withdrawal like that of an animal from its
natural retreat, while the further implications of his unintended
trespass continue to hover above the action until grasped by
the Chorus and drawn down into the single forward thrust
towards *rapprochement* of man and place, in their command to
him: "Make atonement at once to the deities here; they were
the first object of your coming, and you have violated their
sanctuary."[2]

Oedipus asks them to instruct him in the ceremony he must
follow, and their leader proceeds to tell him, lingering with pious
exactness over the ritual details.[3] Then, after everything has
been made plain, Oedipus suddenly says: "I cannot go—for I
am twice disabled, by lack of strength and by lack of eyes"[4];
and his second daughter, Ismene, duly performs the rite on his
behalf.

These happenings from within the play's first Episode anticipate Oedipus's movement to meet death at the close. The later
rite is heralded by a peal of thunder which Oedipus recognises
for the sign promised in Apollo's oracle, and also for a divine
summons; and his manner of responding when the god calls
him to initiate the mystery of his own life's end recalls, through
shock of contrast, the "I cannot go" with which his blindness
and frail old age answered the earlier summons to ritual action.
For now he is inspired to lead them all:

Follow me, my children—this way. Strangely I am become your
guide, as you were mine. Come. Do not touch me. Leave me to
find the sacred tomb where destiny is bringing me to burial in
this land. This way. Come. This way.[5]

[1] ll. 117-26.　　　[2] ll. 466-7.　　　[3] ll. 469-92.
[4] ll. 495-6.　　　[5] ll. 1542-7.

and the action commands an effect of wonderful purity and force as Oedipus sheds all hesitancy in order to direct his human guides, and the ceremonial, and (under Apollo's oracle) his own destiny. The logic of the stage-event is primitive and universal. And inescapable. This is very great drama.

Nevertheless we may—I think we do—misinterpret our certain and shared experience of being deeply moved; for when Sophocles spends his invention on the dramatic solitary, thrusting upon him the individuate and splendid life that must be acknowledged here for Oedipus, the concept of the tragic hero, that ubiquitous critical ghost, is naturally busy—in this instance evoking a Sophoclean proto-Lear. The imaginative focus, as in Shakespeare's fifth Act, has been discovered in a visionary lift of the old king's bruised consciousness, and its rallying in face of the great fact of death. This view falsifies the *Oedipus at Colonus* to a point at which the same view's inadequacy to *Lear* is not worth remarking. For it surrenders the principle of locality, opposing Oedipus to his fate without any regard to the dramatic text in which Sophocles allows Oedipus no interest in death outside "the place where I must die".[1]

Such disrespect for locality is no doubt half wilful: in *King Lear* itself a modern sensibility is aware of inner connection between the play's rushing mental life and the quite extraordinary vagueness of physical setting; the dignity and relevance —to make a more general point—of a man's coming to death are affronted by particularity and the mere material circumstance, and we decline to believe that finding the place may be no less important than, and only formally separable from, the dying there. But in the *Oedipus at Colonus* it is so. The linking of death and Colonus, insistent throughout, is in the end defined and realised at once in the demonstrative simplicities of action, when Oedipus sets out to discover the exact spot at the sanctuary's heart where death is to be found and known. Our sense of locality is fed by glancing precisions like the ones in that otherwise dissimilar play, the *Philoctetes*:

He came to the Threshold where the brazen stairs plunge down to the earth's roots. And here he halted, in one of the many branching paths, near the basin in the rock which commemorates the enduring covenant of Theseus and Peirithous. He stood

[1] l. 1521.

P

mid-way between the basin, the Thorician rock, the hollow pear tree and the marble tomb; and then he sat down and took off his filthy clothes.[1]

A messenger is here describing Oedipus's movements after he has passed out of sight of the audience. The significance of the complex local details (which will have been plain to an Athenian audience) is almost entirely lost to us, but behind such strangely authoritative touches as the hollow pear tree we experience, however obscurely, the religious urgency of Oedipus's progress; to plot this and finally to pin-point the place is a most solemn exercise since the mystery of his death—the "sights which may not be seen" and the "speech which may not be heard"[2]—is to be celebrated here and nowhere else. We are in touch, moreover, with a political as well as a religious urgency. What happens at the moment when Oedipus leaves life is hidden from every human being in the world except Theseus, the king of Athens. Oedipus sends for Theseus to be the sole witness of his passing because, as he explains, possession of his dead body will ensure the safety of Athens in future troubles, and Theseus and the kings after him will "always hold the land unharmed"[3] if each of them cherishes and keeps to himself, then hands on to his successor, the sacred rites attending Oedipus's death and the precise whereabouts of his tomb. These are reciprocal benefits since Theseus has formally admitted Oedipus into Athenian citizenship,[4] thus releasing him from social death in the last hours of his life.

Oedipus comes to Colonus and dies there. The religio-political complex of this local theme—local in the further sense that we have no evidence of a Panhellenic source for the story —is on the one hand acted out by Oedipus and on the other held in still, lyric contemplation by the Chorus in their song (which is perhaps the most famous of all Greek Tragedy's choral songs) praising Colonus, and then, with wider sweep, the whole of Attica. This song recalls the Athenian stranger's declaration of pride in belonging to Colonus, the place which "has a kind of greatness in the hearts of those who live here",[5] and its dramatic relevance will always be undervalued by the commentator whose preoccupation is narrowly aesthetic. Sophocles

---

[1] ll. 1590-7.   [2] ll. 1641-2.   [3] l. 1765.
[4] ll. 1631-41.   [5] l. 63.

of course believes that Colonus and Attica are beautiful, and he says so, but only within a sustaining context of holiness and natural virtue. He writes of the Attic olive tree:

> And our land has a thing all Asia cannot boast of nor the great Dorian island of Pelops bring to birth: the grey-leafed olive, a self-renewing growth, undefeated, the dread of enemy arms and our children's nourisher: the olive, abundant here as nowhere else.[1]

and in his dense statement the economic importance of the olive[2] coheres with its divine origin in Attica,[3] and with its marvellous power of self-renewal shown after the invading Persians had burnt it,[4] and with its commanding of reverence, of religious fear, in the Spartan army during the Peloponnesian war, nearly at an end when Sophocles wrote his *Oedipus at Colonus*. The present is one of very few instances where reference to contemporary events is justified. This song will surely have evoked in its first hearers a bitter and very near memory of Spartan invasion and ravaging of Attica, almost a yearly occurrence in this war—with a counter-thought to the olive's divine and natural resources, and a light prophetic hint of healing after war.

In mattering for itself, locality matters for the man who arrives and dies; Oedipus does not *happen* to die at Colonus, within the dramatic scheme any more than within the religious, and it follows that many of the questions which get asked about his death and earlier life of suffering are simply irrelevant. What is at first sight very strange, lending an air of paradox to all talk of a Sophoclean Everyman, is the singular and favoured end which isolates Oedipus totally. He does not even die like the rest of us; in the conjoining of man and place under the oracle, death's ordinary process is set aside. Nevertheless, it is as im-

---

[1] ll. 694-701.

[2] Olive oil was their principal fat. The tenderness within "our children's nourisher" is precisely that of young growth, and remote from the modern cult of childhood.

[3] The goddess Athena had caused an olive tree to spring up on the Acropolis: this was said to be the parent of olives recognised as sacred in historical times.

[4] I accept Jebb's tentative explanation of αὐτοποιόν.

portant to read the universal human condition on Oedipus's mask as it is to refrain from universalising, *Lear* fashion, the death which the god has devised for him. Oedipus stands for Sophoclean humanity in his blindness and, being blind, in his dependence on those who can see. When the thunder sounds, and he begins to move with mysterious confidence towards his place of death, we do well to recall Sophocles's image of the right-hand trace-horse for the relation of god to man, for Oedipus renders all humanity at the dark limit of life, blind, committed to action (there is no doing nothing in Greek Tragedy), with a god leading.

Guidance of this kind presents us with an exclusion of divine omnipotence and transcendence which is the more impressive for being unargued, after the fashion of an obvious fact of life. The god in the story is not so powerful that the local Furies may not hamper his design; they must be placated, and besought in prayer to be gracious to Apollo. Neither is there any certainty that the leading god will not mislead. Indeed guidance embraces a cross-fertilising doubleness throughout, and it has been one of the major impertinences of criticism to demand that the quasi-Christian and 'civilised' aspect of guidance shall flourish unsupported by fear of divine malice. This means, in the present case, a separation of Oedipus's ultimate self-surrender to the leading god—in any view a great dramatic climax—from his belief that he was "led by gods"[1] into his unintended sins of long ago. But for Oedipus, and Sophocles, and the religious drama, the situation remains intellectually unforced. Partnership is the enormously wide focus of religious affirmation; men share the world with their gods, and the coupling of "prompted by some god and by a sinful heart"[2] in the evil history of the family is no less serious than the joint enterprise of Apollo and Oedipus which is the action of our play. And in neither case is the picture one of helpless human subordination, since the god is like the right-hand trace-horse (very roughly like; in relation to this broad simplicity of mental posture our "intellectually unforced" is and is not a euphemism for chaotic) who does most of the work, but not all.

There is a considerable literature seeking to maintain a refined interpretation of the divine malice that pervades Greek

[1] l. 998.   [2] l. 371.

Tragedy. In thus easing the appalling peril of existence in the tragic world it can only achieve the opposite of its intention; Oedipus's piety is abused, and the crowning objective effect is dulled in which his fortunes are seen to come full circle. "Now the gods are raising you up," Ismene tells him, "whereas before they compassed your downfall"[1]; and this strong and simple rhythm is confirmed by Sophocles's persistent harking back to the events of *Oedipus the King*.[2] It is the rhythm of Mutability, and its full pointing in and through this one life (whereas in Sophocles's earlier plays it falls mainly to the accompanying voice of choral commentary) gives us more than anything else does the sense that Oedipus speaks for mankind.

Acts for mankind is truer to the dramatic object; indeed many of our interpretative troubles arise from the habit of directing attention almost exclusively towards what Oedipus says; for once our scrutiny is shifted and narrowed in this way, a psychological problem arises to eclipse all others. It is that Oedipus discloses one mood or phase of consciousness in which he believes that he ought not to be blamed for the parricide and incest from which his sufferings spring, and another mood in which he sees himself as justly abhorred by gods and men on account of his sins.

The first mood is one of subjective innocence, stated by Oedipus in vigorous and effective argument: I did not intend to kill my father and marry my mother; I could not help doing these things since they were foredoomed; I am not to blame for actions of my ancestors because of which the gods are angry with our family: "Take me by myself and you could not find

---

[1] l. 394.

[2] Although he wishes the casting down followed by the raising up of Oedipus to fall into single focus, Sophocles is not concerned—it is unlike his attitude and method that he should be—to make the two plays tally at all closely. There are narrative discrepancies, and the people are not imagined in continuity. Creon here has nothing in common with the Creon of the first Oedipus play, and this Ismene is very unlike that of the *Antigone*—just as the Odysseus of the *Philoctetes* is very unlike the Odysseus of the *Ajax*. An exceptional and interesting continuity is maintained between Antigone in her own play and in the *Oedipus at Colonus*, particularly in her solitary challenge to the Greek moral principle: Requite evil with evil and good with good. She says in effect, Requite evil with good—at least within the family. See *Antigone*, ll. 510-23; *Oedipus at Colonus*, ll. 1189-91.

any sin to charge me with. . . ."[1] Touching the parricide, there are the two further points that I acted in self-defence and that I was provoked:

> Answer me this one thing: if here and now someone were to come up and try to kill you—you the righteous one—would you ask if he was your father, or would you deal with him out of hand?[2]

Oedipus's question to Creon is as sharp as hatred and forensic skill can make it.[3]

The second mood is one of objective guilt. It rests on the fact of Oedipus's pollution following parricide and incest, a fact undeniable and undenied in the play, and tractable only on the objective plane, through purificatory rites. The horror of Oedipus's defilement lies deep and for the most part hidden; and the moments when Sophocles allows it to appear demonstrate an ample naturalistic tact. The sound of thunder and the lightning flash—Oedipus's signal—throw the uninstructed Chorus into a panic-stricken beseeching of Zeus not to be angry with them "for having looked upon a man of evil"[4]: the moment of terror is also the moment of defilement's exposure. And Oedipus himself bears pathetic witness to what lies within when, forgetful in his strong emotion, carried out of himself by gratitude to Theseus, he asks for physical contact:

> Give me your right hand to touch, my lord; and let me kiss your cheek, if that be a thing a man may do.—But what am I saying? How could I wish you to touch me, miserable as I am and host to all defiling sin?[5]

And so it becomes an anxious critical problem to relate these two moods intelligibly. An obvious and explored procedure has been to discredit one and take an interpretative stand upon the

---

[1] ll. 966-7. See ll. 521-48 and 969-99.

[2] ll. 991-4.

[3] When Oedipus tells the Chorus that they need not fear "my body or my acts; at any rate my 'acts' have been in suffering rather than in doing" (ll. 265-7), I believe he is making a further point of substance—and of the widest moral relevance—in his defence. He is meeting the ancient principle of *drasanti pathein*—the doer shall suffer for the deed, the principle that informs the Aeschylean *Oresteia*—with the suggestion that the deeds for which he has suffered were not really deeds at all.

[4] l. 1483.   [5] ll. 1130-4.

other: we may either degrade subjective innocence to the peevishness of a fretful old man, to an idle self-justifying that spends itself against the hard fact of defilement; or we may construct an "advanced" morality upon Oedipus's argument and protestation (making all we can of the signs of Euripides's influence on the composition of the play), and reduce objective guilt to the conventional, dramatically inert framework which the orthodoxy of the public religious festival demands. The first course founders upon the serious and very patient elaboration with which Oedipus's subjective innocence is affirmed, and not by himself only. The second is completely false to Sophoclean piety—false to its substance and its expression. Comparison with Aeschylus reveals a weakening of interest in collective and inherited guilt, but no mitigation of the objective status of guilt itself. In fact it is the importunacy of the objective in Sophocles—of oracle, sacrifice, burial rite, formal invocation and formal curse; and the objective is nowhere more prominent than in the *Oedipus at Colonus*—that makes his morality and religion appear less anxiously reasoned than Aeschylus's, and more simple-heartedly institutional.

Neither mood can honestly be subordinated to the other; they are both fully developed, and we must accept their co-existence and approximate equality. The question, of course, is how to do so. And here (I have suggested) criticism creates difficulties for itself by scrutinising what Oedipus has to say in near-isolation, instead of allowing it to fall within his coming to Colonus and dying there. This sacred adventure of the man, helped by his god, is the object of imitation (in the Aristotelian sense of *mimēsis*) through the medium of stage-event, and it has been our main contention throughout that the tragic meaning is to be looked for here. Asked what is meaningful in this imitated action, we answer, the rhythm observed by Ismene in her "Now the gods are lifting you up, whereas before they compassed your downfall", and by the Chorus in their final song: "Many and unmerited were his sufferings, but surely a just god will raise him up again."[1] This rhythm is not the child of facile imaginings about the justice which life renders to individuals; the justice is humanity's, and Oedipus receives it within the work of art because he acts for mankind in his blind

[1] ll. 1565-7.

movement towards death, related hopefully and dreadfully towards his gods, himself bearing Mutability's face and form.

Behind the instinctive modern turning towards what Oedipus says, and away from what he does, lies a desire to make total sense of the play in terms of dramatised consciousness, and principally the consciousness of the tragic hero. We gaze down through Oedipus's words in an effort to see how he understands his fate—or how he fails to understand it: in either case a supremely relevant illumination is expected. And what meets our eyes is a fully articulated contradiction of which neither term can be subordinated to the other, and whose very bland-ness and peace make a naturalistic rationale based on Oedipus's tormented self-division the most hopeless critical enterprise of all. Which is not to say that Oedipus's words are irrelevant or nonsensical; rather that their sense and relevance have been lost through a fundamental misplacement of emphasis, and are recovered as soon as the primacy of action is respected. When this happens, non-communication between the subjective and objective moods ceases to be an autonomous dramatic fact and problem, and becomes a service to the action—the kind of service Aristotle had in mind when he said character is to be included for the action's sake.[1]

The two moods are features, so to speak, of the tragic mask, visible side by side. Their non-communication is not mysterious, it is the norm of the Greek masked drama. The mystery is created by ourselves when we seek to validate them in depth, bending them back so that they converge upon a single, stable seat of consciousness, there to be reconciled or there to remain opposed in eloquent inner dialectic. Instead of which they lie calmly printed on the mask. Their service to the action (which is the sense and relevance achieved through their outwardness) consists in pointing the rhythm of "Now the gods are lifting you up, whereas before they compassed your downfall". Objective guilt and subjective innocence work together in this context, the former placing Oedipus firmly in the trough of defilement from which the upward movement of the action rescues him, the latter asserting divinity's continuous, inscrutable and two-

---

[1] Hence the need to insist that Aristotle is not primarily concerned to say that character is less important than action.

way pressure on human life. The fact that Oedipus is being raised by the same gods who struck him down would be less religiously awful to contemplate did not the pattern of their interventions betoken a naked, almost absurd, volcanic expressiveness defeating moral calculation. (Aristotle's view that tragic misfortune should not come about through vice or depravity is closer to the sacred drama's central fear-and-trembling impulse than its immediate connection with *hamartia* and audience-psychology suggests.) When Sophoclean Tragedy comes to rest in the conclusion "Call no man happy until he is dead",[1] the sensitive modern reader is aware that his religious experience, precisely in so far as it is religious, lacks the bottomless, relativistic insecurity which purges this thought, in Sophocles, of the superficial and the sardonic. We know nothing in the least like it. There can be no contact between Christianity or individualistic humanism and a cosmic Mutability which averages out rather as the weather does. And because no contact, no experience of Mutability's compensating application to this or that man's singular fate.

Discussion of the Oedipodean tragic mask leaves on one side questions of naturalism; nobody can confidently guess how close to life the stage-figure will have seemed to Sophocles's first audience. At the same time we must be prepared to argue for a vital general correspondence between the mask and this ancient society's beliefs about the human self, since a dramatic convention does not spring out of nothing, nor, when it determines the principles of presentation, out of something trivial; and so when criticism calls Oedipus untrue to himself in his protestations of subjective innocence, our answer couples the "real" self with the masking convention. With Oedipus as with Antigone (who has also, and often, been called untrue to herself for admitting circumstances in which she would leave a near relative unburied), the discrete and centrifugal self of our early exposition corresponds to the mask as life to artifact. And just as Antigone's quasi-forensic utterance falls, to the Greek understanding, within character, so does that of Oedipus; only its inclusion is of greater consequence in his case since the legalistic strain is much further developed, and it only remains to extend

[1] *Oedipus the King* closes with this sentiment, which is picked up by Deianeira in the opening lines of the *Women of Trachis*.

the discussion to the overall relationship of language to character in Sophocles.

The following words are spoken by Oedipus to his daughters, just before he leaves them:

> My children, this day you lose your father; here and now there perishes all that is I, and you will not any longer bear the burden of tending me—a heavy burden, my children, as I know. And yet one word, quite alone, resolves all this pain. That word is love. Love was the gift you had from me as from no one else, and now you must live out your lives without me.[1]

The reality of love, the solitary word, is at once concrete and linguistic. Like another "little word" for lack of which Oedipus "was left to wander, an outcast and a beggar always",[2] and like the spoken curses which he imagines going ahead "to fight for me",[3] this love enjoys an independence which makes its connection with him who utters it seem tenuous. And in one sense it is tenuous: what renders innocent—sanctifies even—Oedipus's thought of his own love lightening his daughters' labours on his behalf, in an obscure literal acceptance of the work which the one little word has been doing; he is not using the word solely to denote the fact of his love, he is looking at the word as at a half-domesticated life which remains still outward and alien at the moment of appropriation. For utterance *is* appropriation; the word *is* Oedipus's. This aspect of Sophoclean language is of almost continuous importance, and its effect, if we are honest about our response, is a brilliant impenetrability; groping for the people whose words these are, we explore the hard surface of the mask in its linguistic and acoustic dimension.

Our last knowledge of Oedipus is through the messenger's words:

> Theseus is the only human being who can tell how Oedipus died. Certainly no flaming thunderbolt of Zeus took his life, nor did a whirlwind risè suddenly from the sea to carry him off: nothing like that happened just then. It may be a messenger from the gods came to him; or the foundations of the world opened to receive him in love, with no pain. We know he was taken without lamen-

---

[1] ll. 1611-19.
[2] ll. 443-4.
[3] l. 1376. Jebb aptly terms these curses "personal agencies of vengeance".

tation, and not in sickness or suffering. His end was wonderful beyond mortality.[1]

The receding figure of the king is essentially the action coming to rest. Our interest in him is to see what he does and what is done to him, our difficulty is that our informant, the messenger, loses sight of him at the final stage of his acting out what has to be done. This is a visual and surface difficulty, and it is also, because of Oedipus's unique intimacy with the sacred event,[2] ultimate. But so is the action itself of the surface and ultimate; and so is the tragic mask; and so is the messenger's beautifully opaque language of love and pain. And so of course is Colonus, the place where these things happened.

[1] ll. 1656-65. Theseus adds a few words about Oedipus's passing at ll. 1760-7.

[2] Through this intimacy a kind of sacredness attaches to Oedipus himself. "I come to you," he tells the local Athenians, "a holy man, and pious, and a bringer of advantage to this people" (ll. 287-8). When the full glare of religio-dramatic attention is upon Oedipus as the one who is to execute the action, the fact of his pollution is transcended. He becomes like an object dedicated to sacred uses. He comes to "give" (l. 576) his body, at once foul and supernaturally precious, to Athens. The sacredness that invests Oedipus proceeds from the sacred action itself and has nothing to do with his pleas of subjective innocence.

IV: EURIPIDES

1 Euripides's Electra:
A Third Version of the Myth

At once a large discrepancy becomes apparent between Euripides's story and those told by the two older tragedians. When his play opens Electra is no longer living in her murdered father's palace at Mycenae; Clytemnestra has married her off to a peasant farmer in the neighbourhood, and we find her established with him in a smoky cottage, setting off with a pitcher on her head to fetch water, performing the menial tasks proper to the wife of such a man, her hair unkempt and her dress tattered. This is the situation which greets Orestes on his return.

Euripides's version is remarkably bold in its elaboration of the traditional story: we recall that the fifth-century dramatist was free only to alter details. It is also provocative. It displays inventiveness of the kind most likely to annoy Euripides's enemies—"the great pack of the orthodox and the vulgar", as Gilbert Murray tendentiously styled them; and certainly they were many, and certainly their attitude was in the widest sense conservative.

Two fairly full statements of the case against Euripides survive from the fifth and fourth centuries. One of these, indirect and allusive, is Aristotle's *Poetics*. The other is the *Frogs*, a comedy produced by Aristophanes a few months after the deaths of Euripides and Sophocles, in which the issue is cast in the form of a posthumous literary debate between Aeschylus and Euripides, with Sophocles standing by in silent support of the older poet.

The criticisms in the *Frogs* are directed against the Euripidean *œuvre* as a whole, and at the same time they have immediate and obvious application to the development of the Orestes myth which we find him indulging in his *Electra*. Aeschylus repeatedly accuses Euripides—and so does Aristophanes; he scarcely pretends to view the contest impartially—of introducing into the tragic theatre paupers and figures from low life and persons physically and morally deformed; so that the Mycenean farmer

(he is given no name in the play) and his wife Electra in her
new poverty and humble station are just the sort of people
Euripides's opponents have in mind. Attempting to understand
what it is they object to, we do well to consider the most carefully worked of the many gibes and denunciations in the *Frogs*,
and this is an extended parody of a favourite Euripidean form,
the monody or lyrical monologue.[1] The effect of the parody is
irrecoverable in so far as it depends on the taking off of Euripides's musical idiosyncrasies, about which we know almost
nothing. But what remains is well worth having. We are asked
to imagine that the monody is being sung by a poor spinning-
girl who wakes up after a terrifying and ill-omened dream to
ask what her vision of the night may mean, and to set about
ceremonially washing away this "dream sent by the gods" in
an attempt to avoid a calamitous outcome. All in vain, however, for she suddenly realises that the disaster presaged by the
dream has come to pass; while she was busy at her spinning
another girl stole the precious cock which she had intended to
sell at tomorrow's market; and the monody ends with the first
girl in pursuit of the thief, calling jointly upon high divinities
and the lodgers of the house to help her.

The broad conclusion must be that Aristophanes is here
deriding Euripides's lofty treatment of a low incident; the theft
of a barnyard fowl does not measure up to the ample tragic
gestures of the monody. So much is plain. Our troubles begin
when the neo-classical language of decorum is used to discuss
this gross discrepancy of form and content. Of course no modern
commentator believes that Euripides was simply being wanton
in his plays—that he introduced rags and low life in order to
degrade Tragedy; but critics write—I believe they all write—
as if we were witnessing something in the nature of a seventeenth-
century struggle between the ideal of tragic elevation and the
desire to render the life we live from day to day. While not
wholly false, this view is a pernicious distortion of the truth in
that it fails to isolate the central Euripidean intuition of tragic

---

[1] *Frogs*, ll. 1331-63. See also ll. 840-50; 1043-4; 1063-4; 1079-81. At
ll. 771-8 Euripides is accused of showing off before "highwaymen, cut-
purses, housebreakers and parricides", and thus winning their good opinion
in the world below. At ll. 1305-7 the "Muse of Euripides" comes on-stage
in the likeness of a prostitute.

potentiality in the theft of a cock, at the same time obscuring Aristophanes's joke which is to present Euripides in his habitual folly of treating a trivial theme *as if* it were serious.

Our temptation is to elaborate the issue between them because it seems crassly obvious that the loss of a cock *is* serious—for the poor loser. But it is obvious only to a sensibility which Euripides has helped to create, and that is why all neo-classical opposing of high and low must be secondary when we reconstruct the fifth-century debate, being reckoned subordinate to a transforming apprehension of the quality of life flowing within the human individual. The older understanding, not to be compared with the self-conscious and dogmatic elevation of neo-classicism, is reaffirmed by Aristotle, himself in some ways very self-conscious, when he lays down that the action in Tragedy must be serious and that the people in Tragedy must be appropriate. Seriousness and appropriateness are interdependent concepts, as we saw, since for Aristotle the differentiation of individuals is primarily status-determined: kingly actions should be reserved for kings; a slave, because he is a slave, is "entirely worthless"—although he may, within this framework, be a "good" slave. And now Euripides appears with a new interest in, and new reverence for, the humanity of mere consciousness. Consciousness is solitary and inward, and it is also every man's birthright or affliction; and so the particular and the universal begin to emerge on either side of the Aristotelian general, threatening to eclipse his world of type-distinctions. Euripides may have been a little in awe of his own insight, as Socrates was when he found he could teach geometry to a slave.[1] Certainly his discovery is the more momentous of the two, for he was not solely or even primarily concerned with intellect as the common possession of humanity, cutting across status. Nor should we unduly moralise his vision. He is holding to a new apprehension of the human self, and considering how to achieve its representation on the stage.

The spinning-girl of Aristophanes's parody directs us not so much to humble and everyday life as to a brilliantly fresh perception of what human beings are really like, and therefore to

---

[1] *Meno*, 82A–86B. Or rather, Plato exploits the dramatic surprise flowing from Socrates's demonstration that knowledge of geometry is somehow latent in the slave.

a changed estimate of what is important to dramatic art. The girl's meanness of station is not gratuitous; she has to be poor because her feelings upon the loss of her cock would otherwise fail in tragic scope. Conversely, when Aristophanes twits Euripides with dressing his stage-kings in rags "in order that the audience should think them pitiable",[1] he exposes, no doubt inadvertently, Euripides's deeper purpose which is to isolate and emphasise the pathos of ruined fortune in the great. Such pathos is a matter of respect for consciousness, in the keen particularity of its life and in its common, communicable humanity. The poverty and the kingly status are both means to an end, and the novelty of the end sheds light on Aristotle's pronouncement that Euripides is "the most tragic"[2] of the dramatists. This admission, apparently in blank contradiction of the whole tenor of the *Poetics*, is forced on Aristotle by his preoccupation with audience-psychology—this is the most un-traditional aspect of the thesis—and by his stressing of pity, together with fear, as specifically tragic emotions. An unequalled flair for getting at the audience through their sense of the pathetic was something which could not, in the late fourth century, be denied the youngest of the dramatists. And Aristotle does not attempt to deny it; the connection between Euripides's "tragic" stature and his pity-stirring power is explicit in the *Poetics*. (Euripides arouses in him that paradoxical sense of advance into decline which an education in eighteenth-century music leads many of us to experience towards Beethoven.) But he would have said that the new sympathetic intimacy was bought too dear, even if the full price only became known when Tragedy fell into the hands of smaller men than Euripides. The pathetic self, the solitary and inward self, was cultivated at the expense of that godlike impersonal vitality which Aristotle had at the forefront of his mind when he wrote: "Tragedy is an imitation not of human beings but of action and life."

The Greek for human being is *anthrōpos*. In the *Frogs*, Aristophanes allows Euripides to declare that the tragedian ought to speak "*anthrōpeiōs*"[3]—humanly, as befits a man. And once again the quarrel with Aeschylus and Sophocles must not

[1] *Frogs*, ll. 1063-4. Aristophanes is thinking of stage kings like Oeneus, rather than like Telephus, whose rags were a disguise. See *Acharnians*, l. 410 ff.   [2] *Poetics*, 53a30.   [3] l. 1058.

be reduced to an affair of the merits of everyday as against inflated diction. With Electra's farmer husband in the Euripidean version, the essential fact is that the dramatist has deployed human relationships within the story in such a way as to break through the crust of type-distinctions founded on status. Electra has been forced to marry beneath her, and the unexpected outcome is a *bouleversement* in which her husband displays a royal generosity and delicacy in his treatment of her. "Your kindness I reckon godlike",[1] Electra tells him. His is no ordinary consideration, as Euripides makes us understand by his emphasis upon Electra's preserved virginity. The farmer declares:

> Aphrodite is my witness that I have always respected her maidenhood; she is still a virgin. My station is humble, you see, and I shrink from affronting the daughter of a better man by bringing her to bed.[2]

Furthermore, the dialogue is subsequently directed to exclude the assumption that the farmer was moved simply by his fear that Orestes might return one day and punish him for insulting his sister. "He is a virtuous man as well",[3] Electra insists when Orestes finally appears and suggests the lower motive of fear, and she brings him to acknowledge the strange truth himself in the exclamation: "Indeed a noble nature this!"[4]

Electra's husband is still at work in the fields when Orestes and his friend Pylades reach the cottage. He returns at last and rebukes Electra for her slowness in showing hospitality to the strangers: "You should have thrown open our doors to them long ago."[5] The gesture is characteristically generous, and Orestes, constant in his attitude of wide-eyed amazement ("By heaven! is this the man who has been helping you make a fiction of your marriage . . .?"[6]), now embarks on a long meditation:

> So, there is no reliable means of assessing a man's worth; humanity is cross-grained. Before now I have seen nullity fathered by greatness and virtuous children born of vicious parents. Again, I have found dearth in a rich man's soul and an ample soul in a poor man's body. Then what distinguishing principle should one apply in order to judge these matters correctly? Wealth? A useless criterion. Or poverty? The trouble with poverty is that it teaches a man to be bad through pressure of need. Well then, must I

[1] l. 67.   [2] ll. 43-6.   [3] l. 261.
[4] l. 262.   [5] l. 357.   [6] ll. 364-5.

invoke the soldierly virtues? But who would be able to testify to his neighbour's courage in the stress and confusion of battle? It's best not to bother—best to leave such problems alone. For here [*indicating Electra's husband*] is someone who counts for nothing in Argos, one of the crowd, a man with no family reputation to boast of; and yet his personal nobility is evident.[1]

We are likely to find this passage stiff, naive, digressive—and undramatic, because we do not experience the shock which Euripides is playing for when he displays a noble consideration and fineness of nature in Electra's husband; it does not amaze us that the rough exterior of a Mycenean smallholder should conceal a great spirit. (Nor does a tragic treatment of the theft of a poor girl's cock strike us as inherently absurd: in this vital respect we are unappreciative of Aristophanes's parody.) But Euripides will surely have secured from his first audience the response he wanted. They will have been with Orestes as he pondered the mysterious separation of personal merit and exalted status; and when he turned towards the farmer with a demonstrative inflection very characteristic of this writer ("For here is someone . . ."), they will have followed his gaze in awed fascination.

Behind the farmer stands his modest cottage; he and it and Electra and the noble strangers are involved in a persisting interpenetration of merit and status which accords some measure of tonal unity to this indifferent play. Arriving at the cottage, Orestes calls it a hovel fit only for a labourer to live in.[2] And so it is; but it is also Electra's home, and she acknowledges her duty to keep it decent for her husband; it is only right, she tells him, that he should have somewhere comfortable to return to after working in the fields all day[3]: his right and her duty are not affected by the husband's sexual delicacy; the virgin-wife who is a king's daughter reckons herself inescapably the cottager's mistress.

Thus a situation of some intricacy is created by the farmer's

[1] ll. 367-82. My instinct is to understand ll. 377-8 thus: "But who could testify to a soldier's courage from the look of his spear?"—which lends further point to Euripides's contrasting of inner and outer. The verbally close passage at *Supplices*, ll. 846-52, is against me, but not decisively.

[2] l. 252.

[3] ll. 73-6. Electra admits to a second motive in undertaking menial tasks, which is to "show the gods the insult done me by Aegisthus" (l. 58).

inviting Orestes and Pylades into his home. Electra's immediate reaction is one of alarm: "Reckless fool, you know how poor your house is: why did you welcome these strangers here—strangers above your station?"[1] His reply is a sudden ripping open of the status-defined surface of things: "What do you mean? If they are really as noble as they seem, surely they will be equally content with rich or humble fare?"[2] We must be alert to what is momentous in this perception, within a fifth-century framework, if we are to do justice to the farmer's Lear-like discourse on sufficiency and excess which follows almost at once:

> It is on occasions like this, when my hospitality is thwarted, that I perceive the great power of wealth—whether to give to strangers or to spend on the sick body's cure. But the price of our daily bread is a different and small matter, since the rich man's stomach holds no more than his poor neighbour's.[3]

To the "really" noble individual, capable of transcending the rigid correspondence of high living with high station, the farmer now adds his vision of humanity united in its daily needs. Talk of the Euripidean particular and universal ceases, perhaps, to be offensively abstract in the light of this double realisation. And when food for the guests is later brought in ("this tender lamb from my own flock . . . cheese straight from the press, and this flask of old wine"[4]), the precious and confirming scope of the good things of the poor is finely suggested. Euripides's originality does not end with his giving the king's daughter a farmer for her husband.

2 The Unhoused Talent

In his *Electra* Euripides is telling the same story as Aeschylus and Sophocles, the story of Orestes's return and his vengeance-killing of Clytemnestra and Aegisthus: which seems to secure a conviction of arbitrariness and special pleading against the critic who concerns himself first with some aspects of Euripidean divergence. A saving "seems" is here justified, I believe, by the alien dramatic life animating the theme of status and personal

[1] ll. 404-5.   [2] ll. 406-7.   [3] ll. 426-31.   [4] ll. 494-7.

merit, and causing it to resist containment within the traditional story. At the end of the play two divinities, the twin sons of Zeus, appear "over the roof tops"[1] in the stage-crane much favoured by Euripides, and their task is to resolve the affairs of this violent family. They direct Orestes (in a long speech) to Athens, where he is to stand trial for his mother's murder, also telling him to give Electra to his well-born friend Pylades, to be his wife. Electra's present husband, the farmer, is as yet unaccounted for. He is fitted in at the end. Pylades, so the two gods explain to Orestes, "must conduct this titular brother-in-law of yours to Phocis, and there reward him well".[2]

This paying off of the farmer—the only reference to him in the second half of the play—introduces us to a kind of self-refutation within the Euripidean drama; and from now on, as we have already hinted, the language of decorum is bound to be superficial. It is true that Euripides, writing in the fifth century and for presentation at a public religious festival, had no means of giving the farmer his due: for example, he could not confirm his marriage to Electra. But there is no reason to think he wanted to do any such thing. On the contrary, the farmer's unwillingness to consummate his marriage has upon it the mark of endorsement by the dramatist; the farmer is right to refrain, he does not merely display fine feelings by refraining.[3]

The deeper truth is that what Euripides wants to say in his *Electra* is not quite the tale he has to tell. The principal signs of this disunity are the faraway sweetness of the play's choral lyrics, scarcely engaging with the businesslike action of revenge; the perfunctory tone of the solution presented or imposed by Zeus's divine sons; the unassimilated counterpoise of status and merit, intrusive yet manifestly rich. The disunity is by no means complete, which is one reason why this is not among Euripides's worst plays; the farmer-husband disappears, but the cottage itself—the façade before which the entire action is played—grows into very relevant dramatic prominence with the forming of a plan to lure Clytemnestra inside, where Orestes will be

---

[1] l. 1233.   [2] l. 1286-7.

[3] And this in spite of the fact that the farmer's family was not humble in its origins; it has come down in the world: "my good birth", the farmer tells us, "has been lost through its impoverishment" (l. 38). See J. D. Denniston's note on l. 253 for a discussion of wealth in relation to nobility.

waiting to kill her. With Electra's inviting of her mother ("Enter our poor house—and please be careful the smoke-grimed walls don't soil your clothes"[1]), Euripides achieves a fleeting effect of sudden visionary shock such as a mechanical juxtaposing of wealth and poverty could not account for. Nor are we here simply aware of what awaits Clytemnestra within. We are responding to a momentary rallying of the work of art.

Since the issue between Euripides and the older tradition is not *au fond* one of decorum, at least in the familiar neo-classical sense, no great progress can result from scrutinising the humble life of his plays in isolation. The trouble with Electra's husband is not that he is horny-handed, but that the mode of Euripides's observing and presenting of him resists appropriation by the masked drama; the trouble lies within the dramatic individual, in the bare fact of his nursed and exploited consciousness, and it may be found in kings as well as in farmers. We do in fact find it in King Agamemnon, at the heart of the *Iphigeneia at Aulis*.

In that play Euripides is offering the familiar predicament of the Greek expedition against Troy, assembled at Aulis but prevented by contrary winds from setting sail. As in Aeschylus and Sophocles, and as in the wider tradition, the king and commander-in-chief has to sacrifice his daughter to the angry goddess in order to secure a passage for his army. Agamemnon's compulsion is status-defined and status-determined in the Aeschylean version; for one who stands where Agamemnon stands there is nothing else to be done. Sophocles adds the suggestive detail that Agamemnon cannot disband the expedition even if he wants to. But in this third version Agamemnon wavers. Euripides wants us to see him hesitating and changing his mind, and he has written a play which, in one very large aspect, is strictly about the psychology of indecision.

A new secrecy, or possibility of secrecy, is needed by Euripides. In place of the large-featured and public Aeschylean situation where Calchas the seer "proclaimed another remedy to the chiefs",[2] we have to imagine that the dreadful truth is known to very few—perhaps only to Agamemnon and his brother Menelaus and a third chief, Odysseus. This context is required

[1] ll. 1139-40.   [2] *Agamemnon*, ll. 199-201.

in order that Agamemnon's reactions to the news that he is called upon to sacrifice his daughter shall appear (and again we must stress the novelty of Euripides's treatment) private; in order that the twists and turns shall be thrust home to, shall be experienced by the audience as issuing from, the father's solitary and self-collected consciousness. His mental shifts are enormously complicated by any standard the ancient drama could apply. When he heard what Calchas had to say, Agamemnon's first instinct was to give orders to his herald to proclaim the disbanding of the whole army. And this was done.[1] But then Menelaus, by "bringing every argument to bear",[2] persuaded him to change his mind. So he sat down and wrote a letter to Clytemnestra his wife, bidding her send Iphigeneia to Aulis, and pretending at the same time (since he knew she would never agree to the sacrifice) that he wanted Iphigeneia at Aulis because her marriage to Achilles had been arranged.

Now, at the time the action opens, Agamemnon is having third thoughts; an old slave-attendant discovers him composing a further letter in an agony of writing, erasing, rewriting, of sealing and reopening.[3] It transpires that this letter countermands the earlier one and requires Clytemnestra to keep Iphigeneia at home in Argos—"for after all we will celebrate our child's wedding at another time".[4] The slave is commissioned to take the letter, and is on the point of leaving for Argos when Menelaus intercepts him, opens the letter and confronts his brother with its contents.

A long debate ensues in which Menelaus accuses Agamemnon of inconstancy and Agamemnon defends his latest volte-face as a return to sane counsels. They are still quarrelling when a messenger breaks in with the news that Clytemnestra has arrived at Aulis with Iphigeneia and the baby Orestes. This is a decisive blow for Agamemnon; he turns to lamenting his defeat at the hand of Fortune and surrenders his position totally. "Yours is the triumph", he tells his brother, "and mine the bitterness."[5] However, the Euripidean and mental *coup* lies beyond the messenger's startling news, unguessed as yet. Menelaus suddenly announces that he too has faced about; Agamemnon's distress makes him see the justice of the opposing

---

[1] ll. 94-6.   [2] l. 97.   [3] ll. 34-42.
[4] ll. 122-3.   [5] l. 472.

argument: "I abandon my former standpoint. . . . What has your daughter to do with Helen? Let the army be disbanded and leave Aulis. . . ."[1]

Thus it seems likely that Agamemnon will change his mind yet again. And if he could he would; but he cannot, because, as he now tells Menelaus,[2] the whole Greek army mustered at Aulis will compel him to go forward with the sacrifice. At this moment they do not know about the divine demand for Iphigeneia's life, but if he sends her back to Argos, Calchas himself will tell them. Menelaus suggests they kill the seer in order to silence him. Agamemnon replies that Odysseus also knows, and Odysseus is notoriously guileful and a rabble-rouser. Both brothers now abandon hope of keeping the oracles secret. Henceforward Agamemnon's actions are forced, and such psychological interest as hangs on his wavering is lost to the play.

This bare outline of Agamemnon's chequered mental history receives its dramatic substance, its life, from the resources of Euripidean expressiveness; for if the complexity of mental change and contradiction in the *Iphigeneia at Aulis* (a very late play and perhaps unfinished) is without precedent, then so are the pains taken by the dramatist to plot the stages of change and contradiction through facial expression[3] and gesture and the subtle personal language of mood, even when—in fact especially when—concealment of what lies within is being attempted by the stage-figure who thinks and feels. The old slave is summoned to his master in the small hours of the morning. "Why this restless pacing outside your tent, lord Agamemnon?"[4] he asks—which introduces the other signs of insomniac distress: the lighted taper, the tears, the struggle to compose the countermanding letter.[5]

Euripides persists in a thoroughgoing correlation of hidden trouble and telltale manner. "Look me in the face!"[6] is all Menelaus needs say, for he has read the second letter and knows about Agamemnon's "secret scheming"[7]; but Clytemnestra and Iphigeneia are both initially deceived by the pretence of

---

[1] l. 479; ll. 494-5.   [2] l. 514.

[3] Thus Euripides defies the masking convention while seeming to accept it.

[4] ll. 12-13.   [5] ll. 28-48.   [6] l. 320.   [7] l. 326.

impending marriage to Achilles, and with both of them the
duologue of face and heart is played out fully. Iphigeneia
exclaims: "So glad to see me—and yet your gaze is troubled!"[1];
and this observed discordancy prefaces an exchange between
father and daughter in which she draws attention to his
"knitted brow" and "streaming eyes", and he counters vaguely
with talk of the cares which oppress "one who is king and
general too", and with ambiguous mention of his sorrow at the
prospect of being parted from her: he must sail to Troy, but she
too has a "voyage" she must undertake.[2] Then Agamemnon
turns from his daughter to his wife, craving her pardon "if I
showed too much grief at the thought of giving my daughter to
Achilles".[3] For the moment Clytemnestra is satisfied with this
explanation of his distraught appearance. Later she meets
Achilles who tells her he knows nothing about a marriage;
whereupon she discovers the truth of the intended sacrifice from
the old slave-attendant. Agamemnon's grief-stricken aspect is
now accounted for: "Your very silence and all this groaning
are a confession; do not bother to state the truth."[4]

Emotional detail and mobility are intended to expose the
suffering heart which the front of the soldier-king would otherwise conceal. In the *Iphigeneia at Aulis* Euripides departs from
his normal practice of beginning a play with an elucidatory
Prologue, and offers instead a short exchange between king and
slave under the stars of early morning. Its purpose, perhaps not
sufficiently appreciated by commentators who deny Euripides's
authorship of the passage and/or transpose it to a later point,
is to establish the perspective in which we are to see the whole
man. Euripides wants to advance the fact that the king is
human too: first and foremost, at this stage, that he is weary of
command. In his brief, and theatrically loaded intimacy with
the slave, Agamemnon confides:

> I envy you, old man; yes, and I envy every one who is obscure
> and has no fame and lives a life without any danger in it. But I
> envy nobody in high office.[5]

And when the old attendant shows consternation at this statement, he elaborates the wretchedness of a position exposed to

1 l. 644.   2 ll. 645-85.   3 ll. 686-7.
4 ll. 1142-3.   5 ll. 16-19.

the demands of heaven from above and to those of human subjects from below.

Agamemnon's complaint is not merely that kings are called on rather than slaves to sacrifice their daughters in order that foreign expeditions may prosper; he also says that the suffering which comes to all men, the common burden of existence, comes hardest to those who are highly placed:

> Consider the advantage of humble birth! The poor man finds it easy to weep and tell out all his troubles. And the great man has these troubles too, but he—but our lives are ruled by ceremony and we are the people's slaves. So with me: I am ashamed to weep, and again I am ashamed not to weep. . . .'[1]

Indeed, the Euripidean emphasis falls on Agamemnon's common humanity rather than the solitary eminence of his position; he experiences the *same* sorrows as other men, but is less well equipped to contend with them. His disadvantage is not a matter of status, as we have been using the term hitherto, but of the office which attaches to the man. Office comes and goes, the man endures: in fact, humanity has become central, with the result that everybody in the play (with the interesting exception of the correct old slave who rejects Agamemnon's talk about envying the humbly-born with the observation that he finds these sentiments displeasing in a great man's mouth)[2] regards Agamemnon's command of the expedition as a professional appointment which he happens to have secured. To Agamemnon himself it is a "distinction"[3] which he would gladly forgo, while Menelaus alleges in his anger that he curried favour with all and sundry ("keeping open house to every fellow townsman who cared to enter"[4]) in order to gain the generalship. When Clytemnestra asks, indignantly:

> Do you suppose any of your children will come near you, to be made a sacrifice of? Have you thought of that? Or are you only concerned to carry a sceptre around and march at the head of an army?[5]

her view of kingship and military command falls within character, the contemptuous inflection being her own; but she also shares the general mental habit of the play, which is to attach office to the man in such a way that the focus of attention upon

¹ ll. 446-52.   ² l. 28.   ³ l. 85.   ⁴ l. 340.   ⁵ ll. 1192-5.

consciousness is left undisturbed. For this reason it is misleading as well as imprecise to speak of a clash of royal duty and fatherly feeling in the Euripidean Agamemnon, unless we go on to say that the dramatic function of office is to reflect interest upon his humanity by placing it under singular stress. Agamemnon is blinded or corrupted or neutrally and pathetically tormented by his office: the play offers conflicting judgments on this point; and when we come to decide the question for ourselves, Euripides wants us to feel there is only one thing to be done, and that is to scrutinise the man.

The farmer-husband in the *Electra* and Agamemnon in the *Iphigeneia at Aulis* are distinguished from the dramatic individuals of Aeschylus and Sophocles by the kind of interest they solicit. Electra's husband looks a peasant and is a peasant, but we come to see that he is possessed of heroic generosity and tact. Agamemnon looks and is a king and commander-in-chief, the greatest of the great; but we discover he is nursing a secret sorrow which he experiences and responds to it in a fashion that unites him with all humanity. (Contrast the mute Iole in Sophocles's *Women of Trachis*: she is one of a crowd of destitute captive girls, but Deianeira catches something noble in her manner and she proves to be a king's daughter: her rank confirms the personal aura.)

The newness of our interest, as reader or spectator, lies in the effort of penetration which we make in relation to Euripides's people. We stand at the outset where Orestes stands when he contemplates his sister's husband and feels obliged to admit "there is no reliable means of assessing a man's worth". Appearances are deceptive, rank and personal merit may not coincide, and so we use whatever means lie at hand in order to reach the truth. And that penetrative effort at work within ourselves corresponds, we recognise, to a persistent—probably the main —dramatic impulse in Euripides; for the nearest approach to a characteristic tragic attitude in this most diverse writer is surely Medea's cry:

> O Zeus, why have you given us the means to distinguish clearly between true gold and counterfeit, but no sign, no bodily mark whereby to tell the good man from the bad?[1]

[1] *Medea*, ll. 516-19.

Much of his work, particularly his best work, moves between appearance and reality; he sees predicament as the need to distinguish these, and disaster as the failure to do so. This is the bare scheme of the *Hippolytus*, illuminated by Theseus in a declaration which is unconsciously ironical (since he is falsely accusing Hippolytus at the moment he speaks these words) and also central to the tragic action, because Hippolytus dies in consequence of Theseus's misreading of his nature:

> Men should possess some clear test of friendship, some touchstone of souls to show which friend is true and which false. If only humanity spoke with two voices, the one honest and the other politic or random, then the lying voice would be convicted by its opposite and we should not be deceived.[1]

Getting at the truth, distinguishing reality from appearance, is a larger affair than the telling apart of knaves and honest men; our penetrative effort has as many forms as the Euripidean exposition of the fact of consciousness from which, of course, that effort initially proceeds. What the veil of seeming conceals may be a rare moral or intellectual talent, or it may be a kind of commonness, for, as Andromache says, "the seeming-wise are splendid outside, but like the ordinary run of men inside"[2]: in either and any case we pass beyond the veil in order to learn the truth, and in any case we respond to a specifically Euripidean presentation of the human self. We need to labour *penetrative* because all Greek Tragedy—perhaps all Tragedy—occupies itself with life's appearance-and-reality tensions; and yet neither Aeschylus nor Sophocles halts us before the stage-figure in this kind of solemn, intent regard.

Then naturally the individual consciousness is newly to the fore. The *Oedipus at Colonus* of Sophocles and the *Alcestis* of Euripides are both about—"about" in a worthlessly vague sense—the coming of death to a human being, and in asserting as we did that Sophocles's play should be experienced and expounded through action and locality, we adduced the negative argument that attempts to grasp the theme of death through the consciousness of the man about to die are decisively rebuffed. But if we repeat this argument with the *Alcestis* we turn

[1] *Hippolytus*, ll. 925-31.   [2] *Andromache*, ll. 330-1.

the tables on ourselves, for the rewards of an approach through the dying individual's apprehension of death prove to be rich.

Alcestis and her husband Admetus are principally concerned. The god Apollo has contrived to secure Admetus's release from impending death, provided he finds a substitute willing to die in his place. Whereupon Admetus "went in turn to all who were near and dear to him",[1] but could find nobody prepared to die, except his wife. And now the day has come on which Alcestis is to die.

Thus the play's opening is poised, like Sophocles's, on the verge of death. We find the Chorus anxiously speculating in front of the silent palace. Perhaps Alcestis is already dead. The place is deserted; there is nobody to ask. Certainly this silence is ominous, yet cries of lamentation would be expected from within if she were dead, and the customary tokens of death, lustral water and a shorn lock of hair, are not visible at the palace gates. A maidservant appears to resolve their doubts: Alcestis is alive, but only just; she is "at her last gasp".[2] And in this way, and by giving the maid a speech[3] in which she describes Alcestis's ceremonial washing and robing herself for death, her decking of the household altars, her farewell to her bridal bed, her kissing of her children, Euripides prepares for the entrance of husband and wife, the one face to face with death, the other with bereavement.

Outside the palace at last, Alcestis turns her dying gaze upward to the sun and the flying clouds (the association of sunlight and life was always immediate for the Greeks), while Admetus bends over his wife in a selfish agony of loss: "Raise yourself up—don't abandon me."[4] She ignores him, for death is very close, flooding through her consciousness: "I see the boat, two-oared, and the lake, and the ferryman of the dead—Charon, his hand on the boat's pole. He is calling me now: 'Why are you delaying? Hurry! You are keeping me.'."[5] And so the dialogue continues, with Alcestis in the grip of a visible and tangible enemy, and Admetus imploring her: "In heaven's name don't leave me—you can't!"[6]—a bitter-clear and savagely comic refutation of his bartering her life for his own, and also an acting out of the profound psychological truth observed by

---

[1] *Alcestis*, l. 15.   [2] l. 143.   [3] ll. 152-98.
[4] l. 250.   [5] ll. 252-6.   [6] l. 275.

the maidservant: "Our master will know his loss only when he suffers it."[1] For most men the future certainty of death is but a very faint shadow of its presence, and we are not meant to judge Admetus a monster; indeed his response to death now grown terribly immediate in Alcestis's bared consciousness ("I must die. Not tomorrow. Not on the third day of the month. But in one moment they will be saying I am dead"[2]) is to beseech his wife to take him with her.[3] We must not dismiss Admetus altogether or we shall underestimate the moment when he collects himself to explain to his children: "She cannot hear us, she cannot see us; fate has dealt you two and me a crushing blow."[4] We must grant the ironical pointing (modernly brilliant) of that "fate", not merely psychological plausibility but a measure of appeal—and I believe the dramatist invites us to do so—if the play's later realisation of bereavement is to attain its full pathetic stature: when we hear that Admetus has to be restrained from leaping Hamlet-like into the open grave, when he cannot bear to enter his house, remembering how he first brought Alcestis there to the sound of marriage hymns, "holding my dear wife's hand"—the mistressless house with its "floor all covered with dust" and the eloquent empty chair.[5]

Euripides gives us precisely what Sophocles withholds, or rather what Sophocles has not to give: the individual consciousness addressing itself to death, swamped by death; the pitiful, irrational attempt to fend off death from one who is loved and needed; wild promises of faithfulness beyond the grave; the cry of the dying to the living: "Don't you see it's *now* I'm to die"; the whole mentality of loss. That Sophoclean humanity proves "interesting" in an atmosphere of psychological privation we explain by his just referring of the play's human detail to locality and action; these are his means of treating Oedipus's death, and the death-theme is not to be sought in anything that a modern man could meaningfully call Oedipus's state of mind: just as Philoctetes's sufferings (which are very much the subject of that play) are realised in the action of getting him off the island, and in the cave, that marvellously painful dramatic reality. And thus the older of the two great writers and contemporaries works without the kind of inwardness cultivated by the other in the *Alcestis* and elsewhere.

[1] l. 145.   [2] ll. 320-2.   [3] l. 382.   [4] ll. 404-5.   [5] ll. 895-961.

We should probably be right to accord Sophocles some measure of intellectual self-awareness in the plays which he was writing towards the end of the fifth century, a time of rapid change—which is not quite to say that he was conservative or old-fashioned. Scholars observed long ago that there is abundant evidence of his contact with the Sophistic Movement, and we should add that his art remained essentially undisturbed by it. Sometimes we find what looks like Euripidean material embedded in Sophocles's work: the self-defence of Oedipus based on his guiltless mind; Ismene's insistence that Antigone and Haemon, the betrothed pair, are in love, after Creon has said that Antigone's death need not prevent Haemon from marrying because "there are other fields for him to plough"[1]; the taste of Heracles's and Iole's infatuation[2]; the form given to Philoctetes's dilemma: "how can I praise what happens in the world, when praising divine ways I find the gods are evil?"[3]; the two instances—both, perhaps significantly, from the last plays—of a man's word of honour, the personal pledge, being accepted in place of a formal oath.[4] The main interest of these examples is their dramatic inertia; they are modern (from the standpoint of Aeschylean tragedy) but unexploited, as if Sophocles were aware of, and formally admitted, an area of contemporary exploration and self-questioning which nevertheless fails to modify his sensibility at all profoundly.

Oedipus's guiltless mind, which is the most impressive case, leaves us puzzled at the outset by our inability to allow this theme what appears to be its due intellectual, moral and dramatic value in the *Oedipus at Colonus*—by the impossibility of taking it seriously, we are tempted to say—without making nonsense of the play's religious affirmations. Then turn back to the *Frogs*, to a thrust against Euripides which Aristophanes seems to have been specially pleased with since he repeats it, and which became notorious in antiquity beyond the Old Comedy. It is a line from Euripides's *Hippolytus*: "My tongue

---

[1] *Antigone*, ll. 569-70. Ismene's reply points to the unique adjustment of the love-relation: "But there cannot be another love-pledge like theirs."

[2] Sophocles has a lot to say about the power of love, but the situation glimpsed here of an individual "wholly absorbed" (*Women of Trachis*, l. 463) in this passion is extraordinary.

[3] *Philoctetes*, ll. 451-2.

[4] *Philoctetes*, l. 811; *Oedipus at Colonus*, l. 650.

swore, but not my heart."[1] The point of quoting Euripides against himself is not immediately obvious since in his play, as every member of Aristophanes's audience will have known, Hippolytus dies rather than break the solemn religious oath into which he has been tricked—"caught unawares" as he puts it.[2] Nor can we force a better sense on it by ignoring the context of the *Hippolytus* and asserting that Euripides elsewhere or generally in his plays champions this or comparable behaviours; because he does not, and Aristophanes never says he does. Sensible commentators are aware of this problem and proceed gingerly with the subject of Euripides's offensive morality:

> it must not be understood . . . that Euripides was, in any sense whatever, the holder or propagator of immoral principles. But the great civic and social virtues, honour and justice and valour, patriotism and self-devotion, respect to parents and reverence to the gods, and the like—virtues which to Aeschylus, and generally to the Athenians of the old heroic days, were matters of conscience, about which no discussion could be tolerated—were by Euripides brought to the test of "that universal solvent, the wild living intellect of man".[3]

This concentrating of attention upon Euripidean indulgence in independent rational enquiry places Rogers at the heart of the critical tradition of yesterday; his is one of many moderate versions of Euripides the Rationalist. Such intellectualist accounts, like the literature of decorum, are not satisfactory, and for the same reason: they burke the human issue. For what Aristophanes is exposing to ridicule and censure in "My tongue swore, but not my heart", and what he can be sure of communicating to his audience by a mere glance at the line, is an obviously Euripidean address to the human self. Our root concern is not with intellectualism any more than with immorality, but (in the present instance) with something immediately recognisable in a manner of juxtaposing tongue and heart.

Now it is illuminating that Sophocles should be allowed to ponder the mind that does not go with the deed, and allowed

---

[1] *Frogs*, ll. 102, 1471. These references are to *Hippolytus*, l. 612.

[2] *Hippolytus*, l. 657.

[3] Introduction to B. B. Rogers's edition of the *Frogs*.

R

in the most grave religious context of the *Oedipus at Colonus*,[1] but that Euripides should not. Our sense of Sophocles's unanxious, innocent admitting of this material is hereby confirmed, and our efforts to locate Euripides's originality in an unexampled inward-reaching are encouraged. Of course the confirmation and the encouragement are by no means perfectly articulate in Aristophanes; a contemporary account of deep-flowing change never is; but the human reiterations of the *Frogs* are none the less remarkable. The case against Euripides, passionately felt and less than completely understood, is something to which the ruined kings and noble peasants, the emotional freaks, the women and slaves and cripples, are known to be relevant; something that rejects the anarchic and sinister measuring of an event's tragic height against the capacities of the particular suffering and protesting heart and mind.

In further pursuit of this theme we say that Euripides proceeds untraditionally in order to plough up the hard surface of traditional tragic action. Working towards an honest (I mean felt by himself to be true) and also stageable vision of humanity,[2] he explores the outer fringe of his society's experience, where the categories of status fail, and returns with infamous stories. Hence a partnership of the ordinary and the outlandish: the woman who turns tigerish when she is cornered both confounds the type-distinction and affirms the universal womanly trait. Every bosom returns an echo; Euripides is a great pathetic genius—and yet women should not display the manly virtues, say Aristotle and the tradition. The position is one which Hippolytus's talk of tongue and heart indicates sufficiently for the comic purpose of the *Frogs*.

"I am free in heart, though not in name", declares the Euripidean slave.[3] "This woman is a slave, but she has spoken in the language of the free", is Deianeira's commendation of

---

[1] Of course, the general argument is not affected by the possibility that Aristophanes may not have seen or read the second Oedipus play when he wrote his *Frogs*; he will have found nothing unSophoclean in the assertion: "Nobody is evil who sins without meaning to" (Fragment 665).

[2] The whole Euripidean endeavour remains unintelligible unless we revive a world in which the thought that kings and slaves and women and perverts are these things second and human beings first (and is not their humanity sometimes momentous?) begins to command the artist.

[3] *Helen*, ll. 730-1.

the wise old nurse in the *Women of Trachis* of Sophocles.[1] The impenetrability of the stage-figure in Sophocles is linguistically sustained; this estimate of the nurse's disposition comes to rest finally, unenquiringly, in the word. Euripides, on the other hand, uses the word as a tool with which to reach and expose the inward fact; the slave's true nature must be sought within him, just as the Euripidean character who swears to speak the truth "from my heart" (*apo kardias*)[2] is referring to the hidden source of his utterance, and just as Orestes's polemical victory in the following exchange:

> MENELAUS [*sarcastically*]: You of course are a fit person to handle sacred water.
> ORESTES: Why not, may I ask?
> MEN.: And to kill sacrificial victims before battle.
> OR.: Well, are you?
> MEN.: Yes, my hands are clean.
> OR.: But not your heart.[3]

turns on his sudden disclosing of the inward and "real" state of affairs. This is the world of "My tongue swore, but not my heart." "What do they mean," Phaedra asks (and she has just confessed: "My hands are pure but my heart is defiled"[4]), "when they speak of people being in love?"[5] She is groping after the feeling of love, eager to get her hands round it. But when the Sophoclean Oedipus pronounces the "one solitary word" which is the love that eased his children's burden of attendance upon him, he affirms the direct surface-relationship of the play's action and its language.

The continuous hard exterior thus presented receives its visible fulfilment in the mask, the nexus of type-features with nothing behind it. Professor T. B. L. Webster has concluded from his study of drama and the visual arts in the fifth century that "realism develops both in extent and in depth" during this period,[6] and we now take advantage of his learning to proceed a little beyond the lumping together of Sophocles and

---

[1] ll. 62-3. We meet the slave who is free in heart once in Sophocles, in a single-line fragment (940) whose context is completely obscure.

[2] *Iphigeneia at Aulis*, l. 475.

[3] *Orestes*, ll. 1602-4.

[4] *Hippolytus*, l. 317.

[5] *Ibid.*, l. 347.

[6] *Greek Art and Literature: 530-400*, p. 205.

Euripides within a single general tendency; for while the human interest of Sophocles's work is innocently achieved—in the sense of "innocently" already invoked—that of Euripides's work derives from the characteristic penetrative enquiry which, precisely because it forces attention behind the surface show, threatens to destroy the masking convention. The mask becomes one man's face—mobile, simulative, telltale. When Iphigeneia comes to Aulis and Agamemnon meets her with profession of joy, but (she observes) is wild-looking and mysteriously anxious, our ultimate concern is with a discrepancy of inner and outer which brings us back yet once more to Hippolytus's tongue and heart. It may well be that stage-masks used by the two dramatists underwent the same physical changes. The question of use remains, and intelligently to compare the simulations of the *Iphigeneia at Aulis* with those of the *Philoctetes* would be to expound the principle of difference.

The disunity of what Euripides wants to say with the story he has to tell begins, I hope, to be apparent. In his *Electra* we find him fostering into prominence a character (the word seems right at last) who is doomed to remain on the perimeter of the action. The *Iphigeneia at Aulis* indicates a more stubborn difficulty, for there Agamemnon is as central to the action as he is to the dramatist's care, and the disunity persists. It is keenly felt at the long-delayed moment when Agamemnon explains to Iphigeneia the necessity of sacrificing her:

> Some frantic urge possesses the Greek army to sail with all speed to Troy and put an end to the rape of wives from Hellas; and they will kill my daughters in Argos as well as you and me, if I frustrate the goddess's decree. My child, it is not Menelaus who has enslaved me to him; I am not serving Menelaus's pleasure. No, Greece is my compulsion. Whether I want to or not, I must sacrifice you for her: this is the necessity to which I submit. So far as her freedom rests with you, daughter, and with me—Greece must be free; and Greek husbands must not lose their wives to the thieving violence of foreigners.[1]

Whereas a glaring uncollectedness in argument is found throughout Greek Tragedy, only in Euripides does it give

[1] *Iphigeneia at Aulis*, ll. 1264-75.

offence, and this is primarily because of the expectation of coherence (which includes the incoherence of the plausibly deranged *psyche*) already roused in the reader. Euripides cannot achieve success in plotting the course of Agamemnon's mental adventures without making a big moment of their last phase; and our response to what has gone before is the familiar self-preparation of the theatre for a crisis of consciousness and conscience: why should Euripides spin the single volitional thread through Agamemnon's shifts and hesitations unless he is moving towards this end? The actual outcome, in which we find ourselves back as it were inside Greek Tragedy, disappoints us; the king who wished he could cry and tell his griefs like other men is not discoverable in this discourse. Locally, the rhetorical tradition proves stronger than Euripides, and through the entire arc of stage-event, actor and action are at odds. It becomes an aesthetic grievance that Agamemnon should be forced to sacrifice Iphigeneia, for his compulsion gives the lie to our carefully nourished interest in the question: what will Agamemnon do?

Forced moves are without this embarrassing constriction in the work of the two older dramatists; the apparently inescapable logic of determinism is simply not heard where the religious and yielding instinct bathes dramatic action in Necessity. The contextual, atmospheric Necessity of their plays is an enormously reduced force in Euripides—inevitably, since the compelled act is brought home to the agent with a new specificity and persistence: note the inflection of Agamemnon's "whether I want to or not". The necessity, in short, is his, and thereby is initiated the kind of scrutiny of personal circumstance that leads critics, mistaking effect for cause, to speak of Euripides's rationalism. (But we are nearly all of us united in awareness of something thin and "mental" in Agamemnon's argument, and in his gummed-on patriotic sentiment.)

With all large terms drawn from a common cultural stock, alertness is needed to observe difference beneath a surface identity of usage. Necessity is one of these. Another is moderation, a shared tragic feature whose colour becomes distinctively prudential in Euripides. Thus the most important of his eloquent slave-nurses—their function is choric in a novel sense —expounds a technique of moderation which is essentially a defensive, hedgehoglike self-gathering on the part of the vulnerable individual:

> My long life teaches me a lot: I have learned that men should commit themselves only to moderate friendships since love is too strong a draught to strike the soul's marrow undiluted. The bonds of affection should rest light upon mankind, easy to break and easy to tighten.[1]

Her statement is wrenched into superficial accord with the tradition a few lines later, in its final sentence: "Therefore I have less praise for excess than for moderation, and any wise man will agree with me"[2]; but her salutation of the ideal, while conforming to the type of gnomic concluding utterance in Greek Tragedy, is here a superadded piety and lacks the disinterestedness of other voices. She is really talking about the best avoiding action open to single human beings in an uncontrollable and unpredictable world.

In fact Euripidean self-centredness is a revolutionary *modus operandi* which requires us to qualify our ventured generalisations about Greek Tragedy. When we say that Necessity is compatible with great moral suppleness at the level of dramatic fact, Euripides's work must be excepted, at least partially. That moderation has nothing to do with mediocrity is not quite true for the consciousness which fences itself in against life's pain and peers up at the great, and around at the expansive and the uncalculating, in almost complacent anticipation of a tumble—an attitude often supported by the dramatist's carefully planted ironies. Iphigeneia is among the world's "fortunate ones"[3] to the messenger who reports her arrival at Aulis. "Princely is the happiness our princes enjoy" runs the choral song. "Behold Iphigeneia, child of royal Agamemnon. . . ."[4] We are witnessing the first stage of a vast transformation, from acknowledgment that the air in high places is *hubris*-tainted (which is a fact of life) to the imposing of a fall-of-princes pattern (which is a moral distillation).

One and the same self-centredness occasions a drawing in of skirts in anticipation of pain and a directing inward of protest and indignation in response to pain suffered. Hippolytus's

---

[1] *Hippolytus*, ll. 252-7.   [2] *Ibid.*, ll. 264-6.
[3] *Iphigeneia at Aulis*, l. 428.   [4] *Ibid.*, ll. 590-2.

death agony recalls that of the Sophoclean Heracles in the *Women of Trachis*; the mood of tragic extremity seems unremarkable in the following passage until, after his appeal to Zeus, we encounter a series of first-person pronouns charged with the fiercest intimation of personal outrage:

> In heaven's name, you men, touch me gently where my flesh is torn. Who is this standing to the right of me? Come lift me carefully, steadily, and so bear your luckless burden—a man cursed by his father in blind error. Zeus, O Zeus, do you see these things —*me* the reverent and god-fearing, *me* the surpassing chaste, *me* thrust into the deep and yawning place of death. . . .[1]

And then it becomes evident that there is nothing in all Aeschylus and Sophocles genuinely comparable to Hippolytus's reiterated "*me*". Not that protestation of innocence is extraordinary, nor an easily inferred criticism of divine justice (again we insist that Euripides's attitude to religion is not an autonomous problem): what distinguishes Hippolytus—distinguishes him, say, from Prometheus and Philoctetes; they both repay momentary consideration from this point of view—is the breasttapping emphasis of his protest. The Euripidean figure has lost a pure expressiveness which was crucial to the earlier tragic effect, maintaining there an unbroken connection between the naked shout of pain (Antigone's "sharp cry of a bird",[2] Ajax's "deep distressful roaring, like a bull's"[3]) and the reasoned statement; and which made it possible to greet disaster with protestation of innocence, indictment of heaven, prayer for death, invoking of vengeance on enemies: while never—if the vulgarism may be lent precise application—taking it personally.

And in place of lost expressiveness the Euripidean figure gains a knowledge—indignant in Hippolytus's case, in others pitiful and despairing—of his collected, self-determined identity. He becomes an object to his own understanding, and he presents this object to others:

> Then count this a disgrace and show respect towards me; pity me, and, like a painter standing back from his picture, survey me and observe my sorrows closely. I was once a queen, but now I am

---

[1] *Hippolytus*, ll. 1358-66. The repeated "*me*" of the translation seeks to convey the very marked stress achieved by other means in the Greek.
[2] *Antigone*, l. 424.   [3] *Ajax*, ll. 321-2.

your slave; once I was blessed with many and fine children, but I am childless now and old too, cityless, forlorn, most wretched of women.[1]

In the work of the two older dramatists the stage-figure never offers himself as an *exemplum* with the bounded purposefulness of the queen of beaten Troy in Euripides's play. Furthermore Hecuba is not merely a Fallen Prince whose story is instinct with solemn and "tragic" significance. She is also a fallen prince inside a story; awareness of being held suspended in the controlling and defining medium of art informs her invitation to stand back like a painter from his picture in order to contemplate her. At the same time and distinctly, therefore, she is moral object-lesson and aesthetic object. And the business of deciding what conclusion should be spelt out of her sad story, and out of others like hers, occasions us doubt and alteration (which is one reason why the critical tradition has had difficulty making up its mind about Euripides): sometimes the shared Greek sentiment emerges in the text: "No mortal man is happy or fortunate to the last"[2]; and sometimes, as with Hecuba herself, the picture of the fallen prince induces a mood of hesitant questioning much exploited by those who favour Euripides the Rationalist:

What shall I say, O Zeus?—that you keep watch over men? Or that this is a vain fancy vainly held by us who believe in a race of gods, when it is chance that governs mortality? Was not this the queen of wealthy Troy, wife to all-fortunate Priam? And now her whole city has fallen to the spear, and she is a slave and old and her children are dead, and she lies on the ground, poor lady, dust-begrimed.[3]

As always, we should be concerning ourselves less with a particular moral and religious conclusion, or failure to reach conclusion, than with a single, many-sided self-centredness: in the present context, with a self-promotion that advances, as it isolates, the moral object-lesson which is also the aesthetic object. The observed rhythm of Hecuba's fall recalls our discussion of mutability in Sophocles; and now, venturing a crude and external distinction, we say that the most impressive feature

---

[1] *Hecuba*, ll. 806-11. [2] *Iphigeneia at Aulis*, ll. 161-2.
[3] *Hecuba*, ll. 488-96.

of Sophoclean mutability is a kind of non-antithetical double-ness (the wheeling constellation which is one of mutability's likenesses figures together the departure and the return of joy), whereas in Euripides the movement is dominantly one-way, and that way is downward: the Euripidean bent is char-acterised by a fallen-prince *exemplum* such as Hecuba presents. To the objection that King Oedipus's fall is as exemplary as Queen Hecuba's and much more fully elaborated, we answer that the long process of his exposure is not a single downward movement (since it is also the process of Thebes's healing), and that the word *exemplum* is inadmissible because it declares a distinct moralising intent and way of looking at the stage-figure which Sophocles's play is without. Precisely its uncategorised life running through the work of art makes Sophoclean muta-bility an interpretative sheet-anchor on the one hand, and on the other a pattern, harmonic rather than linear, whose meaning commentary must find formidably immediate. What is sayable about the pattern seems not worth saying.

The progressive exposure of Oedipus has nothing in common with the penetrative impulse of Euripides's work: that is why the horrors of *Oedipus the King* constitute an experience of utter calm, a blazing serenity—indeed like watching the stars; and it is also why Euripides fails to liberate his tragic intelligence in the articulation of a cosmic tune: *impersonal* he might call this joy-and-sorrow music, with a new pejorative stress born of his commitment to the dramatic individual and to consciousness. But, working with masks and a venerated story, he lacks the means of successful reform. Tragedy is an imitation of action and life, or of human beings; the mask carries the action, or the act waits on the agent. Euripides goes some way towards embracing Aristotle's rejected alternative: he appropriates Necessity to the man who finds himself compelled; he inclines the religio-moral ideal of the Mean towards a prudential counselling of moderation addressed to single vulnerable souls; he isolates the sufferer in Tragedy, as framed aesthetic object and as moral object-lesson; he awakens in the sufferer himself the indignation of self-defined innocence; he gives to the action that downward thrust which is often and wrongly thought typical of Greek Tragedy, and, in so far as mutability's two-way movement survives, he conceives it antithetically—as a sudden veering of the wind that brings good fortune after bad,[1] or bad after good[2] (the wind can only blow in one direction at one time); he is resourceful to palpate the fact of consciousness. But he cannot go the whole way. He cannot transform a spread-out, maplike revelation into a drama of inwardness.

Euripides's access of interest in human beings (if we may retain for a moment Aristotle's simple-seeming dichotomy) is also a failing confidence in action, since the old sufficiency is hereby questioned. Drained of a human plenitude which had been of the surface while not superficial, action will have appeared newly bare and poor, and Euripides dealt with this situation by attempting to infuse interest into what was becoming, for him, mere event. His various measures—he was ingenious—are thus a labour of complete pioneering seriousness, and we have no reason to think he was in earnest only where he has proved successful. Thoroughly bad plays like *The Children of Hercules* offer a medley of superficial attractions which it seems at first sensible to assume were idly concocted; but this impression vanishes when the critical vision is purged of two and a half millennia of hindsight. For the faults which we recognise and denounce as vulgarity, staginess and the rest, while they are faults indeed, were not carelessly or cynically entertained.

Clearly defined terminal climax, so impressively absent in the older drama as a whole, becomes a felt need in Euripides; and so his *Helen* and his *Iphigeneia in Tauris* both move towards exciting, ship-borne getaways. The classical unravelling (*lusis*)[3] of the action has veered and narrowed towards a theatrical *dénouement* which in these two plays must be narrated, of course; but in the *deus ex machina*—the god who appears aloft in the stage-crane to rescue and resolve, Euripides sees the opportunity in play after play of coupling visual sensation with climactic event. And these plays are among his failures or marred successes. In the *Andromache* and the *Orestes* and the *Electra*, a superimposed, hustled inruption of the deity is simply

[1] As in *Electra*, ll. 1147-8. This image is followed immediately by one of the tide's turning (ll. 1155). Thus the antithetical stress is maintained. Contrast the Sophoclean constellation and the Sophoclean sea.

[2] As in *Hercules Mad.* l. 480.

[3] Aristotle's term. See Chapter XVIII of the *Poetics*.

damaging; but in recognising this we should discount the
commonly alleged wish of Euripides to poke fun at popular
religion. His errors lie within the sphere of dramatic calculation, as they also do with Medea's clumsy crane-borne epiphany
at the end of her play, where religion is plainly not in issue.

The intended import of the visible scene is often pitiful. When
the dead child Astyanax is carried on-stage upon his dead
father's sweat-stained shield,[1] it is the insistent ocular prompting that makes this moment Euripidean; he is deliberate about
impact in a way his predecessors were not. Often the emotion-
nudging directions of his text ("Give o give them your hand,
children, and they must give you theirs; come close to them"[2];
"Look, Hecuba! do you see Andromache borne this way on an
alien chariot? And clasped to her beating breast is Astyanax
her darling, Hector's child"[3]; "Lay the blind man's hands on
the ill-starred faces of his sons"[4]) look like the lardings of a
clumsy sentimentalist to us who judge the pseudo-pathetic
effect on its own merits, with no mitigating regard to Euripides's
attempt at a visual shoring-up of weakened tragic action. But
this second is the fundamental concern, at least partially identi-
fied by Aristotle in his discussion of *opsis*[5]; for while he acknowledges the emotional appeal of visible appearances,[6] he also
condemns *opsis* on the *a priori* ground that it is inartistic,[7] and
by this he means that it usurps the action's function of arousing
pity and fear. As always, he is maintaining action's purity and
sufficiency, and the question of quality in these matters—of true
and false visual pathos—never engages his attention: whereas to
us it matters very much whether Euripides's eye-taking and
tear-jerking effects are well managed. We do not find the veiled
Alcestis inartistic. We want to discriminate.

It must be obvious that the present essay leans heavily upon
failure to find coherence in Euripides's work, of the order of

[1] *The Trojan Women*, l. 1119.
[2] *The Children of Hercules*, ll. 307-8.
[3] *The Trojan Women*, ll. 568-71.
[4] *The Phoenician Maidens*, l. 1699.
[5] Usually translated "Spectacle"; but we cannot be sure whether
Aristotle has the whole *mise en scène* in mind, or just the physical and visible
get-up of the stage-figures.
[6] *Poetics*, 50b17.   [7] *Ibid.*, 53b1-8.

those distinct coherences which the two critical fictions of the
Aeschylean norm and Sophoclean mutability were intended
to explicate. Clearly, too, oblique homage is being rendered
Euripides when we postulate so momentous a clash of tradition and the individual talent behind the confusions of his
surviving work; a massive dislocation, unlike an ordinary mess,
can be perpetrated only by a great writer. We avail ourselves
of Macaulay's surprising insight: "The sure sign of the general
decline of an art is the frequent occurrence, not of deformity,
but of misplaced beauty"[1]; and in so doing we stress "frequent"
and "beauty" as much as we stress "misplaced".

Therefore the truth is remote from what many people once
believed: that Euripides was a pamphleteering genius who
perforce, or by guileful choice, cast his radical message into an
acceptable tragic mould. On the contrary, Euripides wanted to
write plays, and to suspect an ulterior motive is to misinterpret
our dim awareness that he was in difficulties with the received
dramatic form. Again, more than twice as much of Euripides
has come down to us as of Aeschylus or Sophocles, and yet we
feel that our record of the youngest tragedian is singularly
incomplete. And this is because of the disruption caused by his
way of apprehending the human self. If every line he wrote
had been preserved, I believe our impression of incompleteness
would persist not greatly changed, and then it would cease to
be a matter for argument that the source of this impression is
to be found within the unfocussed talent itself.

The judgment that our record is fragmentary, like the judgment that Euripides's worst work shows that he sometimes
failed to take his art seriously, lacks penetration; and so does
the wider sweep of exegesis and critical appraisal. It is unprofit-
able to oppose sophistic versions of Euripides's religion with
the rich store of reverence in his plays; we need to put our finger
on perceptions like "To recognise our friends is a god"[2] before
we can cut through the weary debate about belief and arrive at
his interest in divinity as a fact of mind (which does not mean
fiction of mind). The much-canvassed question whether Euripides
was for or against women (of course he was both) scratches the
surface of the *Medea* and the *Alcestis* and the *Hippolytus*, all three
of which gain formidable impetus from the ability of their

[1] Essay on Machiavelli.   [2] *Helen*, l. 560.

women to unsettle received antitheses; bravery and cowardice, selflessness and rapacity, stir as though threatening to change places, and wisdom and folly are on the move too; and sex violently eludes domestication by the defining masculine intelligence. Similarly with the clash of aristocratic and plebeian attitudes. And similarly with academic discussion of changes taking place in a region that has been artificially separated from the people and the sentiments; we hear about Euripides's advance into "true" soliloquy as if this were first and foremost an affair of dramatic technique, and fundamentally arbitrary, rather than of consciousness and the locked world of the self. Wilamowitz put modern criticism in his debt by challenging the bourgeois-realist and pamphleteering versions of Euripides, but he encouraged new confusions by speaking, rather in the idiom of a German admirer of Shakespeare, of the dramatist's genius for character-portrayal; and in place of the "soldier of rationalism" (for Verrall's *Euripides the Rationalist* had distinguished counterparts in Germany and France[1]) we have been offered a bewildering number of alternatives: *Euripides the Irrationalist*[2], *the Idealist*,[3] *der Mystiker*,[4] the Devout,[5] the Religious Fantasist,[6] the Pure Poet[7]; and much small-scale speculation of the *Euripides, ein antiker Ibsen?* variety.

Macaulay's "misplaced beauty" remains our most reliable guide. We find room for almost everything here, including the rationalism; for it should not be denied that Apollo's presentation of the Trojan War as a divine remedy against overpopulation[8] *is* Euripidean, as well as charmingly pointed: all this must go in, without that stress on the "cannibals impute cannibalism to their gods"[9] range of sentiments which gave us our ancient Voltaire. Euripides's lyrics are suspiciously separable, often, from the plays they belong to, but they are also very fine, especially in their evocation of quietness (*hēsuchia*) and

[1] The work of Nestle and Decharme, for example.
[2] By E. R. Dodds (*Classical Review*, 1929).
[3] By R. B. Appleton (*Classical Review*, 1918).
[4] By H. Reich (*Festschrift C. Lehmann-Haupt*).
[5] André Rivier, *Essai sur le tragique d'Euripide*.
[6] L. H. G. Greenwood, *Aspects of Euripidean Tragedy*.
[7] E. Howald, *Die griechische Tragödie*.
[8] *Orestes*, ll. 1641-2.
[9] *Iphigeneia in Tauris*, ll. 386-90.

"green joy".[1] And while the final dramatic achievement is a scattered one, a whole range of mask-piercing and even, at the end of his life, mask-exploiting effects (the smiling mask of the Stranger in the *Bacchantes* is meant to be inscrutable; it is a modern mask) declares Euripides's huge originality. In fact, the greatness of the *Bacchantes* rests in a vivid spirituality which we encounter in three or four earlier plays, and particularly in the *Alcestis* with its "Boldly stretch out your hand and touch the stranger"[2] at the dead wife's return; and which, by convincing us that what we see happening on the stage is true in another sense, forbids the bald conclusion that Euripides was unable, finally, to bend Greek tragic action his own way. In this high matter he has naturally not had his due; but the misplaced beauties have received justice from the critical tradition, and we let them be.

3 Coda

One implication of the last chapter deserves a moment's thought. It is that we feel ourselves imaginatively closer to Euripides than to Sophocles.

There are only two undoubted changes of scene in the extant drama, and one of these occurs in Sophocles's *Ajax*[3] when the tent concealing the disgraced soldier at the start, and from which he emerges to face the new day, gives place to the setting which he has chosen for his suicide. He now enters (we must imagine a deserted stretch of beach near Troy), bearing a sword which he presses into the sand and then contemplates in soliloquy, his eye on its upturned point:

> *He's firm in the ground, my Slayer. And his cut*
> *(If I have time even for this reflection)*
> *Should be the deadliest. For, first, the sword*
> *Was Hector's gift, a token of guest-friendship,*
> *And he of all guest-friends my bitterest foe;*
> *Here, too, it stands, lodged in this hostile ground*
> *Of Troy, its edge made new with iron-devouring stone.*

[1] *Bacchantes*, ll. 866-7.   [2] l. 1117.

[3] The other is in Aeschylus's *Eumenides*, when Orestes leaves Apollo's temple at Delphi and comes to Athens, where his trial takes place.

And, last, I've propped it, so, with careful handling,
To help me soon and kindly to my death.[1]

Which indicates the complexity that attends all judgment as to
relative nearness; for the death of Ajax is much more like the
last Scene of *Othello* than is anything in Euripides. And it is
more like at a level where we grope among the profoundest
vitalities of western art.

The onrush of calm at Ajax's death, which is also a kind of
tolling cosmic voice, points the need to be a little less vague
than heretofore about definitions of the stage-figure in Greek
Tragedy. Comparison of Sophocles with Aeschylus, especially
in their treatment of the Orestes myth, was meant to demonstrate among other things the increased dramatic energy generated through the promotion of the individual figure in the
former's work; and comparison of Euripides with Sophocles
also traced an increase—in solicited dramatic interest, this
time, not in dramatic energy—through Euripides's many-sided
concern with the inward fact of consciousness.

Sophocles's achievement was to realise privacy. The public
nature of the Greek literary self before he wrote his tragedies
(which quasi-Romantic interpretation of the ancient Lyric has
done more than anything else to obscure) was fully sustained
by Aeschylus, and may be seen as the informing principle of
his human creation. It is a bond uniting the pageant-outward-
ness of his conspicuous mutes (the Champions in the *Seven
against Thebes*, the Jurors in the *Eumenides*) with the articulate
figure's power—and frequent disposition—to address the Universe. Prometheus stands over against Nature in massive
stability:

O air of heaven, O swift-winged breezes, O river-water, O
countless laughter of the sea's waves, O Earth, mother of all, and
all-seeing eye of the sun—on you I call. . . .[2]

[1] ll. 815-22, in Mr John Moore's translation (*The Complete Greek Tragedies*,
edited by David Grene and Richmond Lattimore: University of Chicago
Press, 1957).

[2] *Prometheus Bound*, ll. 88-91. The magnificent pre-pastoral strength of
Aeschylus's images from nature (after the storm which overtook the Greek
fleet on its way home from Troy "we saw the Aegean sea aflower with dead
bodies": *Agamemnon*, l. 659) belongs to his public imagination.

whereas Philoctetes broods amply upon the fluid love-hate relationship of the cave and other natural features of the island to himself. Nature exists *for*—in the eye of—Sophoclean man with entirely new reference to self, which is why, when Philoctetes and Ajax[1] bid farewell to the scenes of their long hardships, and when the more complex reciprocities of the *Oedipus at Colonus* are declared, the world of *The Prelude* seems suddenly much less remote, as if the sensibility of the race had taken a giant stride. And what is new here is a containment of the human individual that brings within imagination a manner of appropriating relationships such as leads us to call them personal. It is an affair of total Nature—of life first and only second of nature-poetry—and therefore it is omnipresent in the Sophoclean drama.

Our earlier account of the 'personal' sharing out of the one myth between Orestes and Electra and Clytemnestra told only part of this story: the rest is implicit in Aristotle's bare statement that Sophocles was responsible for the introduction of the third actor into Greek Tragedy.[2] And it was also Aristotle who distinguished a drama of characterful action from a drama of humanity, thus establishing the basis for our own differentiation between Sophoclean privacy and Euripidean inwardness, and for our observing just now, with Ajax and Othello, how privacy endures.

Inwardness gives us, as privacy does not, our modern category of the subjective. When Orestes saw the Furies in the *Oresteia*, he was not experiencing an hallucination: he was polluted. But when the Euripidean Orestes *thought he saw*[3] the Furies, he knew that his guilty "conscience"[4] lay at the back of the apparition. It would be hard to exaggerate the importance of this change. It is, at the same time, a change which by-passes Sophocles in his main dramatic strength and interests. Euripides

---

[1] *Ajax*, ll. 412-27.

[2] *Poetics*, 49a19. The three-way stress, interaction, adjustment, that becomes possible when three speakers are on the stage with the Chorus (Aeschylus took the third actor from Sophocles, but not the suppleness that conceived the Jocasta-Creon-Oedipus exchange at *Oedipus the King*, l. 634) was an almost entirely neglected study until the younger Wilamowitz's *Die dramatische Technik des Sophokles* was published posthumously in 1917.

[3] *Orestes*, l. 408.

[4] *Ibid.*, l. 396.

moves far away from his contemporary when he plays—trifles almost—with the story of the phantom-wife Helen in order to devote a tragedy to the theme of Illusion; and when, in the *Bacchantes*, he achieves a double representation, teasingly simultaneous, of faith and superstition.

What happened after the *Bacchantes*, which was written towards the end of Euripides's life, nobody can say, for the plays are lost; and we should not forget that among his contemporaries and juniors Ion and Agathon were reckoned very great tragedians in antiquity, and that Horace believed, as did many other Romans, that the perished tragic literature of his people succeeded better than their Comedy. (Nor should that Comedy's closeness to its Greek model, nor the surviving fragments of Greek New Comedy, nor *The Bad-Tempered Man*,[1] lead us to underestimate our considerable ignorance as to the long aesthetic evolution set on foot by Euripides and profoundly affecting not only stage-practice but the idea of fiction itself, in its separateness from history and myth, and in its literary status.)

But our present limited purpose is to suggest certain originalities and continuities in imaginative creation, and this is not rendered vain, surely, by our surrounding ignorance, or by the known and half-known facts of the larger history of mind. That the difference between me and not-me was as inconceivably primitive an observation for Homer as it is for us, does not touch the newness of the dramatic subjective in Euripides. Nor does the development over centuries in what I have called the discrete and centrifugal self of ancient Greece.[2] The cautious thing to say is perhaps that Euripides broke with a convention which imposed formal limits on the idea of personality in

[1] Menander's play is our only more or less complete specimen, recently discovered, of post-Aristophanic Greek Comedy. It disappoints the high hopes which the surviving fragments of Menander had justified. Presumably his *Bad-Tempered Man* is juvenile.

[2] I do not feel in any serious way at odds with Rohde or with Snell, German historians of the Greek mind who narrate a long slow process. But there must be disagreement between my own attempt and all forms of gradualism in the literary scholarship or the criticism of Greek Tragedy— and disagreement persists even where my debt is large, as it specially is (on the crucial theme of self-expression) to Leo's *Der Monolog im Drama* and Schadewaldt's *Monolog und Selbstgespräch*.

S

Tragedy (which was an action of genius). In any case I am not
suggesting that inwardness sprang upon the Greeks fully armed
from Euripides's head. And there are other worlds for study
beyond Greek Tragedy in which the flowering of inwardness
mainly concerns Socrates, while in others it concerns St Paul,
in others Hamlet, in others the nineteenth and twentieth
centuries, while in others it is aboriginally Semitic, and in
others it has never happened. But we hold fast to the firmness
and fulness and the power to command comprehension and
assent in the ancient audience (and dimly in ourselves) that
make a ponderable object of the human self in the Greek
masked drama—an object to which our distinguishing of public
and private and inward refers. Of course art presents a vast
human wealth beyond this scheme (Homer's small boy frightened by the glitter of his father's helmet has been with us from
the beginning), although in admiring the force and justice of
apparently unconnected perceptions we are sometimes responding to hidden neighbourhood. Krook's nameless male
lodger of the early chapters of *Bleak House* is found dead in his
room ("He must be buried, you know"):

> So the little crazy lodger [Miss Flite] goes for the beadle, and the
> rest come out of the room. "Don't leave the cat there!" says the
> surgeon: "that won't do!" Mr Krook therefore drives her out
> before him; and she goes furtively down-stairs, winding her lithe
> tail and licking her lips.[1]

The unexpressed fear of dishonour to the corpse draws its
strength from the same source as the story of Antigone's
attempt on behalf of her brother's body lying exposed on the
Theban plain, and it contrasts grotesquely with the Victorian
death-rhetoric of Dickens awake.

It is true that Shakespeare learned more history from
Plutarch than most men could from the whole British Museum,
and it is a truth deserving the widest application: I mean it
should be allowed to illuminate the bigness of effect which all
great writers are able to secure by way of the simple and seem-
ingly casual in their work. When Henry James tells us that the
face of Ralph Touchett, while he lay dying, was "as still as the

---

[1] Chapter XI.

lid of a box",[1] I do not think it fanciful to affirm that the
novelist has intuitively grasped the significance of the Greek
masked drama for the civilisation that comes after it. He is in
the tradition of literary interplay between privacy and inwardness which began when Sophocles and Euripides were competing against one another at Athens. He is more *in* the
tradition than modern writers who have consciously abandoned
the roundedness and stability of the nineteenth-century fictional
character—than Lawrence, and Pirandello with his hall-of-
mirrors devices for the human image, and Brecht. He is much
more *in* the tradition than Yeats and Synge and the lesser
Hellenizers. And he can do more *about* the tradition than
Matthew Arnold, who lamented the departure of Greek tragic
action, intelligently, but with insufficient analytic power.

This is a tradition which all cruder forms of historical study
misapprehend, because modern men are able to conceive of
human privacy only in terms of inwardness; and so such
developments as that of ancient portraiture from an extreme
of idealisation towards the individual likeness, and of the tragic
mask from a bare statement of type-features towards an exactness of correspondence with the individual stage-figure such as
the older theatre never attempted or desired,[2] are always interpreted one way—the way of inwardness. No need to search

---

[1] *The Portrait of a Lady*, Chapter LIV.

[2] This process indicates a progressive subversion of the classical function
of the mask; the multiplying and refining of the type-distinctions which the
mask is able to present (Donatus describes no fewer than forty-four masks)
is essentially late antiquity's assimilation of the mask to the face beneath it.
At the same time, to abandon the masking convention altogether would be
unthinkable. Thus a stage-figure in Roman Comedy who wishes to disguise
himself might put on a travelling hat or a cloak, but he would not change
his mask. The mask is still the *persona*, the ultimate dramatic entity, and to
change a mask would be like disguising a character in the modern theatre
by bringing on another character in his place. (Those who assume that
masks were occasionally changed in classical Greek Tragedy have failed, as
I think, to be serious about masking. Lessing probably states the correct
principle for solving problems of staging like the blindness of Oedipus when,
commenting on the two-sided mask—one grey and one black eye—mentioned in Pollux, he says that after the blinding the actor would present
only the grey eye to his audience: see Jebb-Pearson, *The Fragments of
Sophocles*, vol. I, pp. 177-8; and on two-sidedness generally, Chapter
Thirteen—"Le dédoublement de la représentation"—of Claude Lévi-
Strauss's *Anthropologie structurale*.)

further for the cause of our imposing the tragic hero on Aristotle. Theophrastus, indeed, who succeeded Aristotle in the headship of the Peripatetic School, defined Tragedy as a "change in a hero's fortunes",[1] and it may be that we have here a rarely exact indication of the parting of the ways in the late fourth century, with Aristotle telling his students that Tragedy is not an imitation of human beings, and with those students— or some of them—unmoved and sceptical in the light of their experience of Euripidean creations like Medea[2]: at a time, too, when the visible presence of the stage-figure is becoming newly and "heroically" magnificent, and virtuoso acting is on the increase.

Of course we have no business saying that Aristotle was right and his pupil Theophrastus was wrong; all our effort must be bent to the contrasting of Medea's centrality to her play with King Oedipus's to his, apart from which the granting or withholding of the title of hero is quite empty. And it would be rash to assume that the interest of such contrasting is purely antiquarian. Cordelia's radiant privacy of being, her individuality without inwardness, moves us immediately—but it causes critical chaos later on. The point is not that she seems to have stepped out of Sophocles, but that she was always in Shakespeare.

I believe that a number of false estimations of the amplest European sort, like the under-rating of the Spanish drama and the over-rating of the French, flow from failure to recognise the continuing life-in-art, on both sides, of the opposed formulations of Theophrastus and Aristotle. Inflexibility in attitude to the projection of the self in literature brings with it an unhealthy dogmatism, often unconscious, about the nature of drama.

> MENELAUS: My hands are clean.
> ORESTES: But not your heart.

The Euripidean riposte, traced through Seneca:

---

[1] ἡρωικῆς τύχης περίστασις. The phrase is preserved in Diomedes, *De Poematibus*, 8, 1 (*Comicorum Graecorum Fragmenta*, ed. Kaibel, 57).

[2] Since when writer after writer (M. Pohlenz, for example: *Die griechische Tragödie*, 2nd edn., p. 258) has affirmed that with Medea we get inside a woman's nature as never before in Greek Tragedy.

ATREUS: Natos ecquid agnoscis tuos?
THYESTES: Agnosco fratrem.[1]

ought not to dominate consideration of the Renaissance to the
extent it has. In one sense we have been too linguistic, and in
another not enough; for our understanding of rhetoric embraces
the punch-line, the gnomic and the sententious, and the processes of bombastic refinement, but scarcely those moments of
sudden visionary denial of the third dimension when Shakespearean dialogue is transported into a world of acoustic
mask-wearing:

LEAR: Lend me a looking-glass;
   If that her breath will mist or stain the stone,
   Why, then she lives.
KENT: Is this the promis'd end?
EDGAR: Or image of that horror?
ALBANY: Fall and cease.
LEAR: This feather stirs; she lives.

The shared-out spoken word is all. Who, listening, seeks edit-
orial guidance upon the end of the world? While beyond—or
beside—the human and linguistic issues is the conceptual
poverty of action, cramping discussion of Shakespeare, and
the drama, and the novel, and whole phases of our literature.
(Goethe's "In the beginning was the Deed" affords at least as
good an introduction to European and even English Romanticism as does the feast of inwardness promised in the books: much
harm has been done by blundering applications of the distinction drawn between poetry as "expression of personality"
and poetry as "escape from personality" in the most influential
critical essay of our century, Mr Eliot's *Tradition and the
Individual Talent*.)

For all this, Greek Tragedy does not cease to be very alien.
If Turgenev's boy impelled in love—impelled as by a push
from behind—to jump down into the road from a high wall,[2]

---

[1] *Thyestes*, ll. 1005-6. Thyestes has been feasting on his children, and
Atreus brings in their heads for his brother to "recognise". He answers:
"I recognise my brother."

[2] *First Love*, Chapter XII. The passage is noted by Lord David Cecil in
his Introduction to Sir Isaiah Berlin's translation.

and if Heathcliff obeying his "natural impulse" to catch his
enemy's child at the foot of the stairs and save him from hurt,[1]
appear to act in a strangely rich and meaningful (and Romantic!)
way, we must speak first of their gesture of truth to the deeper
self, and only second—and then with caution—of the instinctive
action's vestigial autonomy in modern literature. And if Alec
D'Urberville's feeding strawberries to Tess:

> and, presently, selecting a specially fine product of the "British
> Queen" variety, he stood up and held it by the stem to her
> mouth.
> "No—no!" she said quickly, putting her fingers between his
> hand and her lips. "I would rather take it in my own hand."
> "Nonsense!" he insisted; and in a slight distress she parted her
> lips and took it in.[2]

imparts something of the fierce economy, the sharpness, of
Greek tragic action, this is because the naïve directness of
Hardy's talent forbids us to employ the language of sexual
symbolism: the male outrage before us here is somehow the
thing itself.

It turns out to be our bad luck that Greek Tragedy is superficially intelligible in a modern way. To quote in translation
Aeschylus and Euripides for the benefit of a largely Greekless
public, and then to put the leading question: "Is it too much to
say that in all these strangely characteristic speeches of Orestes,
every line might have been spoken by Hamlet", is not rendered
harmless by the quaint follow-on: "and hardly a line by any
other tragic character except those directly influenced by
Orestes or Hamlet?"[3] On the contrary, the meaning of the
ancient drama for ourselves is best fostered by our mustering
what awareness we can of its near-inaccessibility. We cannot
recover the discrete and centrifugal self by taking thought, or
undo the tremendous shock of change suffered by our civilisation when Greek inconstancy, which is sometimes another name

---

[1] *Wuthering Heights*, Chapter IX.

[2] *Tess of the D'Urbervilles*, Chapter III.

[3] Gilbert Murray, *The Classical Tradition in Poetry*, p. 212. By no means
all classical scholars imagine that the fifth-century tragedians thought more
or less as we do. Already, in this book's second section, we have met and
quarrelled with a primitivist school of Aeschylus criticism.

for Greek inspiration,[1] gave place to the Roman "Be true". But thinking is still preferable to not thinking; and thinking (of this kind) is not at all seriously dependent on modern specialised scholarship. In fact the older achievements of learned and speculative imagination point the way clearly enough for the amateur, who does not feel tempted to underrate—still less ignore—them for no better reason than that they are now seen to be locally vulnerable, and who does not need reminding that Rohde's *Psyche* still stands, substantially, and so does Glotz's *La solidarité de la famille*; and that Hegel on the masked drama was not altogether head-in-air (his understanding far surpassed Nietzsche's); and that Fustel de Coulanges overstated his case, but not grossly:

> Pour connaître la vérité sur ces peuples anciens, il est sage de les étudier sans songer à nous, comme s'ils nous étaient tout à fait étrangers, avec le même désintéressement et l'esprit aussi libre que nous étudierions l'Inde ancienne ou l'Arabie.
>
> Ainsi observées, la Grèce et Rome se présentent à nous avec un caractère absolument inimitable. Rien dans les temps modernes ne leur ressemble. Rien dans l'avenir ne pourra leur ressembler.[2]

[1] As it was with Alcibiades; and Alcibiades offended far more by his sacrilege than he did by his treachery. For an indication of the many and important theoretical aspects of Greek inconstancy, see A. W. H. Adkins, *Merit and Responsibility: a Study in Greek Values.*

[2] *La cité antique*, Introduction.

INDEX

Abresch, F., 87

Adkins, A. W. H., 279

Aeschylus, Section II and Chapter 1 of Section III *passim.* Also 11, 15, 18, 42-3, 52, 61-2, 159-60, 162, 164, 166, 170-2, 174, 181, 206, 210, 231, 247, 253, 257, 261, 263, 268, 271-2, 278

Works:

Agamemnon, Section II, Chapters 2, 3 and 4, *passim.* Also 148, 157, 247, 271

Eumenides, Section II, Chapters 3 and 4, *passim.* Also 73, 150, 270-1

Libation-Bearers, Section II, Chapters 3 and 4, *passim.* Also 73, 141-4, 146-8, 153-4, 158-9, 162, 173, 192

Niobe, 93

(Oresteia), Section II, Chapters 2, 3 and 4, *passim.* Also 42-3, 70-2, 141-2, 149-52, 156, 162, 206, 230, 272

Persians, 72, 80, 86, 109, 130, 171

Philoctetes, 141, 218

Prometheus Bound, 71-2, 128, 157, 263, 271

Seven against Thebes, 71, 118, 131, 148, 157, 171, 206, 271

Suppliant Women, 65-7, 69-70, 120, 128, 133

Agathon, 29, 40, 273

Alcibiades, 279

Anagnōrisis (Recognition), 15-16, 57-8, 213

Anscombe, G. E. M., 60

Antiphanes, 61

Appleton, R. B., 269

Areopagus, Council of, 112

Aristophanes, 50, 239-42, 256-8

Aristophanes of Byzantium, 177

Aristotle, Section I *passim.* Also 67-8, 115, 117, 160-2, 165-6, 176, 188-91, 194, 198, 211, 213, 220, 231-3, 239, 241-2, 265-7, 272, 276

Works:

Concerning the Poets, 21-2, 50

De Anima, 26

Eudemus, 26

Nicomachean Ethics, 15, 24, 26, 34, 37

Poetics, Section I *passim.* Also 67-8, 161-2, 189-91, 200-1, 266-7, 272

Politics, 21

Rhetoric, 15, 39, 41, 50, 53, 56

Arnold, Matthew, 275

Austen, Jane, 183

Beethoven, Ludwig van, 71, 242

Blake, William, 41

Bowra, C. M., 196

Bradley, A. C., 81, 211

Brahms, Johannes, 69'

Brecht, B., 275

Brontë, Emily, 278

Butcher, S. H., 12

Bywater, I., 14, 17-20, 41-2, 47, 49

Castelvetro, L., 31

Change of Fortune in the *Poetics,* 13-16, 19-20, 39, 48, 57-8, 62, 189

Christianity, 15, 32, 39, 54, 60, 128, 169, 175, 191, 195, 209, 233